Applied Concept Mapping

Capturing, Analyzing, and Organizing Knowledge

Applied
Concept
Mapping

Capturing, Analyzing,
and Organizing Knowledge

Brian M. Moon ■ Robert R. Hoffman
Joseph D. Novak ■ Alberto J. Cañas

CRC Press
Taylor & Francis Group
Boca Raton   London   New York

CRC Press is an imprint of the
Taylor & Francis Group, an **Informa** business

CRC Press
Taylor & Francis Group
6000 Broken Sound Parkway NW, Suite 300
Boca Raton, FL 33487-2742

Printed in the United States of America on acid-free paper
10 9 8 7 6 5 4 3 2 1

International Standard Book Number: 978-1-4398-2860-1 (Hardback)

Library of Congress Cataloging-in-Publication Data

Applied Concept Mapping: Capturing, Analyzing, and Organizing Knowledge / editors, Brian Moon ...et al.
    p. cm.
Includes bibliographical references and index.
ISBN 978-1-4398-2860-1
    1. Social sciences--Methodology. 2. Information visualization. 3. Management. I. Moon, Brian M. II. Title.

H61.A6793 2011
300.22'3--dc22
                                                     2010027609

Visit the Taylor & Francis Web site at
http://www.taylorandfrancis.com

and the CRC Press Web site at
http://www.crcpress.com

Dedications

Brian M. Moon, to his loves—Alyson, Skyler, Jayden, and Foster

Robert R. Hoffman, to his loving family—Robin, Rachel, and Eric

Joseph D. Novak, For Joan

Alberto J. Cañas, to Carmen: "With you, Concept Mapping has been a lifelong adventure"

Contents

SECTION I   Practitioners' View

SECTION II   Recent Case Studies and Results

SECTION III   Pushing the Boundaries

Preface

In small pockets of industry around the world over the past two decades, practitioners have been applying Concept Mapping to solve problems. They have improved on Joseph Novak's original conception, developed methods and technologies to enhance the process, and have demonstrated the impacts of their approaches. Concurrently, the successes of Concept Mapping in educational systems have multiplied. Millions of school children around the world engage in the kind of meaningful learning Novak originally intended with Concept Maps. Along the way, the needs of both communities—corporate and educational—converged on the path forged by interconnecting computers to create an elegant knowledge modeling kit—CmapTools—that enables Concept Mapping on a large scale and realizes the full potential of the Internet.

This book is intended to mark a tipping point. With an emerging generation of computer-savvy Concept Mappers set to take their place in the workforce in the coming years, we hope that this book will provide the impetus to encourage them to continue to apply and extend what they have learned in school to the problems of the workplace. We envision a world in which the most perplexing problems can be conceived, analyzed, and solved using Concept Maps, without the problem solver having to explain to other people what Concept Mapping is. We know of no other method that can so ably and efficiently help people crystallize their ideas, doing so in a form that practically begs to be connected to other knowledge. *Applied Concept Mapping: Capturing, Analyzing, and Organizing Knowledge* offers a glimpse at what is possible when practitioners adopt and apply techniques inspired by Concept Mapping. We can only imagine what is possible once the tipping point is "tipped."

The editors would like to express their gratitude to the contributors. In a historical and very genuine sense, it is the personal experience of the authors that *is* the story of Applied Concept Mapping. We have learned a great deal in reviewing their work as well as those whose work we reviewed but did not include.

Apart from the content covered in this volume, we know of other exciting examples of Applied Concept Mapping. However, much of the work is protected by proprietary rights or security classifications. Indeed, a good deal of our best work has been reserved for our clients. We are thankful to the sponsors and clients who have allowed these contributions to be presented in print.

We acknowledge the staff at the Institute for Human and Machine Cognition (IHMC) and all of the government sponsors who have contributed to the development of CmapTools, especially the U.S. Department of Defense and NASA.

We extend our appreciation to Michael Sinocchi and the staff at Taylor and Francis for their support and encouragement throughout the publication process.

We thank Jill Jordan for providing proofreading support, drawing on her career as an English teacher.

Finally, three of us wish to express our deep indebtedness to Joseph D. Novak, whose life's work has inspired us and thousands of others to improve the worlds in which we work. Joe's shoulders are giant indeed.

Brian M. Moon
Robert R. Hoffman
Joseph D. Novak
Alberto J. Cañas

Editors

Brian M. Moon is the co-founder and chief technology officer of Perigean Technologies LLC, Fredericksburg, Virginia. He holds a BA in psychology from Miami University, Oxford, Ohio, and an MSc in sociology from the London School of Economics and Political Science, United Kingdom. From 1996 to 2000, Moon provided social science support to legal defense teams. He joined the staff of Klein Associates Inc. in 2000 to apply naturalistic methods to the solution of problems in software engineering, organizational and workplace design, and training. In 2007, Brian founded Perigean Technologies with his wife, Alyson, to help organizations improve through smarter use of their own knowledge and to help improve the way knowledge moves through organizations. Perigean Technologies' clients have included Westinghouse Electric Company, the New York Power Authority, the Defense Advanced Research Projects Agency, TNO, the Federal Bureau of Investigation, General Dynamics Advanced Information Systems, and Sandia National Laboratories. Moon has served on the program committee for International Conferences on Concept Mapping (CMC 2004, 2006, 2008, 2010), and is the owner of the Applied Concept Mapping Group at LinkedIn. He has published extensively on topics concerning knowledge management and methodology.

Robert R. Hoffman is a senior research scientist at the Florida Institute for Human and Machine Cognition (IHMC), Pensacola, Florida. He is recognized as one of the world leaders in the field of cognitive systems engineering and Human-Centered Computing (HCC). He is a Fellow of the Association for Psychological Science and a Fulbright Scholar. His PhD is in experimental psychology from the University of Cincinnati, where he received McMicken Scholar, Psi Chi, and Delta Tau Kappa honors. Following a postdoctoral associateship at the Center for Research on Human Learning at the University of Minnesota, Hoffman joined the faculty of the Institute for Advanced Psychological Studies at Adelphi University, Garden City, New York. He began his career as a psycholinguist, and founded the journal *Metaphor and Symbol*. His subsequent research leveraged the psycholinguistics background in the study of methods for eliciting the knowledge of domain experts. Hoffman has been recognized internationally in disciplines including psychology, remote sensing, weather forecasting, and artificial intelligence; for his research on human factors in remote sensing; his work in the psychology of expertise and the methodology of cognitive task analysis; and for his work on HCC issues in intelligent systems technology and the design of macrocognitive work systems. He is a co-editor for the Department on Human-Centered Computing in *IEEE: Intelligent Systems*, is editor for the book series, "Expertise: Research and Applications," and a co-founder and track editor for the *Journal of Cognitive Engineering and Decision Making*.

Joseph D. Novak is a professor emeritus, Cornell University (Ithaca, New York), and senior research scientist at IHMC. Completing graduate studies at the University of Minnesota (Minneapolis) in 1958, Novak taught biology at Kansas State Teachers College at Emporia, 1957 to 1959, and biology and teacher education courses at Purdue University (West Lafayette, Indiana), 1959 to 1967. From 1967 to 1995, he was professor of education and biological sciences at Cornell University where his research focused on human learning, educational studies, and knowledge creation and representation. He has developed a theory of education to guide research and instruction, first published in 1977 and updated in 1998 and 2010. He is author or co-author of 29 books and more than 140 book chapters and papers in professional books and journals. His *Learning How to Learn* (with D. Bob Gowin) published in 1984 has been translated into eight languages. He has consulted with more than 400 schools, universities, and corporations, including recent work with Procter and Gamble, NASA, the U.S. Navy, and the Electric Power Research Institute. His recent book, *Learning, Creating, and Using Knowledge: Concept Maps as Facilitative Tools in Schools and Corporations* (Routledge, 2010), is being translated into three foreign languages. He has received a number of awards and honors, including a 1998 honorary doctorate from The University of Comahue, Nuquen, Argentina; honorary doctorate, Public University of Navarra, Pamplona, Spain, in 2002; honorary doctorate from the University of Urbino (Italy) in 2006; and the first award for contributions to science education from the Council of Scientific Society Presidents.

Alberto J. Cañas is co-founder and an associate director of IHMC. He received a BS in computer engineering from the Instituto Tecnologico de

Monterrey, Mexico, an M. Math degree in Computer Science, and a PhD in management science, both from the University of Waterloo, Canada. He has taught at the Instituto Tecnologico de Costa Rica, Tulane University (New Orleans, Louisiana), and INCAE (in Costa Rica). In the late 1980s, he served as the director of IBM's Latin American Education Research Center in Costa Rica. From 1989 to 2005, he was a faculty member of the Computer Science Department at the University of West Florida (Pensacola). His research and development at IHMC has included uses of computers in education, knowledge management, knowledge acquisition, information retrieval, and human–machine interface—all leading to the development of CmapTools. Cañas has served as the co-chair for the CMC 2004, 2006, 2008, 2010, and has published and lectured throughout many countries in North and Latin America, Europe, Africa, and Asia.

Contributors

Phillip J. Ayoub
The Pennsylvania State University
State College, Pennsylvania

David Barberá-Tomás
Universidad Politécnica de Valencia
Valencia, Spain

Barbara L. Bowen
Sound Knowledge Strategies
Port Townsend, Washington

Patricia Bradley
Environmental Protection Agency
Key West, Florida

Alberto J. Cañas
Florida Institute for Human and
    Machine Cognition
Pensacola, Florida

John W. Coffey
University of West Florida
Pensacola, Florida

Barbara J. Daley
University of Wisconsin–Milwaukee
Milwaukee, Wisconsin

Natalia Derbentseva
Defence R&D Canada–Toronto
Toronto, Ontario, Canada

Carrie Ann Desnoyers
Milwaukee, Wisconsin

Thomas C. Eskridge
Florida Institute for Human and
    Machine Cognition
Pensacola, Florida

William Fisher
Environmental Protection Agency
Gulf Breeze, Florida

Hector Gómez-Gauchía
Universidad Complutense de
    Madrid
Madrid, Spain

Jeffery T. Hansberger
Army Research Laboratory
Suffolk, Virginia

Andrew G. Harter
Security Analysis and Risk
    Management Association
Arlington, Virginia

Jim Harvey
Environmental Protection Agency
Gulf Breeze, Florida

Robert R. Hoffman
Florida Institute for Human and
    Machine Cognition
Pensacola, Florida

Acacia Z. Kuenzer
Federal University of Paraná
Curitiba, Paraná, Brazil

Wilson L. Lanzarini
The Petrobrás University
Rio de Janeiro, Brazil

Bennet Larson
Jenzabar, Inc.
Raleigh, North Carolina

Michael R. Lovell
University of Wisconsin–Milwaukee
Milwaukee, Wisconsin

David R. Mandel
Defence R&D Canada
Toronto, Ontario, Canada

Ron McFadyen
University of Winnipeg
Winnipeg, Manitoba, Canada

Michael D. McNeese
The Pennsylvania State University
State College, Pennsylvania

Brian M. Moon
Perigean Technologies LLC
Fredericksburg, Virginia

Joseph D. Novak
Cornell University
Ithaca, New York
and
Florida Institute for Human and
    Machine Cognition
Pensacola, Florida

Ronald A. Perez
University of Wisconsin–Milwaukee
Milwaukee, Wisconsin

Ernesto de los Reyes-López
Instituto de Gestión de la
    Innovación y del Conocimiento
Valencia, Spain

John E. Rogers
Environmental Protection Agency
Gulf Breeze, Florida

Marc Russell
Environmental Protection Agency
Gulf Breeze, Florida

**Mónica Elizabeth Edwards
Schachter**
Instituto de Gestión de la
    Innovación y del Conocimiento
Valencia, Spain

Jan Maarten Schraagen
TNO
Soesterberg, The Netherlands

Nathaniel E. Stern
University of Wisconsin–Milwaukee
Milwaukee, Wisconsin

Austin Tate
University of Edinburgh
Edinburgh, Scotland

Eleonora B. Taveira
The Petrobrás University
Rio de Janeiro, Brazil

Josine van de Ven
TNO
Soesterberg, The Netherlands

Andrea White
University of Melbourne
Melbourne, Australia

Susan H. Yee
Environmental Protection Agency
Gulf Breeze, Florida

Introduction and Overview of the Book

Brian M. Moon, Robert R. Hoffman,
Joseph D. Novak, and Alberto J. Cañas

All life is problem solving.

Karl R. Popper

Applied Concept Mapping is the application of Concept Mapping to problem solving in the workplace. We mean problem solving in the most general way possible, invoking Popper's perspective. By workplace, we mean to be inclusive of all aspects of commerce and governance. This conception of Applied Concept Mapping makes for two important distinctions. First, it references Concept Mapping, a theoretically and scientifically grounded diagrammatic method of knowledge representation developed by Joseph D. Novak that is distinct from other similarly named or otherwise loosely acquainted methods. Second, the designation of Applied Concept Mapping serves to contextualize, which distinguishes the application from Concept Mapping's deep roots in educational settings. An example Concept Map is presented in Figure I.1.

The first distinction on the kinds of diagramming is highly important. Indeed, there are many approaches to "mapping intellectual landscapes" (cf., Okada, Shum and Sherborne 2008), "idea mapping" (cf., Sibbett 2010) and "visual thinking" (cf., Roam 2009a and 2009b) for business purposes. Few if any, however, are grounded in as extensive a theoretical and scientific base as Concept Mapping. Since its first formulation by Joseph D. Novak and colleagues at Cornell University in the 1970s, Concept Mapping has been subjected to empirical evaluation—both experimental and naturalistic—by researchers in settings ranging from schoolhouses in third world countries, to the world's most respected consumer products companies, to the halls of government.

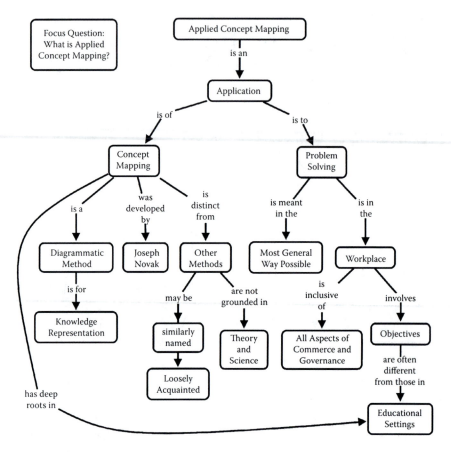

FIGURE I.1
Applied Concept Mapping.

The second distinction is important to clarify the intention for this volume. Practitioners in applied settings have taken Novak's basic approach and the lessons learned in research settings, and extended and innovated them in the service of solving vexing problems in the workplace. It is the difference of the objectives in these settings that makes necessary the distinction from educational settings. While learning is always an outcome of problem solving activities, it is not the only one, as the contributors to this volume ably demonstrate.

Our introduction of Applied Concept Mapping begins with a review of its roots and concludes with an overview of the global expansion over the past two decades. Following the introduction, we provide an overview of the book.

ROOTS OF APPLIED CONCEPT MAPPING

Joseph Novak has described the process that leads to the creation of Concept Mapping and its application in education (Novak and Gowin, 1984; Novak, 2010).

One of the earliest applications of Concept Mapping into workplace settings was a project aimed at improving communication effectiveness, which was conducted by Novak and his colleagues at Cornell on behalf of Eastman Kodak in 1990 (cf., Bennet and Frazier, 1990). Mazure's (1989) and Frazier's (1993) dissertation work suggest that the roots of Concept Mapping as an educational strategy were spreading and beginning to take hold in applied settings in the early 1990s, specifically in therapy with substance abusers and creating shared understanding as a basis for the cooperative design of work changes and changes in working relationships, respectively.

Yet the roots were not only springing from Cornell University. In parallel with Novak's work, following Novak's sabbatical leave at the University of West Florida in 1987, Alberto Cañas and Kenneth Ford at The Institute for Human and Machine Cognition (IHMC) began the development of software to facilitate the process of constructing Concept Maps in a collaborative environment. Sponsored by IBM, their development effort began linking schools in Latin America before the Internet reached these countries, utilizing IBM's corporate computer network (Cañas et al., 1995).

THE DEVELOPMENT OF CmapTools

The growth of the Internet and the emergence of new models for sharing, collaboration, browsing, retrieval, and publishing offered by the World Wide Web introduced new possibilities for the use of Concept Mapping, and led IHMC to develop the software suite CmapTools (Cañas et al., 2004). The software was designed with the objective of going beyond facilitating the construction of computer-based Concept Maps, enabling users to collaboratively build Concept Maps from distant locations, to hyperlink Concept Maps and associated resources into "knowledge models," and to easily publish the results, several years before Wikis and Blogs were introduced. The use of CmapTools quickly extended to hundreds of thousands of users throughout the world, who soon found innovative uses for Concept Mapping beyond the until-then traditional uses in education.

GROWTH OF APPLIED CONCEPT MAPPING

By the 1990s, interest in Concept Mapping began to take on the feel of a full-fledged movement, with the epicenter shifting to IHMC. In the early 1990s, Concept Maps were being used during the knowledge elicitation stage of building NUCES, a nuclear cardiology expert system (Ford et al., 1996). This was followed by the initiation of a collaboration between IHMC and the U.S. Navy that led to the development of the first version of CmapTools and its first applied use in the construction of a training system for electronic technicians, El-Tech (Coffey et al., 2003). At the NASA Glenn Research Center in Cleveland, Ohio, Cmaps were used to capture, represent, and preserve institutional memory of senior scientists with regard to launch vehicle systems integration (Coffey, Moreman, and Dyer, 1999).

With the advent of CmapTools, it was possible to create extensive knowledge models, i.e., sets of Concept Maps hyperlinked to other Concept Maps and related resources. One of the first major applications of knowledge modeling was conducted on behalf of the U.S. Navy. Hoffman et al. (2000) created the System To Organize Representations in Meteorology: Local Knowledge (STORM-LK). The system is a collection of Concept Maps and associated media (video, satellite image, and a text Web page) that visually represent the knowledge needed for weather forecasting in the Gulf of Mexico, as elicited from experts from the U.S. Navy's Meteorology and Oceanography Command in Pensacola, Florida.

Geoff Briggs at NASA Ames Research Center began in the late 1990s the construction of a large knowledge model on the exploration of Mars, which is, to date, still being extended by the author and available on the Web (http://cmex.ihmc.us) (Briggs et al., 2004). Beyond its intrinsic value, the project offers a concrete demonstration of one of the fundamental—indeed radical—ideas underlying the use of Concept Mapping in the field of knowledge engineering. Namely, that a domain expert can construct extensive knowledge models without the need for a knowledge engineer performing the elicitation and modeling.

As CmapTools and Concept Mapping realized successes in the United States, their application globally also expanded. Basque et al. (2004) conducted a large-scale knowledge acquisition effort using Concept Maps at Hydro-Québec in Canada. Hoffman et al. (2001) sought to help the government of Thailand preserve one its national treasures—the oral traditions in silk weaving—by creating knowledge models based on data from interviews with people in the Thai craft villages.

By the time of the First International Conference on Concept Mapping in 2004, the application of Concept Mapping had been empirically evaluated for efficiency and effectiveness as a knowledge elicitation method (Hoffman et al., 2002) and a method to solve problems in the workplace (Freeman, 2004).

Chief among these problems was the growing concern over capturing and preserving knowledge in many institutions that were at risk due to the aging and retiring populations in many Western countries. In the United States, Coffey and Eskridge (2004) Applied Concept Maps and CmapTools at a nuclear power plant for knowledge elicitation and institutional memory preservation. In setting forth guidelines for capturing valuable undocumented knowledge from energy industry personnel, the Electric Power Research Institute (2002) cited Concept Mapping as a primary method for this process. EPRI's guidelines laid the groundwork for a series of IHMC-facilitated workshops in which Concept Mapping for this purpose was employed with personnel from Progress Energy, Southern Company, South Texas Project Electric Generating Station, Rochester Gas and Electric, TXU Energy, DTE Energy, Ontario Power Generation, Public Service Company of New Mexico, Nebraska Public Power District, Exelon, Detroit Edison, CANDU Owners Group Inc., Entergy, the Institute of Nuclear Power Operations, Diablo Canyon, and Energy Northwest/Columbia Generating Station. In this industry, Concept Mapping has since been successfully deployed at the Tennessee Valley Authority (Coffey and Eskridge, 2008), the Westinghouse Electric Company (Moon and Kelley, 2010), Southern Company, and the New York Power Authority (Perigean Technologies, 2010). As the workplace problem of mitigating lost knowledge is a demographic one, it is likely that knowledge modeling in the utilities industry will likely continue into the foreseeable future (Moon, Hoffman, and Ziebel, 2009).

Building on their rapidly accumulating experiences in Concept Mapping and knowledge modeling in varied settings, both Coffey (2006) and

Hoffman (in Crandall et al., 2006) delineated guidance and stepped through techniques for new practitioners of Applied Concept Mapping. As Concept Mapping continued to flourish, though, it became apparent that applications were not restricted to capturing knowledge. Fourie and Schilawa (2004) researched the value of Concept Maps for knowledge management in the German banking and insurance industry, and concluded that Concept Mapping was a good method for knowledge acquiring and sharing in areas such as investment strategies, portfolio management, and customer relations. Based on their research at Lafitt SA, a Spanish prosthesis company, de los Reyes-López and Barberá (2004) showed that Concept Mapping can be a powerful tool in organizational learning, particularly in the generation of knowledge, the dissemination of it at the intraorganizational level, and the transformation of it into organizational conduct.

By the mid-2000s, some practitioners were beginning to innovate on and press the boundaries of the basic principles and techniques of Concept Mapping. Brewer and McNeese (2004) explored spatiality in Concept Maps. Derbentseva et al. (2004) found that the structure of the Concept Map influences the type of relationships that are likely to be constructed in a proposition that links two concepts together. Castro et al. (2006) developed a methodology for developing ontologies within the biological domain. Moon (2004) introduced a blended method approach for understanding teams and teamwork by merging a team cognitive task analysis method of Wagon Wheeling with Concept Maps.

In 2005, Fourie reviewed the state of "computer-based Concept Mapping tools in business," focusing exclusively on CmapTools. He stated:

> Although the uses have been expanded in the business world ... Concept Maps and Concept Mapping tools are mainly being used on the level of knowledge management and collaboration, to improve shared understanding, to enhance team and group performance, and to facilitate training. Although not prominent in the literature ... Concept Maps and Concept Mapping tools are also used for project management and product innovation and design. It must, however, be noted that Concept Maps and Concept Mapping tools in the business context have primarily being used or are planned to be used for knowledge management, which is understandable due to the excellent knowledge modeling capabilities of CmapTools. There is no doubt that to survive in a very competitive business environment, businesses will have to improve their capability to create and share

new knowledge. ... Computer-based Concept Mapping tools can enhance this creation and sharing, *inter alia* by overcoming the traditional linear method of capturing and presentation of knowledge; facilitating brainstorming and planning sessions; improving the sharing and presentation of knowledge, as well as the level of collaboration (p. 12).

Indeed, even more applications have been added to Fourie's list in the past several years. These include strategic intent in South Africa (Fourie and Westhuizen, 2008) and strategic planning in Colombia (Preciado et al., 2008); group decision making in the United States (Coffey, 2004); anthropological research in France (Cahuzac and Le Blanc, 2004); socioecosystem management in Nepal, Pakistan, and Tibet (Salerno et al., 2008); engineering technical report writing in Columbia (Ramírez et al., 2008); and social science research in Israel (Kozminsky et al., 2008), to name but a few.

As the list suggests, applications have not only been in service of commercial interests. Indeed, representatives from many government agencies have shown great interest in Concept Mapping. In the United States, the Department of Defense has sponsored numerous efforts that Applied Concept Mapping on behalf of its missions. These have included efforts aimed at large-scale transformation of operations (Moon et al., 2006), tactical uses (Kaste, Heilman, and Hoffman, 2007), mission planning (Hoffman and Shattuck, 2006), information visualization (Cañas et al., 2005; Moon and Hoffman, 2008; Moon et al., 2008), fostering shared mental models and teamwork performance (Blickensderfer et al., 1997), and job task analysis within the Navy (Dumestre, 2004). Moreover, the U.S. government, in particular the U.S. Navy, the Department of Defense, and NASA, has been the primary sponsor for the development of CmapTools at IHMC. To address the needs of some of these organizations, CmapTools was extended to support secure communication, encryption and certificates, and a version of CmapTools (the CmapTools Ontology Editor [COE, http://www.ihmc.us/groups/coe/]) was developed for the editing and creation of ontologies.

The international community of Concept Mappers has established biennial conferences to share developments, findings, and ideas, including ideas about applications and business strategies (CMC 2004, 2006, 2008, 2010). The 2004 conference in Pamplona, Spain, marked a pivotal point for

Applied Concept Mapping. For the first time, practitioners from around the world began sharing their experiences, innovations, and findings. The second conference was held in Costa Rica in 2006, and by the third conference in 2008 in Estonia and Finland, the global presence of Concept Mapping had been established. Papers and posters were presented from Europe (Turkey, Northern Ireland and Ireland, United Kingdom, Greece, Scotland, Portugal, Italy, Malta, Latvia, Austria, Hungary, Norway, Sweden), Asia (Japan, India, Taiwan, Malaysia, Republic of Korea, Singapore), Middle East (Iran), Australia, and the Americas (Mexico, Venezuela, Columbia, Argentina, Costa Rica, Cuba, Panama, Brazil, Canada, and the United States). The fourth conference took place in Chile in 2010. Of particular note was a video presentation highlighting many applications of Concept Mapping at *Cirque du Soleil*, to include logistics planning, knowledge codification, and ideation (Simard, 2010). While the majority of the published work at the conferences has focused on educational applications, an expanding number have reported on work in applied settings. The germination in classroom settings will likely flower into applied settings in the decades ahead.

Having introduced the topic of Applied Concept Mapping, we now turn to this volume—its themes and organization, and notes about figures.

THEMES OF THIS VOLUME

Several themes run through the volume. First, the material presented continues the trends in Applied Concept Mapping discussed above in a number of ways. Our contributors demonstrate the continuation of many of the same sorts of commercial and governance applications. They offer solutions to creating a common lexicon, designing complex engineering products and cognitive systems, improving intelligence and organizational learning, implementing software systems, managing ecosystems and related goods and services, and understanding business models. In doing so, they reflect the versatility of Applied Concept Mapping.

A second theme of the book is the variety of interpretations of Concept Mapping. It would seem that there are Concept Maps and there are "Novakian" Concept Maps. What makes for "Novakian" Concept Maps can be learned, presumably, from Joseph Novak's definition of what a Concept Map is. And yet, there is variety among Concept Maps. For instance, some have opted away from the semihierarchical structure, finding benefit in center-focused representations. All of the Concept Maps presented in the chapters of this book show most of the hallmark features of "Novakian" Concept Maps, which are detailed in Chapter 1. Indeed, the principal criterion of selection of chapters for this volume was just this.

But, here too we find some variety. Sometimes links are used to capture numerical relations (e.g., confidence levels) between concepts. Some start and/or end with the hallmark features of "Novakian" Concept Maps, but introduce other processing methods that distort the Concept Map or diverge from the hallmark features for specific purposes. In each case, the contributors offer substantive reasons for why their particular Concept Maps diverge, where appropriate. Ultimately, Applied Concept Mapping is about the practical.

The integration of theory, application, assessment, and personal experience is a third theme of the chapters in this book. Each contribution blends these elements in order to tell a story. Some stories center on theoretical considerations, using application and assessment as a means of testing theory. For others, application has been the focus of the work, and assessment and personal experience provide windows into the success of the applications.

Assessment is an important consideration for Applied Concept Mapping. While several empirical studies have looked at the efficiency (Hoffman et al., 2002) and effectiveness (Freeman, 2004; Fourie et al., 2004; Moon and Hoffman, 2008) of using Concept Maps in applied settings, the impact on any given effort is often very difficult to measure. The chief reason for this is that clients' and sponsors' interest in Applied Concept Mapping lies in solving the problem, not in assessing the process or finely measuring the outcome. Nevertheless, most contributions to this volume include outcome feedback on the value of Applied Concept Mapping, including both anecdotal and systematically obtained results. We view this theme as necessary for driving further innovation.

A fourth theme of the chapters in this volume is the challenges in introducing Concept Mapping into applied settings. The challenges are many. Some are to be expected, e.g., those associated with breaking corporate traditions and bringing in new ways of doing work and new tools. But some may surprise, e.g., the high skill level necessary. One must personally experience the "light bulbs going off" when realizing that it is easy to make Concept Maps yet not so easy to make good ones.

A fifth theme is the use of CmapTools. This was a second principal criterion of selection of chapters for this volume. While Concept Maps can be digitally created using any number of tools, CmapTools has been explicitly developed to enable creation and sharing of Concept Maps. The software, as well as extensive documentation and relevant research publications, is available for *free* download at the IHMC Web site, http://cmap.ihmc.us. To be direct about it, we would not want readers who might not know otherwise to get the impression that this book is merely an advertisement for a software package. At the same time, this book highlights the highly flexible capabilities of the CmapTools. In this Introduction, we have already noted the valuable contribution the software has made in applied settings. In addition to being free, it is fortunate that the CmapTools "sell" themselves.

The last theme is really the entire theme of the book. With these contributions, we see Applied Concept Mapping taking root in commercial and government enterprises. With each problem solved, and each new introduction, the practitioners of Applied Concept Mapping continue to establish it as a legitimate tool for doing business. In many ways, however, Applied Concept Mapping remains a work in progress. New approaches to problem solving are being innovated in the workplace. Several contributors note the direction of their future work. Indeed, we have devoted one section of this volume to highlighting where boundaries can and are being pushed.

ORGANIZATION OF THE BOOK

There are many ways to organize the story of Applied Concept Mapping. It would be reasonable to organize by theory, techniques, and case studies, but as we noted above, our contributors routinely merge these aspects of their work, and rightly so. Geography could be another way to think about the landscape of applications, as the United States, Canada, Australia, Spain, Brazil, Scotland, and The Netherlands are represented here. But given the international flavor demonstrated above, we know this is only a small sample of the worldwide use of Applied Concept Mapping.

Workplace sectors could be another advanced organizing scheme, as the book contains contributions from the service technology, goods production, not-for-profit, and government sectors. Within these sectors are contributions touching on a variety of domains, including healthcare and medicine, electric utilities, intelligence analysis and military, petrochemical, environmental sciences and management, financial services, consumer and industrial products, law, security, risk management and emergency response, and associations. Many of our contributors have worked across several of these domains. Still another scheme could be application areas, which include knowledge elicitation, transfer, and management; lexicon and ontology development; modeling; training and organizational learning; product, software, cognitive systems, and organizational design and engineering; stakeholder engagement; analysis; and distributed planning. Figure I.2 combines these schemes to provide a cursory overview of the content of the volume, and demonstrate the many crosslinks within the content.

We have chosen to organize the volume around the perspectives and experiences of our contributors. Thus, Section I presents a collection of chapters representing Practitioners' Views—narratives, guidance, and reviews of applications from career Concept Mappers. Each of the contributors in this section has logged many hundreds of hours in developing, conducting, and evaluating Applied Concept Mapping.

In Chapter 1, Applying Educational Tools and Ideas in the Corporate World, Joseph D. Novak and Alberto J. Cañas recount the emergence of Applied Concept Mapping and CmapTools from their perspectives as founders of Concept Mapping and co-founder and an associate director of the Institute for Human and Machine Cognition, where he had led the development of CmapTools. Their story adds much depth and personal color to the roots of Concept Mapping section above.

With Chapter 2, Skills in Applied Concept Mapping, Brian M. Moon, Robert R. Hoffman, Thomas C. Eskridge, and John W. Coffey go beyond previous descriptions of the processes of Concept Mapping to bring into high relief the nature of the skill involved in Concept Mapping for a variety of purposes and across different settings.

Michael D. McNeese and Phillip J. Ayoub provide a unique perspective on two decades of methodological development in their Concept Mapping work in Chapter 3, Concept Mapping in the Analysis and Design of Cognitive Systems: A Historical Review. Their reflections drive home the theme of the interpretations of Concept Mapping, and they show how their interpretations have arisen from pragmatic concerns.

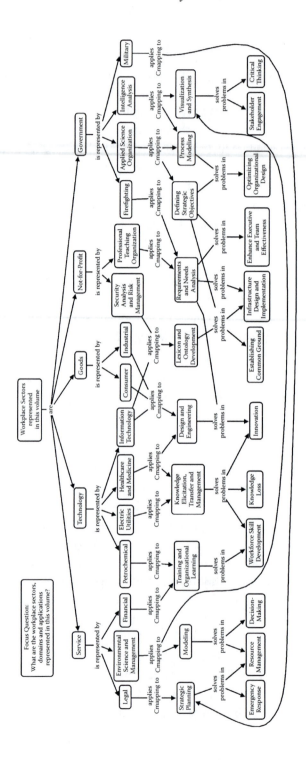

FIGURE I.2
Volume content with crosslinks.

In Chapter 4, Concept Maps: Tools to Enhance Executive and Team Effectiveness, Barbara L. Bowen shares several case studies and, most importantly, results and impacts from her work as a Concept Mapping practitioner. The contribution helps set expectations for the potential outcomes of Applied Concept Mapping.

Similarly, Bennet Larson details a number of his case studies using Concept Mapping, though for quite different applications, in Chapter 5, Concept Mapping on the Road: Applied Business Concept Mapping in Software Implementation and Training Consulting.

Section II focuses on Recent Case Studies and Results, and presents in-depth examinations of specific applications and their results. Notably, many of the contributing teams include career practitioners, working alongside domain and industry experts to solve real-world problems.

In Chapter 6, Using Concept Maps to Improve the Practice and Organization of Intelligence in Canada, Natalia Derbentseva and David R. Mandel present the results of their effort to introduce Concept Mapping into the defense and security community. Their chapter provides an empirical look at how a potential user community envisions applications of Concept Mapping.

Andrew G. Harter and Brian M. Moon, in Chapter 7, Common Lexicon Initiative: A Concept Mapping Approach to Semiautomated Definition Integration, offer a methodological review of their original approach for using Concept Mapping to develop a common lexicon. It provides a first-of-its-kind, step-by-step method for moving toward consensus in meaning across a diverse group of practitioners.

From Australia, Andrea White shows how Concept Mapping was used with and compared to other modeling methods in Chapter 8, The Use of Concept Mapping in Ecological Management: A Case Study Involving Grassland Ecosystems. White clearly demonstrates that Concept Mapping has a place among other widely used methods for conceptual modeling.

Robert R. Hoffman, Jan Maarten Schraagen, Josine van de Ven, and Brian M. Moon put Concept Mapping to use for TNO, the government-funded applied science organization in The Netherlands, and they describe a number of applications in Chapter 9, Influencing the Business Model and Innovations of a Research Organization through Concept Mapping. The chapter is also a good example of Concept Mapping taking root in an organization.

Chapter 10, Concept Mapping Ecosystem Goods and Services, revisits the domain of ecosystem management. Susan H. Yee, John E. Rogers, Jim

Harvey, William Fisher, Marc Russell, and Patricia Bradley offer a look at how they used Concept Mapping to synthesize and visualize large amounts of complex information in the service of developing shared understanding.

In Chapter 11, Concept Mapping in Corporate Education: Experiences at Petrobrás University, Acacia Z. Kuenzer, Wilson L. Lanzarini, and Eleonora B. Taveira provide an overview of the adoption of Meaningful Learning and Concept Mapping into the corporate university of an international energy company. The chapter highlights the epistemological rationale, and details how Concept Mapping has impacted their corporate learning program.

Barbara J. Daley, Michael R. Lovell, Ronald A. Perez, and Nathaniel E. Stern, in Chapter 12, Using Concept Maps within the Product Design Process in Engineering: A Case Study, show the evolution of Concept Mapping in the course of the design process. Specifically, they illustrate how designers' sense of the engineering process and evolving design change are changed by Concept Maps.

Finally, with Chapter 13, Improving Organizational Learning with Concept Maps: A Business Case Study, David Barberá-Tomás, Mónica Elizabeth Edwards Schachter, and Ernesto de los Reyes-López return to the roots of Concept Mapping to explore and demonstrate how meaningful learning can be applied at the organizational level using Concept Maps.

Section III is titled Pushing the Boundaries. Contributors to this section have in different ways explored what is possible, and where the boundary conditions lie, with Applied Concept Mapping.

In Chapter 14, Conceptual Mapping as the First Step of Data Modeling, Hector Gómez-Gauchía and Ron McFadyen show how an attempt to solve one problem using Concept Maps, i.e., conceptualizing database design, led to the need to introduce a highly structured approach to address linguistic differences and merge Concept Mapping with known modeling approaches. The chapter presents and assesses what is possible on both fronts.

In Chapter 15, Concept Mapping in Virtual Collaboration Environments, Brian M. Moon, Jeffery T. Hansberger, and Austin Tate report on experimentation integrating Concept Mapping into 3-D virtual environments. They offer a suite of lessons learned from the effort, and guidance for forging into these growing terrains.

The volume closes with a personal narrative from Carrie Ann Desnoyers in Chapter 16, Vying for the Use of CmapTools in Corporate Training, which chronicles her attempts at importing Concept Mapping using CmapTools into a corporate environment. Inclusion of this story in Section III serves to remind us how challenging some of the most basic boundaries to adoption continue to be.

NOTES ABOUT THE FIGURES

It should by now be appreciated that diversity is a notion that ought to be invoked when thinking about Applied Concept Mapping. There is no such thing as a "right" or "perfect" Concept Map, or even a "proper" application of Concept Mapping. We believe the flexibility of Applied Concept Mapping is one of its key strengths.

That said, publication imposes certain requirements for conformity. For our contributors, the use of grey scale in figures was one such requirement. Many of the Concept Maps that appear in the chapters were originally created in color, and use of color was a vital component for problem solving or knowledge portrayal. Where possible, the contributors have provided Internet addresses to their Concept Maps, where they can be viewed in full color. Additionally, all figures can be viewed at this volume's companion Website—www.appliedconceptmapping.info.

Most of the Concept Maps were created with CmapTools, and many of the Concept Maps included in their original form links to other resources. We did not impose a requirement to strip the Concept Maps of their resource links in the figures so that the interconnectedness of Concept Maps and their resources could be displayed. Thus, many of the Concept Maps include icons, such as those shown in Figure I.3. Where allowable, the contributors have provided Internet addresses to their Concept Maps, where the resource links are active and can be used to explore other resources.

FIGURE I.3
Resource icons.

Finally, many of Concept Maps presented are examples of "works in progress." The contributors have chosen to share working products to illustrate how the Concept Maps have been useful at places along the continuum of their work. Thus, many of the Concept Maps may appear unfinished. In reality, no Concept Map is ever finished. Knowledge, problems, and solutions are constantly in flux.

FINAL REMARKS

We opened this introduction and overview with a quotation from one of the most important of the philosophers of the twentieth century, Karl R. Popper—"All life is problem solving" (Popper, 1999). It fits well with the theme of the volume. Popper came to this perspective in much the same way Applied Concept Mapping has come to take it on. He began his career as a school teacher, certified to teach mathematics, physics, chemistry, and biology. In service of his school teaching, he mastered the craft of cabinet-making, and it was while working at a cabinetmaker's bench that he arrived at his first solution of a philosophical problem: the origin of the Western system of classical music: tonality, harmony, and counterpoint. The story, Popper said, was indicative of how he lived his entire life:

> I become acquainted with a subject, maybe superficially to start with, then more deeply because I am fascinated by some problem. Then—in some cases soon, in other cases after some years, perhaps even after some new problems in other fields have begun to interest me more—a problem or an idea may crystallize in my mind and lead to intense work; that means, I begin to think intensely about the problem, I try to clarify it, simplify it, often in the light of a new idea, and the problem may considerably change its character. A tentative solution may turn up; and upon further intense work, this solution may change considerably, in interaction with the changing problem. Sometimes all of this happens only in my mind, and the proposed solution is never written down; or it is written down fifty years later … At other times, I may write down notes at various stages of the process, or *I may draw a diagram* … [But] sometimes I forget my result for years—or, worst of all, forever (emphasis added, p. 154).

Popper did not recommend his way of working: "On the contrary, I wish to discourage all my listeners from adopting so hazardous a method" (though he also noted that it served him quite well, 1999, p. 154). We not only recommend it, we strongly encourage it, especially that part about drawing a diagram. Applied Concept Mapping is about finding problems, doing the intensive work to clarify and simplify them, and viewing them in light of other problems, *all while drawing the diagram*, so that the solutions are not lost but carried forward and connected to others.

REFERENCES

Basque, J., B. Pudelko, and M. Léonard. 2004. Collaborative knowledge modeling between experts and novices: A strategy to support transfer of expertise in an organization. In *Concept Maps: Theory, Methodology, Technology, Proceedings of the First International Conference on Concept Mapping*, eds. A. Cañas, J. Novak, and F. González. Pamplona, Spain.

Bennett, P. W. and K. Fraser. 1990. *Using concept maps to improve communication effectiveness at Kodak*. Department of Education, Cornell University, Ithaca, NY.

Blickensderfer, E., J. A. Cannon-Bowers, and E. Salas. 1997. Theoretical bases for team self-corrections: Fostering shared mental models. In *Advances in Interdisciplinary Studies of Work Teams*, Vol. 4, eds. M. M. Beyerlin, D. A. Johnson, and S. T. Beyerlein. Greenwhich, U.K.: JAI Press.

Brewer, I. and M. McNeese. 2004. Expanding concept mapping to address spatio-temporal dimensionality. In *Concept Maps: Theory, Methodology, Technology, Proceedings of the First International Conference on Concept Mapping*, eds. A. Cañas, J. Novak, and F. González. Pamplona, Spain.

Briggs, G., D. Shamma, and A. J. Cañas, et al. 2004. Concept Maps applied to Mars exploration public outreach. In *Concept Maps: Theory, Methodology, Technology, Proceedings of the First International Conference on Concept Mapping*, eds. A. Cañas, J. Novak, and F. González. Pamplona, Spain.

Cahuzac, H., and B. Le Blanc. 2004. From intuitive mapping to concept mapping: An application within an anthropological urban field study. In *Concept Maps: Theory, Methodology, Technology, Proceedings of the First International Conference on Concept Mapping*, eds. A. Cañas, J. Novak, and F. González. Pamplona, Spain.

Cañas, A., K. Ford, and J. Brennan, et al. 1995. Knowledge construction and sharing in quorum. Paper presented at the Seventh World Conference on Artificial Intelligence in Education, Washington, D.C.

Cañas, A. J., G. Hill, et al. 2004. CmapTools: A knowledge modeling and sharing environment. In *Concept Maps: Theory, Methodology, Technology, Proceedings of the First International Conference on Concept Mapping*, eds. A. Cañas, J. Novak, and F. González. Pamplona, Spain.

Cañas, A. J., R. Carff, and G. Hill, et al. 2005. Concept Maps: Integrating knowledge and information visualization. In *Knowledge and Information Visualization: Searching for Synergies*, eds. S. O. Tergan and T. Keller. Heidelberg/New York: Springer Lecture Notes in Computer Science.

Castro A. G., P. Rocca-Serra, R. Stevens, C. Taylor, K. Nashar, M. A. Ragan, and S. A. Sansone. 2006. The use of concept maps during knowledge elicitation in ontology development processes—the nutrigenomics use case. *BMC Bioinformatics* 25 (7): 267.

CMC 2004, 2006, 2008, 2010. Available online at http://cmc.ihmc.us.

Coffey, J. W. 2004. Facilitating idea generation and decision making with concept maps. *Journal of Information and Knowledge Management* 3 (2): 179–192.

Coffey, J. 2006. In The Heat Of The Moment ... Strategies, Tactics, and Lessons Learned Regarding Interactive Knowledge Modeling with Concept Maps. *Concept Maps: Theory, Methodology, Technology, Proceedings of the Second International Conference on Concept Mapping*, eds. A. Cañas and J. Novak. San Jose, Costa Rica.

Coffey, J. W., Cãnas, A. J., Reichherzer, T. et al. 2003. Knowledge modeling and the creation of El-tech: A performance support system for electronic technicians. Expert systems with applications, 25(4): 483-492.

Coffey, J. W. and T. C. Eskridge. 2004. A Knowledge Retention Pilot Study in the Nuclear Power Industry: Activities, Achievements, and Challenges. Technical Report to the Electrical Power Research Institute (EPRI), Palo Alto, CA.

Coffey, J., D. Moreman, and J. Dyer. 1999. Institutional memory preservation at NASA Lewis Research Center. In *Proceedings of the HBCU/OMU Research Conference* (Historically Black Colleges and Universities/Other Minority Universities) Conference. John H. Glenn Reseearch Center, Cleveland, OH. April 25–26.

Coffey, J. and T. Eskridge. (2008). Case studies of knowledge modeling for knowledge preservation and sharing in the US nuclear power industry. *IJKM* 7 (3): 173–185.

Crandall, B., G. Klein, and R. R. Hoffman. 2006. *Working minds: A practitioner's guide to cognitive task analysis.* Cambridge, MA: MIT Press.

de los Reyes, E. and D. Barberá. 2004. Los mapas conceptuales como herramienta de aprendizaje organizaciaonal: Aproximación a un marco teórico y presentación de resultados parciales de un proyecto. In *Concept Maps: Theory, Methodology, Technology, Proceedings of the First International Conference on Concept Mapping,* eds. A. Cañas, J. Novak, and F. González. Pamplona, Spain.

Derbentseva, N., F. Sayafeni, and A. Cañas. 2004. Experiments on the effects of map structure and concept quantification during concept map construction. In *Concept Maps: Theory, Methodology, Technology, Proceedings of the First International Conference on Concept Mapping,* eds. A. Cañas, J. Novak, and F. González. Pamplona, Spain.

Dumestre, J. 2004. Using CmapTools software to assist in job task analysis. In *Concept Maps: Theory, Methodology, Technology, Proceedings of the First International Conference on Concept Mapping,* eds. A. Cañas, J. Novak, and F. González. Pamplona, Spain.

Electric Power Research Institute (2002). *Guidelines for capturing valuable undocumented knowledge from energy industry personnel,* Palo Alto, CA. 1004663.

Ford, K. M., J. W. Coffey, and A. J. Cañas, et al. 1996. Diagnosis and explanation by a nuclear cardiology expert system. *International Journal of Expert Systems* 9: 499–506.

Fourie, L. 2005. Computer-based concept mapping tools in business. Paper presented at the Proceedings of the San Diego International Systems Conference, San Diego State University.

Fourie, L., J. Schilawa, and E. Cloete. 2004. The value of concept maps for knowledge management in the banking and insurance industry: A German case study. In *Concept Maps: Theory, Methodology, Technology, Proceedings of the First International Conference on Concept Mapping,* eds. A. Cañas, J. Novak, and F. González. Pamplona, Spain.

Fourie, L. and T. van der Westhuizen. 2008. The value and use of concept maps in the alignment of strategic intent. In *Concept Mapping: Connecting Educators: Proceedings of the Third International Conference on Concept Mapping,* eds. A. Cañas, P. Reiska, M. Åhlberg, and J. Novak. Tallinn, Estonia and Helsinki, Finland.

Fraser, K. M. 1993. Theory based use of concept mapping in organization development: Creating shared understanding as a basis for the cooperative design of work changes and changes in working relationships. PhD diss. (unpublished), Cornell University.

Freeman, L. A. 2004. The power and benefits of concept mapping: Measuring use, usefulness, ease of use, and satisfaction. In *Concept Maps: Theory, Methodology, Technology, Proceedings of the First International Conference on Concept Mapping,* eds. A. Cañas, J. Novak, and F. González. Pamplona, Spain.

Hoffman, R. R., J. W. Coffey, and K. M. Ford. 2000. A case study in the research paradigm of human-centered computing: Local expertise in weather forecasting. Report on the contract "Human-Centered System Prototype." Washington, D.C.: National Technology Alliance.

Hoffman, R. R., J. W. Coffey, M. J. Carnot, and J. D. Novak. 2002. An empirical comparison of methods for eliciting and modeling expert knowledge. Paper presented at the Meeting of the Human Factors and Ergonomics Society, Baltimore, Maryland.

Hoffman, R., R. Hewett, D. Shamma, A. Orway, and J. Yerkes. 2001. The Thailand National Knowledge Base Demonstration Project. Available online at http://cmapskm.ihmc.us/rid=1052620868542_1172726424_3865/Demonstration Project Top Map.cmap.

Hoffman, R. and L. Shattuck. 2006. Should we rethink how we do OPORDS? *Military Review*. March/April: 100–107.

Kaste, R., R. Heilman, and R. R. Hoffman. 2007. Concept map value propagation for tactical intelligence. Paper presented at the 12th International Command and Control Research and Technology Symposium: Adapting C2 to the 21st Century." Newport, RI. June.

Kozminsky, L., N. Nurit, E. Kozminsky, and B. Gurion. 2008. Using concept mapping to construct new knowledge while analyzing research data: The case of the grounded theory method. In *Concept Mapping: Connecting Educators: Proceedings of the Third International Conference on Concept Mapping,* eds. A. Cañas, P. Reiska, M. Åhlberg, and J. Novak. Tallinn, Estonia and Helsinki, Finland.

Mazur, J. 1989. Using concept maps in therapy with substance abusers in the context of Gowin's theory of educating. Master's thesis (unpublished), Cornell University.

Moon, B. 2004. Concept maps and wagon wheels: Merging methods to improve the understanding of team dynamics. In *Concept Maps: Theory, Methodology, Technology, Proceedings of the First International Conference on Concept Mapping,* eds. A. Cañas, J. Novak, and F. González. Pamplona, Spain.

Moon, B., A. Pino, and C. Hedberg. 2006. Studying transformation: The use of Cmaptools in surveying the integration of intelligence and operations. In *Concept Maps: Theory, Methodology, Technology, Proceedings of the Second International Conference on Concept Mapping,* eds. A. Cañas and J. Novak. San José, Costa Rica.

Moon, B., R. Hoffman, and L. Shattuck, et al. 2008. Rapid and accurate idea transfer: Evaluating concept maps against other formats for the transfer of complex information. In *Concept Mapping: Connecting Educators: Proceedings of the Third International Conference on Concept Mapping,* eds. A. Cañas, P. Reiska, M. Åhlberg, and J. Novak. Tallinn, Estonia and Helsinki, Finland.

Moon, B. and R. Hoffman. 2008. Rapid and accurate idea transfer: Presenting ideas with concept maps. Scientific and Technical Final Report. Contract No. W31P4Q-08-C-0229. Washington, D.C.: Defense Technical Information Center.

Moon, B., R. Hoffman, and D. Ziebell. 2009. How did you do that? *Electric Perspectives Magazine* 34 (1). Edison Electric Institute, Washington, D.C.

Moon, B. and M. Kelley. 2010. Lessons learned in knowledge elicitation with nuclear experts. Paper presented at the 7th International Topical Meeting on Nuclear Plant Instrumentation, Control and Human Machine Interface Technologies, Las Vegas, NV.

Okada, A., S. B. Shum, and T. Sherborne. 2008. *Knowledge cartography: Software tools and mapping techniques.* London: Springer.

Novak, J. and D. Gowin. 1984. *Learning how to learn*. New York and Cambridge, UK: Cambridge University Press.

Novak, J. 2010. *Learning, creating and using knowledge: Concept maps as facilitative tools in schools and corporations*, 2nd ed. New York: Routledge.

Perigean Technologies LLC. 2010. Available online at www.perigeantechnologies.com.

Preciado, D., L. Gallo, and A. Tenorio. 2008. The concept map as a tool for designing a competitiveness and innovation system for Cauca – Colombia. In *Concept Mapping: Connecting Educators: Proceedings of the Third International Conference on Concept Mapping*, eds. A. Cañas, P. Reiska, M. Åhlberg, and J. Novak. Tallinn, Estonia and Helsinki, Finland.

Popper, K. 1999. *All life is problem solving*. London: Routledge.

Ramírez, C., W. Flórez, and R. Barros. 2008. Concept maps: A strategy for the development of technical reports on industrial engineering problems. In *Concept Mapping: Connecting Educators: Proceedings of the Third International Conference on Concept Mapping*, eds. A. Cañas, P. Reiska, M. Åhlberg, and J. Novak. Tallinn, Estonia and Helsinki, Finland.

Roam, D. 2009a. *The Back of the Napkin: Solving Problems and Selling Ideas with Pictures*. Portfolio: New York.

Roam, D. 2009b. *Unfolding the Napkin: The Hands-On Method for Solving Complex Problems with Simple Pictures*. Portfolio: New York.

Salerno, F., E. Cuccillato, and R. Muetzelfeldt, et al. 2008. Concept maps for combining hard and soft system thinking in the management of socio-ecosystems. In *Concept Mapping: Connecting Educators: Proceedings of the Third International Conference on Concept Mapping*, eds. A. Cañas, P. Reiska, M. Åhlberg, and J. Novak. Tallinn, Estonia and Helsinki, Finland.

Sibbett, D. 2010. *Visual Meetings: How Graphics, Sticky Notes and Idea Mapping Can Transform Group Productivity*. Wiley: Hoboken, NJ.

Simard, J. 2010. *Cirque du Soleil Concept Mapping*. Video Presentation at the Fourth International Conference on Concept Mapping. Viña del Mar, Chile. October 6.

Section I

Practitioners' View

1

Applying Educational Tools and Ideas in the Corporate World

Joseph D. Novak and Alberto J. Cañas

CONTENTS

INTRODUCTION

Concept Mapping originated within the education community as a tool to assess the understanding of elementary school science students. Soon after, it became clear that a tool that facilitates the expression of one's knowledge and understanding for any topic—in a simple graphical format that is easy to comprehend by others—could be used by people of all ages and for all purposes, and in all types of organizations beyond schools. Thus, Concept Mapping, as we describe it, began to be used in corporations some 20 years ago. The use of Concept

Mapping worldwide took a huge leap some years later with the marriage of Concept Mapping to technology, particularly the Internet and the Web. Today, this union enables the collaborative construction, easy sharing, and publishing of Concept Maps, making Concept Mapping feasible at large scale within organizations.

In this chapter, we cover the origins of Concept Maps, what Concept Maps are, and the initial attempts by Joseph Novak to use them in the corporate world. We then describe how the potential for Concept Mapping gave rise to the features in the CmapTools software, and concomitantly, how the development of CmapTools accelerated the adoption of Concept Mapping in the workplace. We conclude with thoughts about the necessity for continuing to apply education ideas in corporate worlds.

DEVELOPMENT OF CONCEPT MAPPING

Upon completion of his PhD studies at the University of Minnesota in 1957, Novak took a position in the Biology Department at Kansas State Teacher's College. The position allowed him to continue his research interests in both biology and in education. It was his belief then, as it remains today, that significant improvements in education require better theoretical foundations, and that research in education needed to be more theory based, as it is in the sciences (Novak, 1963). The major problem he saw then was that the only learning theory common in education was behavioral learning theory. He saw little relevance for this theory for human leaning in schools or other settings. Moreover, behavioral psychology was deeply rooted in positivistic epistemology that sought to establish "laws" of learning. Novak was much more inclined to an epistemology of the kind described by James Conant (1947) as "evolving conceptual schemes." Fortunately, Ausubel's cognitive theory of learning was published in 1963 (Ausubel, 1963), and Kuhn's *Structure of Scientific Revolutions* was published in 1962 (Kuhn, 1962). Novak's group quickly adopted ideas from these and related works to guide their research and instructional innovation programs.

In 1965, while on sabbatical leave at Harvard University, Novak began developing audio-tutorial lessons (Postlethwait, Novak, and Murray, 1964) to teach science to first-grade children, providing them with hands-on experiences with science materials and audio-guided instruction (Novak, 1972). Together with his graduate students, Novak continued to develop such lessons after he moved to Cornell University in 1967. When they had a sufficient number of these lessons developed, they launched a long-term study to see how instruction in basic science concepts in grades one and two would influence later learning of science. The biggest challenge in their longitudinal study was how to record and observe changes in students' understanding of science concepts. Novak's team came up with the idea of transforming interview transcripts with children into hierarchically arranged concept and propositional statements, thereby showing explicitly the concepts and propositions these students had acquired. Thus was born the Concept Map tool as shown in Figure 1.1. It allowed the research group to follow cognitive changes in children's science knowledge over time in a highly precise way (Novak, 2004). Novak soon found that Concept Maps were also a powerful tool for helping people learn (Novak and Gowin, 1984), helping teams solve problems, and do better research, and archiving knowledge (Novak, 1998; 2010).

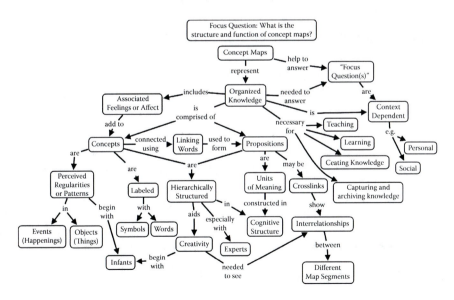

FIGURE 1.1
Concept Map showing the key features of Concept Maps.

Fundamentals of Concept Maps

There are other forms of representation for knowledge, many of which are described by Jonassen and his colleagues (Jonassen et al., 1993). Most of these are not based on an explicit theory of human learning, lack clear epistemological foundations, and fail to make a clear explication of the basic building blocks of knowledge, namely concepts and propositions. We define *concept* as a perceived regularity or pattern in events or objects designated by a label (usually a word or two words). Concepts are what children begin to acquire soon after birth, and by age three all normally developing children have a functional knowledge of several hundred concepts. Moreover, they begin to combine two concepts into simple statements about a thing or event and form propositions. *Propositions* are really the *basic units of meanings* people form, and consist of two concepts joined by linking words to make a meaningful statement. Unfortunately, many knowledge representation tools have concepts or nodes linked with lines, but with no words to indicate the relationship between the concepts or nodes. Still other forms of maps may have a limited set of links, such as "can be," "is a," "kind of," etc., and have been introduced only recently, most often in the context of computerized diagram making. While they offer more opportunity for computer manipulation, they fail to express precise meanings that characterize knowledge or expertise in any field.

Concept Maps are usually structured hierarchically, with more general, more inclusive concepts higher in the structure. This arrangement is consistent with Ausubel's contention that knowledge is stored hierarchically in cognitive structure and more recent studies on expert knowledge and cognitive structure properties (cf., Bransford et al., 1999). These ideas are represented in Figure 1.1. Concept Maps that possess these properties are sometimes referred to as "Novakian" Concept Maps in recognition of his pioneering work.

APPLICATION TO THE BUSINESS WORLD

As the use of Concept Mapping in education expanded, so did interest from other sectors of society. In 1990, Professor Alan McAdams of the Johnson Business School at Cornell University and Novak, together with their students, began working with corporations to demonstrate how communication between senior managers, section managers, and employees might be improved with the use of Concept Maps. Working with the vice president for sensitized components manufacturing for Eastman Kodak, they transferred a presentation made to managers and employees into Concept Maps. By doing so, they demonstrated that critical concepts and relationships between concepts had been omitted. They also showed that these omissions were evident in Concept Maps made from interviews with section managers. Thus began a series of projects with various business groups using the Concept Map tool to help with corporate communications, interpreting customers' explicit and tacit wants, and organizing knowledge for problem solving.

Promising as these small projects appeared to be, none of the corporations chose to implement the use of the Concept Mapping tool on a wider scale. It became obvious that introducing significant new ideas in corporations was even more difficult than working with schools, as others have since learned (cf., Chapter 16). Nevertheless, it was also obvious that the ideas and tools could have significant benefits to corporations.

Proctor and Gamble™

In 1993, Novak attended meetings in Cincinnati, Ohio, sponsored by Procter and Gamble (P&G) to introduce university professors and administrators to corporate practices, such as Total Quality Management (TQM). One of the presenters was Larry Huston, who later became vice president for Knowledge and Innovation for P&G. He indicated that P&G was seeking ways to make research and development (R&D) work more efficiently, but so far they had made only modest progress. Huston was searching for new tools. As Huston was leaving the auditorium, Novak handed him two papers (Novak, 1990a; 1990b) and suggested that these papers describe tools that might be useful to his R&D people. To his surprise, Novak had a phone message from Huston when he returned to his room at lunchtime inviting him to come to Huston's office. Novak spent most of the afternoon with Huston and his assistant explaining how Concept Maps and vee diagrams could facilitate research productivity, citing some of the work he had done with Kodak and Corning corporations.

However, Novak did not get an invitation to meet with a P&G research team until late December in 1993. He learned later that he was the last of a dozen or more consultants who were brought in to "show their tools," including everything from de Bono's Six Thinking Hats' method for fostering creativity to several forms of mind mapping. When Novak met with a team of 18 R&D staff on December 28, they appeared resigned to hearing about another boring bag of tricks. Within an hour, however, the team had reviewed some of the key principles and the theory behind Concept Maps, and even began to define a good "focus question" for the problem the team had been given some two years ago. By late afternoon, all 18 R&D people had collectively produced a large Concept Map dealing with the new paper product they were charged to produce. As a consequence of capturing most of the conceptual and propositional knowledge pertinent to their problem, this research team saw that one of the approaches they had been pursing could not possibly work and other pathways appeared more promising. They also realized that they were missing a specific kind of chemist whose ideas they needed on this team. Within two months, the team had produced a prototype of the new product, and was ready for limited consumer testing.

Thus began a five-year collaboration between Novak and P&G. Working mostly with R&D teams early on, Novak found that the procedures he and his colleagues had evolved worked very efficiently. Novak found, for example, that by conducting consultations with a team leader prior to a meeting with the entire team, one or two good focus questions could be identified for the team's problem and five or six "top" concepts for a Concept Map. This preliminary work enabled the team to produce a "global" Concept Map to clearly state the team's problem. Typically, two to four subteams were then identified based on each individual's expertise. Team members were assigned to subteams to Concept Map in more detail some section of the "global" Concept Map. When subteams completed their work (usually in one to two hours), the entire group met together to review the Concept Maps, and to suggest ways to combine the work of the subgroups and revise the "global" Concept Map for the project. Novak found that participants could progress in one day from an orientation to Concept Mapping, discussion of the project focus question, preparation of a preliminary "global map" for the project, subteam Concept Mapping, and refining the global map.

All of the Concept Mapping was done using Post-it' notes placed on butcher paper with linking lines and words added as the Concept Map took shape. A P&G staff member or Novak's associates would later render

FIGURE 1.2
A subteam working on a Concept Map using Post-it notes.

the Post-it note maps to digital Concept Maps using Inspiration™ software, and these digital maps would be shared with all team members. The team leader would frequently seek additional input and suggestions on the evolving Concept Map, sometimes including other experts who were not present during the team meeting. Figure 1.2 shows an example of team members working on Post-it-based Concept Maps.

What was impressive was how efficiently the whole process used expensive staff time and how productive the Concept Maps proved to be. After numerous successes with R&D teams, P&G began using Concept Maps to help with other problems, for example, how to write better applications for approval of a product by the U.S. Food and Drug Administration (FDA). The FDA Concept Map came about following a presentation of a Concept Map on vaginal infections to the CEO of P&G, John Pepper, and several vice presidents. Pepper said he could see immediately from this Concept Map that vaginal pH and *lactobacillus* were important to consider because so many links went into and out of these concepts. Pepper said he had spent the morning talking to FDA people, and thought there was a need to improve the way P&G prepared new applications to the FDA. One of the team leaders from an earlier project was asked to prepare a Concept Map on dealing with the FDA, and in a few weeks he had a highly useful map, which included ideas that were new to him even though he had been writing such applications for 20 years. Subsequently, he used this Concept Map to instruct new P&G staff members on the preparation of FDA applications.

Another area where P&G found the process of preparation of Concept Maps to be helpful was in bringing together staff people from R&D and from marketing. These groups traditionally use very different concepts in their work, and frequently their communication is quite poor. By bringing marketing and R&D personnel together in the same room and building Concept Maps together, R&D personnel came to understand better the consumer needs and desires, and marketing personnel came to understand some of the technical issues in new product development. The net effect was that both groups felt they were empowered with the knowledge acquired in the Concept Map building process and the numerous, clearly focused conversations that took place during the sessions.

With the many successes he had experienced in training P&G personnel to use the Concept Mapping tool, Novak had hoped that he could move into another phase of work where management teams would build Concept Maps to deal with management problems, as he had successfully done at Kodak. Unfortunately, the opportunity to engage on these issues was not presented. Novak completed his work with P&G in December 1998, having passed along much expertise in Concept Mapping to P&G personnel.

Concurrent with Novak's work in the business world, advances in computer-based Concept Mapping were underway at the University of West Florida.

DEVELOPMENT OF THE CmapTools SOFTWARE

Following Novak's sabbatical at the University of West Florida in 1986 to 1987, Ken Ford and Bruce Dunn became interested in using Concept Maps to elicit expertise. Trained in artificial intelligence (AI), Ford recognized that Concept Maps were a powerful tool for capturing and representing expert knowledge, the first requirement for creating an effective expert system (Ford et al., 1991). An early project involved the capturing of the expertise of a cardiologist (Dr. Jim Andrews) and the knowledge required to interpret computer images of coronary functions in a technique called First Pass Functional Imaging. This project demonstrated that Concept Maps could be used to capture expertise in cardiology and facilitated the development of NUCES, a rule-based training program for cardiologists in the use of Dr. Andrews' methods (Ford et al., 1996). More importantly, NUCES showed the use of Concept Mapping as a navigation tool, whereby icons underneath the concept linked to other Concept Maps and resources, such as videos, images, and texts (Cañas et al., 1994). Thus, having the set of Concept Maps and associated resources served as the explanation component for the expert system (Ford, Cañas, and Coffey, 1993). The Concept Maps in NUCES, however, were hard-coded; there was no Concept Map editor in the system.

As part of Project Quorum, a joint partnership between the University of West Florida and IBM Latin America in 1993, Cañas led the development of software that networked schools throughout Latin America. The network enabled collaboration among students using modems and IBM's Corporate Network before the Internet arrived in some of those countries (Cañas et al., 1995a; 1995b). In addition to providing each student in every participating school with an e-mail address and the possibility of collaborating with other students through the sharing of Logo-based projects using LogoWriter˚ and MicroWorlds, e-mail, and discussion forums, the team developed a Concept Mapping editor that facilitated collaboration among students. The work spawned numerous innovations, to include Knowledge Soups (Cañas, Ford, and Novak et al., 2001) for sharing propositions and the Giant (Reichherzer, Cañas, and Ford et al., 1998), a software agent that collaborates with students during knowledge construction. The Quorum software later became an IBM product named Colabra, but was quickly taken out of the market when IBM Latin America drastically cut its funding for education.

The experience acquired from the use of Concept Maps for knowledge elicitation and as a navigational tool for a large corpus of resources in NUCES, and the innovative ideas for collaborative Concept Mapping from Quorum, served as the basis for the development of a new set of software tools for editing, sharing, and publishing Concept Maps. It had been demonstrated that Concept Mapping was as powerful a tool when used with elementary school children as with high performance experts. This potential user base called for tools that were both easy to learn and powerful. Moreover, the explosive growth of the Internet and the possibilities offered by the new World Wide Web called for simple mechanisms for publishing and sharing of Concept Maps on the Web. The challenge was to bridge the gap between the complexity of what was possible and the simplicity that was necessary.

CmapTools: A KNOWLEDGE MODELING AND SHARING KIT

With initial funding from the U.S. Navy and initially aimed at supporting online, just-in-time training, Cañas and his research team began the development of CmapTools (Cañas et al., 2004a) in 1997. The initial version of the software was successfully tested with the construction of El-Tech, a proof-of-concept, rule-based system to train electronic technicians for the Navy. In El-Tech, the Concept Maps were used as the explanation component and were organized as a "knowledge model," a collection of Concept Maps and linked resources about a particular topic (Coffey et al., 2003).

Collaboration with NASA provided additional funding to continue the development of the software into version 2. The focus of this wave of design was Concept Mapping that could be used by scientists at NASA's Astrobiology Institute at the Ames Research Center in Mountain View, California. To the basic features for constructing Concept Maps was added functionality for sharing Concept Maps among users in distant locations and in various types of collaboration.

Throughout the new millennium, CmapTools' use started to extend fast through the educational and corporate communities around the world. Its development continued with support from the Department of Defense, the government of Panamá, and Microsoft° Corporation.

Underlying the development of CmapTools has been a set of design principles.

The Design Principles of CmapTools

CmapTools was designed with several key objectives in mind. First, the software was to have a low threshold and a high ceiling: Myers, Hudson, and Pausch (2000) refer to the "threshold" as how difficult it is to learn how to use a system, and the "ceiling" as how much can be done using that system. Experience has shown that users can be constructing a Concept

Map within five to ten minutes of their encounter with the software. Even users who have never used a computer, or even a keyboard or a mouse, can begin building Concept Maps once they feel comfortable with the devices. The extensive use by learners and professionals that have been globally demonstrated and are the topic of this volume clearly demonstrates CmapTools' tremendously high ceiling.

Knowledge Models

The second objective was to provide extensive support for the construction of large knowledge models. An in-depth mapping of any domain implies the construction of huge maps that are usually unmanageable, or the decomposition of the domain into a more manageable set of linked maps. In CmapTools, a set of Concept Maps and associated resources about a particular domain is referred to as a "knowledge model" (Cañas, Hill, and Lott, 2003; Cañas et al., 2005). CmapTools aims at supporting the development of knowledge models of all sizes, without limitations of where the resources and maps physically reside.

As part of the initial development work with NASA, Geoff Briggs from the Center for Mars Exploration at NASA's Ames Research Center started developing "Mars 2001," a large knowledge model about Mars that covers all aspects of the planet. The knowledge model continues to be updated and currently includes over 300 Concept Maps and thousands of linked resources (http://cmex.ihmc.us) (Briggs et al., 2004). Briggs' works showed that CmapTools could indeed support the development of such large knowledge models.

To establish the relationships between Concept Maps in a knowledge model, CmapTools facilitates the linking of Concept Maps through simple drag-and-drop operations, making it easy to construct a navigation environment where the users follow links from one Concept Map to another. In the same way, the user can establish links to all types of resources (e.g., images, videos, sound clips, texts, PowerPoint˚ slides, MSWord˚ documents, PDFs, etc.) that are related to and complement the information in the Concept Map. Such resources can reside anywhere on the Internet, intranets, and even local computers. The links are depicted as small icons underneath the concepts or linking phrases (shown in the Introduction of this book). The icon itself portrays the type of resource targeted by the link, and labels are displayed explaining each link when the icon is clicked, making it easy for the user to decide whether to follow the link or not. As

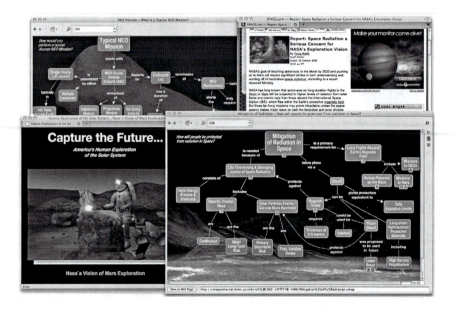

FIGURE 1.3

A knowledge model developed using CmapTools showing Concept Maps and linked resources.

an example, Figure 1.3 shows several windows opened as a result of navigating through a knowledge model on human space exploration.

On the Concept Map about "mitigation of radiation in space" (Figure 1.3), a small icon underneath the concept "Missions to NEOs" can be seen on the top right of the figure. This icon, depicting a Concept Map, indicates there is one or more links to Concept Maps *about* "Missions to NEOs." By clicking on one of these links, the Concept Map on the top left of the figure is opened and displayed (Typical NEO Mission). In the same way, clicking on the "video" icon under the concept "Missions to Mars" opens a Web page with a video as displayed on the lower left window "Capture the Future …." The top right window is a Web page on radiation hazards that was also opened through a link in the Concept Map.

Figure 1.3 also shows how styles can be used to provide a more stylized and professional look to the Concept Maps, including background images for the Concept Map and for concepts. The Concept Maps in their original colors show the use of colors for the background, for concepts, for the texts, etc. To create a knowledge model such as this, users simply "drag-and-drop" the different resources (e.g., the URL for a Web page, the file for an image or video, etc.) onto the concepts and fill in the label that will be requested in a dialog box.

If the Concept Maps are stored in a Place, i.e., a server computer running the CmapServer software that is part of the CmapTools suite, the Concept Maps are automatically converted to Web pages. The links to resources behave exactly the same way on the Web pages as they do in CmapTools. In this way, the knowledge model becomes a Web site that can be navigated by anyone with a Web browser. Most knowledge models are published by storing them on CmapServers, without the participation of a Webmaster, technician, or programmer.

Editing Concept Maps stored on a computer or stored on a CmapServer is completely transparent. CmapTools provides a Views window that allows the user to organize the collection of Concept Maps and resources in folders, whether on a computer or on the server. Because of the way that CmapTools handles links between resources, moving the files around in the folders does not break any links, and, thus, users do not have to worry about lost "URLs" or paths to resources as when constructing regular Web pages. Moving Concept Maps and resources from the personal computer to the CmapServer is done through simple drag-and-drop operations across folders.

Publishing of Concept Maps by means of a CmapServer provides a simple mechanism to not only share and make public large knowledge models, but is also an effective way to publish Concept Maps from meetings, proposals, projects, specifications, etc. Users who need to modify these Concept Maps would use CmapTools, and users who only need to "read" them can use any Web browser.

Collaboration and Sharing

A third design principle concerns ease with which knowledge models can be shared and collaboration can be established. The CmapTools client is designed to automatically locate all Places (CmapServers) that have registered with a Directory of Places and allows users, through appropriate permissions and authentication, to access the Concept Maps and resources on those Places from anywhere on the Internet. Through the permissions mechanism, users can share folders and their contents, allowing teams distributed geographically to collaboratively build Concept Maps and knowledge models. If the team members open and try to edit a Concept Map on a CmapServer at the same time, a synchronous collaboration session is established that allows the team members to modify the map concurrently, communicating through a chat window that is part of the collaboration. (Voice communications can be handled through other means, e.g., phone or Skype™ connection.) In addition, CmapTools allows users to annotate each other's Concept Maps through Annotations, which simulate Post-it notes on the Concept Map. Users also can add a Discussion Thread to a concept or a linking phrase to go deeper into the discussion. Through the sharing of folders on the CmapServers, the synchronous collaboration, annotations, and discussion threads, the users have a rich collaboration environment with which to build their Concept Maps and knowledge models.

Other Features

The CmapTools suite includes many other features that can only be mentioned here. All Concept Maps stored in *publicly available* CmapServers are indexed, and an aggregated index allows users to search for Concept Maps worldwide. The Web site—http://www.cmappers.net—provides an interface to the aggregated index, which contains hundreds of thousands of Concept Maps. Of course, CmapServers hosted on corporate intranets are not publicly available, and any folder on a CmapServer can be password protected. Also on the security side, SSL (secure sockets layer) communication, together with PKI (public key infrastructure) certificates and LDAP (lightweight directory access protocol)-based authentication have been added for use in corporate environments.

The CmapTools client allows the user to search the Web, the index mentioned above, and any CmapServer to which users have access for Concept Maps, resources, or Web sites that are related to the selected concept within the context of the Concept Map. The context provides enough information to generate a query to Google that provides results that are more relevant than the regular queries users submit when searching the Web (Carvalho et al., 2001).

Similar tools that take advantage of the semantics provided by the Concept Map include access to a WordNet thesaurus and a concept Suggester that mines the Web and suggests possible concepts to add to the Concept Map (Cañas et al., 2004b).

A presentation module in CmapTools allows full-screen, stepwise display of a Concept Map for presentations in meetings, and a module has been added to CmapTools to convert it into an ontology editor, the CmapTools Ontology Editor (COE) (Hayes et al., 2005).

With the ongoing development of CmapTools, people all over the world have the opportunity to create, share, and present Concept Maps to the world. We conclude with our thoughts about why we believe this opportunity is important in the business community.

EDUCATION IDEAS IN THE CORPORATE WORLD

Human beings think with concepts. We organize our concepts in the cortical regions of our brain in a form psychologists call *cognitive structure*. But, human beings also have feelings and they act and react to objects and events they encounter. Truly competent people successfully integrate their thinking, feeling, and acting. They achieve this through a process we call *meaningful learning*, and this process depends both on the quality of the organization of knowledge in the learner's cognitive structure and the degree of commitment the learner has to integrate new concepts and propositions with existing relevant concepts and propositions.

Unfortunately, so much of school learning and corporate "training" relies primarily on rote memorization of information. Rote learning does almost nothing to help integrate thinking, feeling, and acting, nor does it build powerful knowledge structures. Building Concept Maps is not only a powerful way to capture and organize knowledge, it is also a process that encourages meaningful learning and a better understanding of the nature of knowledge and the nature of human learning. For some four decades, Novak has worked to make a science out of education and to develop a theory of education to guide this science (Novak, 1977). Simply stated, his theory of education is: *Meaningful learning underlies the constructive integration of thinking, feeling, and acting leading to empowerment for commitment and responsibility.*

If a corporation wants to enhance the power, commitment, and responsibility of its workers, it must seek to do everything possible to enhance meaningful learning by its workers at all levels of the organization. Meaningful learning, at its highest levels, becomes the engine for creativity.

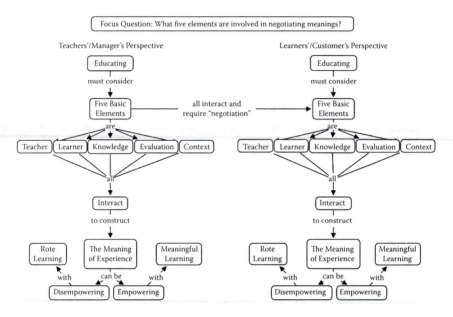

FIGURE 1.4

In Novak's theory of education, five elements are involved in every educative event and these need to be successfully negotiated between the teacher or manager and the learner or employee.

To encourage creativity we must encourage meaningful learning. Concept Maps can play a powerful facilitating role in this process (Novak and Gowin, 1984; Novak, 1998; 2010).

Meaningful learning is a profound concept. *Learning* is one of five elements involved in Novak's theory of education, the others being *teacher/manager* (good managers are good teachers), *context* of learning/managing, *knowledge*, and *evaluation*. All five of these elements interact, and it takes a very skillful teacher or manager to orchestrate education/management to optimize the effects of all five elements, as suggested in Figure 1.4. Moreover, we need to be aware of the learner's or employee's ideas on each of these elements, and there needs to be a *negotiation of meanings* between the teacher or manager and the learner or employee.

We can also consider customers as both learners and teachers, and skillful managers learn how to maximize learning from customers (cf., Lafley and Charan, 2008). In all of our work with corporations, we have found the theory of education we have been developing for work in education to be equally valid and useful in corporations. One might suggest, as many of our colleagues and clients have, that theory may be "fine in universities, but in the business world we need to deal with real practices." But as Kurt Lewin (1951) has pointed out, "There is nothing so practical as a good theory." Good theories *explain why* things work, or fail to work.

Almost every author of business and management books today recognizes the importance of knowledge in every enterprise. We live on what Friedman (2005) calls the *Flat Earth*, where neither mountains nor seas limit the flow of knowledge, goods, and services. On the Flat Earth, almost anything can be made anywhere and shipped anywhere, including knowledge, and the latter moves with the speed of light on the Internet and other transmissions. For a corporation to compete successfully in the Flat Earth economy, it is essential that every employee be encouraged to become highly effective at integrating their thinking, feeling, and acting.

It is our belief that we now know enough about the nature of learning, the nature of knowledge, the process of creating new knowledge, and ways to enhance meaningful learning to transform the way schools and corporations educate and empower their workers. What remains to be overcome is the inertia of schools and corporations to new ideas and new ways of learning. The most successful companies in the latter half of this century will have succeeded in doing this, and maybe our schools also will transform to achieve human empowerment.

REFERENCES

Ausubel, D. P. 1963. *The psychology of meaningful verbal learning*. New York: Grune and Stratton.

Bransford, J., A. L. Brown, and R. R. Cocking. 1999. *How people learn: Brain, mind, experience, and school*. Washington, D.C.: National Academy Press.

Briggs, G., D. Shamma, and A. J. Cañas, et al. 2004. Concept maps applied to Mars exploration public outreach. In *Concept Maps: Theory, Methodology, Technology, Proceedings of the First International Conference on Concept Mapping*, eds. A. J. Cañas, J. Novak, and F. González. Pamplona, Spain.

Cañas, A. J., K. M. Ford, and J. W. Coffey. 1994. Concept maps as a hypermedia navigational tool. Paper presented at the Seventh Florida Artificial Intelligence Research Symposium (FLAIRS), Pensacola, FL.

Cañas, A. J., K. M. Ford, and G. Hill, et al. 1995a. Quorum: A collaborative network for Latin American schools. Paper presented at the 12th International Conference on Technology and Education (ICTE '95), Orlando, FL.

Cañas, A. J., K. M. Ford, and G. Hill, et al. 1995b. Quorum: Children collaborating throughout Latin America. Paper presented at the Sixth IFIP World Conference on Computers in Education, Birmingham, U.K.

Cañas, A. J., K. M. Ford, and J. D. Novak et al. 2001. Online concept maps: Enhancing collaborative learning by using technology with concept maps. *The Science Teacher,* 68 (4): 49–51.

Cañas, A. J., G. Hill, and J. Lott. 2003. Support for constructing knowledge models in CmapTools. Technical Report No. IHMC CmapTools 2003-02. Pensacola, FL: Institute for Human and Machine Cognition.

Cañas, A. J., G. Hill, and R. Carff, et al. 2004a. CmapTools: A knowledge modeling and sharing environment. In *Concept Maps: Theory, Methodology, Technology, Proceedings of the First International Conference on Concept Mapping,* eds. A. J. Cañas, J. Novak, and F. González. Pamplona, Spain.

Cañas, A. J., M. Carvalho, and M. Arguedas, et al. 2004b. Mining the Web to suggest concepts during concept map construction. In *Concept Maps: Theory, Methodology, Technology, Proceedings of the First International Conference on Concept Mapping,* eds. A. J. Cañas, J. Novak, and F. González. Pamplona, Spain.

Cañas, A. J., R. Carff, and G. Hill, et al. 2005. Concept maps: Integrating knowledge and information visualization. In *Knowledge and Information Visualization: Searching for Synergies* (pp. 205–219), eds. S.-O. Tergan and T. Keller. Heidelberg/NY: Springer Lecture Notes in Computer Science.

Carvalho, M. R., R. Hewett, and A. J. Cañas. 2001. Enhancing Web searches from concept map-based knowledge models. In *Proceedings of SCI 2001: Fifth Multiconference on Systems, Cybernetics and Informatics* (pp. 69–73), eds. N. Callaos, F. G. Tinetti, J. M. Champarnaud, and J. K. Lee. Orlando, FL: International Institute of Informatics and Systemics.

Conant, J. B. 1947. *On understanding science: An historical approach.* New Haven, CT: Yale University Press.

Coffey, J. W., A. J. Cañas, and T. Reichherzer, et al. 2003. Knowledge modeling and the creation of El-Tech: A performance support system for electronic technicians. *Expert Systems with Applications* 25 (4): 483–492.

Ford, K. M., A. J. Cañas, and J. Jones, et al. 1991. ICONKAT: An integrated constructivist knowledge acquisition tool. *Knowledge Acquisition* 3: 215–236.

Ford, K. M., A. J. Cañas, and J. W. Coffey. 1993. Participatory explanation. In *Proceedings of the Sixth Florida Artificial Intelligence Research Symposium,* eds. D. D. Dankel and J. Stewman. Ft. Lauderadale, FL: FLAIRS.

Ford, K. M., J. W. Coffey, and A. J. Cañas, et al. 1996. Diagnosis and explanation by a nuclear cardiology expert system. *International Journal of Expert Systems* 9: 499–506.

Friedman, T. *The world is flat: A brief history of the twenty-first century.* New York: Farrar, Straus and Giroux.

Hayes, P., T. C. Eskridge, and R. Saavedra, et al. 2005. Collaborative knowledge capture in ontologies. Paper presented at the K-CAP'05, Banff, Alberta, Canada.

Jonassen, D. H., K. Beissner, and M. Yacci. 1993. *Structural knowledge: Techniques for representing, conveying and acquiring structural knowledge.* Hillsdale, NJ: Erlbaum.

Kuhn, T. S. 1962. *The structure of scientific revolutions.* Chicago, IL: University of Chicago Press.

Lafley, A. G. and R. Charan. 2008. *Game changer: Now you can drive revenue growth and profit growth with innovation.* New York: Crown.

Lewin, K. 1951. *Field theory in social science; selected theoretical papers.* New York: Harper & Row.

Myers, B., S. E. Hudson, and R. Pausch. 2000. Past, present, and future of user interface tools. *ACM Transactions on Computer-Human Interaction* 7 (1): 3–28.

Novak, J. D. 1963. A preliminary statement on research in science education. *Journal of Research in Science Teaching* 1 (1): 3–9.

Novak, J. D. 1972. The use of audio-tutorial methods in elementary school instruction. In *The Audio-Tutorial Approach to Learning* (pp. 110–120), eds. S. N. Postlethwait, J. D. Novak, and H. F. Murray. Minneapolis, MN: Burgess.

Novak, J. D. 1977. *A theory of education.* Ithaca, NY: Cornell University Press.

Novak, J. D. 1990a. Concept maps and Vee diagrams: Two metacognitive tools for science and mathematics education. *Instructional Science.* 19: 29–52.

Novak, J. D. 1990b. Concept mapping: A useful tool for science education. *Journal of Research in Science Teaching.* 27(10): 937–949.

Novak, J. D. 1998. *Learning, creating, and using knowledge: Concept Maps as facilitative tools in schools and corporations.* Mahwah, NJ: Lawrence Erlbaum Associates.

Novak. J. D. 2004. Reflections on a half century of thinking in science education and research: Implications from a twelve-year longitudinal study of children's learning. *Canadian Journal of Science, Mathematics, and Technology Education* 4 (1): 23–41.

Novak, J. D. 2010. *Learning, creating and using knowledge: Concept Maps as facilitative tools in schools and corporations,* 2nd ed. New York: Routledge.

Novak, J. D. and Gowin, D. B. 1984. *Learning how to learn.* New York: Cambridge University Press.

Postlethwait, S. N., J. D. Novak, and H. Murray. 1964. *An integrated experience approach to learning with emphasis on independent study.* Minneapolis, MN: Burgess.

Reichherzer, T. R., A. J. Cañas, K. M. Ford, and P. J. Hayes. 1998. The giant: A classroom collaborator. Paper presented at the Proceeding of the Fourth International Conference on Intelligent Tutoring Systems (ITS). San Antonio, TX.

2

Skills in Applied Concept Mapping

Brian M. Moon, Robert R. Hoffman, Thomas C. Eskridge, and John W. Coffey

CONTENTS

INTRODUCTION

We begin this chapter with a widely held truism: Concept Maps are easy to make and use. Indeed, kindergarten-aged children have been shown to have not only the facility to make Concept Maps independently, but also to benefit from their impacts on learning and metacognitive control skills (Cassata-Widera, 2009). The basic steps for creating a Concept Map have been widely described (cf., Novak, 2010; Novak and Cañas, 2008):

1. Define a focus question
2. Identify the key concepts
3. Spatially arrange the concepts by some notion of inclusiveness or priority ("set up the parking lot")
4. Create links
5. Revise spatial arrangement accordingly
6. Create crosslinks
7. Iterate

Crandall et al. (2006) describe what are essentially the same steps for when practitioners seek to help experts articulate their expertise. These steps hold true regardless of the medium, be it paper and pencil, white board and marker, or computer screen, keyboard, and mouse. Indeed, creating, sharing, and editing Concept Maps using CmapTools is an activity that children and adults throughout the world have found both easy and fun. These steps also hold true for collaborative Concept Mapping, i.e., situations in which one or more people co-create a Concept Map.

Were it not for ease of creation and use, we suspect the global use of Concept Mapping would not have grown over the past three decades, spreading from classrooms to boardrooms, migrating from butcher paper to the Internet. The ease of Concept Mapping is its greatest strength. The most powerful ideas are often the simplest.

And, yet, as practitioners with thousands of hours of Concept Mapping experience between us, our eyebrows are drawn upward when we hear the truism uttered. What we really hear is: "(*Good, Novakian*) Concept Maps are (*not so*) easy to (*efficiently and effectively*) make and use." Moreover, facilitating others in making good Concept Maps is even more difficult. Concept Mapping is not just a procedure, it is a skill set.

This chapter pulls back the curtain on the process of Concept Mapping to reveal the otherwise surreptitious skills that reliably and efficiently yield good Concept Maps. By doing so, we believe Concept Mapping can be differentiated from other approaches to knowledge diagramming that use combinations of graphical and textual elements to represent or express meanings, but are neither theory- nor tradecraft-based. It is one thing to create a diagram or picture, it is another to create precise and integrated meanings.

Our context for the chapter is in applied settings; specifically in using CmapTools-based Concept Mapping to solve problems. We draw on our extensive experience in creating Concept Maps for many purposes, in using Concept Mapping to help others articulate and organize their knowledge and reasoning strategies, and in training others to become Concept Mappers and use CmapTools.

We begin by covering the hallmark features of good, Novakian Concept Maps. Next, we highlight the knowledge and skills that individuals need for Concept Mapping. We then discuss the skills that Concept Mappers must develop so that they can create a Concept Map as a team, i.e., one facilitator and one recorder. We close by briefly mentioning skills that enable Concept Mapping "on-the-fly" in brainstorming and other types of group sessions.

THE FEATURES OF GOOD, NOVAKIAN CONCEPT MAPS

Novak and Cañas (in Chapter 1) describe the basic features of Concept Maps by using a Concept Map. Crandall et al. (2006, pp. 51–54) expanded and refined this basic set to include several additional features that can be used to characterize Concept Maps as "good" and further differentiate Concept Maps from other types of diagrams.

Table 2.1 shows, in column 2, the five basic hallmark features, and four refinements of the basic features suggested by Crandall et al. in column 3.

Our experiences have led us to identify additional features of good Concept Maps, particularly in watching novice Concept Mappers create their first Concept Maps (these are shown in column 4). Unlike the five hallmark features, these additional features can be taken as heuristics, and used to assess the "goodness" of a Concept Map. Application of these heuristics is a key skill in Concept Mapping.

TABLE 2.1

Features of Good Novakian Concept Maps

Features	Novak and Cañas	Crandall et al.	Moon et al.
Elements	Concepts that are labeled with words and/or symbols	Straightforward expression, i.e., no tacit meaning in the elements of the Concept Map (e.g., using color or symbols to code meaning)	Properly formulated focus question, e.g., dynamic- (Miller and Cañas, 2008), functional- (Derbentseva, Safayeni and Cañas, 2006), process-, and/or declarative-inducing questions
	Focus question guides the generation of ideas and questions that the Concept Map is to explain.		
	Linking words and/or phrases that connect the concepts	Unrestricted semantics, i.e., no restrictions on what types of relations can be represented	Diversity in linking words and/or phrases
	Propositions, i.e., simple and meaningful expressions that are the concept–link–concept "triples"	Propositions can be read as "stand alone," enabling propositional coherence (described in detail below)	Use of arrowheads to direct meaning and attention
Structure	Hierarchical structure	Explicit rationale for the "*semi*-hierarchical" structure, i.e., the more general or most important concepts appear toward the top and provide the context or the "big picture" for the Concept Map, while the more particular concepts tend to appear toward the bottom, with the use of crosslinks	Minimally intersecting connections, i.e., no more than three intersections per Concept Map
	Crosslinks that show interrelationships		Balanced structure, i.e., mostly proportionate spatial arrangement
			Connection-necessitated distance, i.e., lines only long enough to make a connection
Usability and Aesthetics			Viewable and legible sizing of the Concept Map and its elements
			Content-appropriate aesthetics

Hoffman coined the term *propositional coherence* to refer to how well individual propositions stand alone as expressions, and, simultaneously, to what extent the entire Concept Map is comprised of such interconnected expressions. Thus, a concept–link–concept "triple" either is or is not a proposition. A Concept Map is or is not propositionally coherent; it is coherent if all triples can be read as propositions. This distinctive feature is important primarily for clarity in the Concept Map, and it also enables ease for linking in new concepts and propositions as the Concept Map expands. Moreover, it identifies "run-on" or "string" propositions as an undesirable feature, an example being:

This book → is about → Concept Mapping → in → applied settings.

Pulling apart the triples, we have as a second triple:

Concept Mapping → in → applied settings,

which is not a proposition. To make the string propositionally coherent, one would need to create two propositions:

This book → is about → Concept Mapping, and
Concept Mapping → is used in → applied settings.

Of course, not every feature will apply to every Concept Map, and there are many reasons why a skilled Concept Mapper may choose to deviate from them when crafting a Concept Map. Indeed, as we describe below, one skill in Concept Mapping is the ability to know when and how to diverge from these features. Moreover, individual preferences may sometimes trump the heuristics. The use of arrowheads on connectors is a classic example. Some prefer them because they guide the eye and reinforce the order of reading the Concept Maps. Others do not because they believe the structural conventions are powerful enough to convey the order.

With all of these features of good Concept Maps in mind, we now turn to the knowledge and skills that proficient Concept Mappers bring to the task of creating them. First, we discuss the necessary knowledge about Concept Mapping. Next, we delineate the skills of an individual Concept Mapper, and then the skills in team Concept Mapping and Concept Mapping "on-the-fly."

KNOWLEDGE ABOUT CONCEPT MAPPING

The Concept Map practitioner must be, first and foremost, familiar with the research base underlying Concept Mapping. Gaining a deep familiarity is no small feat because the literature is vast and even summary reviews are extensive (cf., the reference list compiled by the Institute for Human and Machine Cognition (IHMC) at http://cmap.ihmc.us/Publications/ReferenceList.php). It is, at this time, an individual journey. There are a few academic programs that employ professors and instructors who are steeped in the research; however, most of these are focused on Concept Mapping in educational contexts. As far as we know, there is no formal academic training program on Concept Mapping or its applications. While we can imagine what such a program might entail and we routinely deliver workshops to train professionals in Applied Concept Mapping, it is difficult to conceive where an academic program would best be housed in the traditional academic department structure. The arts and sciences department, in particular, the social, psychological, and organizational sciences, seems appropriate. However, reasonable arguments could be made for engineering, business, and information technology departments.

In any event, exploration of the underlying theory of Concept Mapping, an introduction to the variety of methods and applications, and the architecture and features of CmapTools are available in the literature. A novice Concept Mapper would do well to review Novak's publications (especially Novak, 2010), the proceedings of the conferences on Concept Mapping (cmc.ihmc.us), the homepage for CmapTools (cmap.ihmc.us), and, of course, this book.

We turn now to the skills and knowledge of the individual Concept Mapper.

THE SKILLS OF THE INDIVIDUAL CONCEPT MAPPER

By individual Concept Mapper, we mean an individual practitioner who creates Concept Maps for many purposes. These purposes can include Concept Mapping one's own knowledge, working with another to co-create a Concept Map, transforming prose or some other format into Concept

Maps, analyzing a set of propositions culled from other sources, or creating a knowledge model for use as a presentation or Web site. We distinguish these purposes from Concept Mapping activities that are traditionally performed as a team, e.g., knowledge elicitation, and those done in group settings, e.g., idea generation. With these different purposes come different roles, task responsibilities, and thus skills, as we will discuss. In the next section, we reflect on some methods for gaining skill at Concept Mapping.

Gaining Skills

As a novice Concept Mapper learns about Concept Mapping, practice in creating them plays a critical role. For many of the required skills, solitary practice in Concept Mapping is not only necessary, but nearly sufficient for mastery. One can learn a great deal about the utility of the heuristics simply by attempting to develop a Concept Map of what one already knows about the world, or what might already be captured in other forms, like text documents. Indeed, many of the heuristics were developed through our own trial-and-error practice sessions, using CmapTools to create Concept Maps that meaningfully expressed our intents. While practice without coaching or other means of feedback can be limiting no matter what the skill, creating Concept Maps while thinking through the heuristics can be a good means of gaining an appreciation for and even honing some of the critical Concept Mapping skills.

While solo practice is always beneficial, above we say it is "nearly sufficient" because feedback is crucial. Showing one's Concept Maps to others, particularly those who are familiar with the topic addressed by the Concept Maps, can be invaluable for one's skill development. There are few experiences more enlightening than showing someone a Concept Map and seeing the palpable signs of "map shock" on their face. Asking what makes sense and what is concerning the reviewer should always be the next step.

Solitary practice, however, will not afford the experience necessary to learn many of the particular skills, especially those necessary for co-creating Concept Maps. To learn these skills, a Concept Mapper must practice with others. It cannot be understated how different are the tasks of creating one's own Concept Map, without the pressures of time and performance, and co-creating a Concept Map with another, i.e., the "knower." The skills discussed in the following section are reflective of this setting, and many apply when creating one's own Concept Maps.

Co-creating a Concept Map is different still than working in a team to co-create a Concept Map with a knower. The skills involved in these settings can only be learned through practice, preferably in low-risk situations. Our preferred approach for introducing these settings is to have teams of two or three practice with each other, each serving as the knower, while the others take on the role of Concept Mapper or a Concept Mapping team.

We turn now to the individual skills. We group them by categories for ease of discussion, but not to artificially separate them. Skilled Concept Mapping involves imparting these skills simultaneously and continuously. Indeed, doing so is the overarching skill of Concept Mapping.

Articulation

This set of skills focuses on the abilities to clearly articulate the key elements in a Concept Map, i.e., the focus questions, concepts, linking words, and propositions. The formulation of the focus question establishes the initial direction of the development of the Concept Map. How it is stated can impact the way that the knower thinks to describe the knowledge, e.g., as dynamic or declarative, process or function (cf., Derbentseva, Safayeni, and Cañas, 2006; Miller and Cañas, 2008). Also, it is often the case that a Concept Map started under one focus question becomes a Concept Map about a different focus question, as the knower and Concept Mapper explore the knowledge. The skilled Concept Mapper must recognize when to refocus the question or start a new Concept Map with a new focus question, and judge whether to return to the original focus question.

Articulating, i.e., expressing distinctly, the key concepts in answering the focus question is the role of the knower, as is crafting the linking words and phrases. The proficient Concept Mapper, however, should be able to augment the knower's language capacity to express concepts and links in their clearest, most concise forms. Help from the Concept Mapper can take the form of suggesting synonymous terms, capturing a verbose statement in a quip, and sensing that the knower is thinking and allowing the thoughts to coalesce. CmapTools can assist the Concept Mapper in the suggestion of terms that might be added. The CmapTools Suggester (Cañas et al., 2004) analyzes the concepts in the map and searches the Web for pages that mention the same concepts. Additional concepts that appear on the Web pages but not in the developing Concept Map are presented in a list to the Concept Mapper as concepts that could possibly enhance the scope of the map.

Related is the skill of recognizing that concepts are latently described in links, and vice versa. In the English language, many words can serve as both nouns (i.e., concepts) and verbs (i.e., linking words or phrases). The skill lies in seeing, for example, that there is a concept of googling in the proposition: "We → googled → Something." The concept is "hidden" in the linking word and, thus, can be "pulled out" of the link, a process that opens up the prospect of linking the concept to other concepts:

We → used → Google,
We → discovered → Something, and
Google → can find → Something.

By pulling out Google as a concept, other areas of exploration become available. What else can Google find? Or do? Is there anything that Google cannot find?

This example also demonstrates the skill of thinking in propositions, which is probably the most challenging individual Concept Mapping skill to learn. Propositions are not sentences, they describe relationships. Above, we discussed the idea of propositional coherence. The Google example shows how a skilled Concept Mapper can translate a seemingly simple sentence of three *words* into a Concept Map comprised of three *propositions*. Many people who are new to Concept Mapping will attempt to write sentences by alternating words in concepts and linking phrases, creating "strings." Experienced Concept Mappers will consider, and help the knower consider, the propositional representation of any given statement. This includes deciding how to express the intended meaning of the knower's statements in concepts and linking words or phrases, while minimizing their verbosity and leaving open pathways for other extending connections to them.

Related to the skill of unpacking latent concepts is the skill of seeing invisible concepts that create opportunities for *differentiation* and *subsumption*. Differentiation is about distinguishing subconcepts and their relations; subsumption is about seeing how previously unrelated concepts actually fall under a higher order concept. Application of this skill is most necessary when spatially arranging the concepts by some notion of inclusiveness, categorization, importance, or priority. Such notions may be proffered by the knower, or not. It may fall to the Concept Mapper to see that several concepts "fall under" categories, or lend themselves to a priority structure, or seem to be different than the others. The developing Concept Map can highlight when such opportunities arise. A concept with a "fan" of six or seven concepts linked by a common linking phrase will often be an indicator that there may be one or more intermediate concepts that should "sit between" the concepts and create new layers of abstraction. Ultimately, the knower's schemes are what matters, and the Concept Mapper's vision for the Concept Map can only be inspirational. However, the rewarding feeling of throwing light on hidden concepts can be enjoyed by both the Concept Mapper and the knower.

The next skill lies in executing the proper role in co-creating a Concept Map with a knower.

Role

Highly functioning teams include members who not only know their own roles, but have a deep appreciation for the other roles and people on the team, and thus can adapt their contributions to the roles and styles of others. This skill is a must in professional Concept Mapping with a knower. The Concept Mapper must appreciate that his/her role is to help the knower create the Concept Map. To do so, the Concept Mapper must first orient the knower to Concept Mapping. The knower "must be helped to understand what will transpire in the sessions and why the process is carried out as it is. A briefing regarding the goals of the work, accompanied with a review of preliminary Concept Maps, can help the expert to gain this understanding" (Coffey, 2006, p. 3).

Throughout the Concept Mapping session, then, the Concept Mapper must continuously manage the attention of the knower, directing it to the Concept Map. At times, the process must be explained again. The Concept Mapper must coach but not impose upon the knower by providing instruction, feedback, and, most importantly, encouragement, about the process and his/her participation.

A distinction that we find challenging for novice Concept Mappers to make and maintain is that between the role of co-creator and learner. Many Concept Mappers get caught up in the knower's knowledge, struggle to understand the nature of the knowledge, and shift into the role of learner.

This turns the focus on themselves and how well they understand what the knower is expressing. In the highly complex and technical domains in which we have worked, e.g., nuclear technology (Moon and Kelley, 2010; Hoffman and Moon, 2010; Coffey and Eskridge, 2008), this shift would have crippled our capacity to co-create. We are not nuclear scientists, yet our role has been to help nuclear scientists create Concept Maps of their knowledge, much of which they hold tacitly. A Concept Mapping session is not a training session, and the Concept Mapper is not there to learn.

Of course, we do learn quite a bit as a consequence of the Concept Mapping sessions, and it is always helpful in developing a rapport with the knower when we can demonstrate early in the session that we have a working understanding of the lexicon of their highly specialized field, or at least the experience of the knower. We rarely enter a session without having bootstrapped ourselves (Crandall et al., 2006, p. 38; cf., Coffey, 2006), at least minimally, in the domain and the organization in which the knower works. The professional Concept Mapper may create a few basic parking lots and/or Concept Maps prior to a session to aide in the bootstrapping process, and may even share these with the knower as a means of introducing Concept Mapping. But once the session starts, the focus must quickly, directly, and invitingly be shifted to the knowledge of the knower, and getting that knowledge into the Concept Map. The last thing a Concept Mapper wants to create is a Concept Map describing the knowledge they have of the knower's domain. A well-crafted Concept Map will bear the hallmarks of a good Concept Map, populated by the content of the knower.

The next skill is facility at using CmapTools.

CmapTools Facility

With any specialized practice comes the need for skill at using tools. CmapTools has been developed to support creating and sharing Concept Maps by anyone. No special training is necessary to start Concept Mapping. Indeed, much like the home page for Google, the primary interface, i.e., the Concept Map itself, was designed for simplicity and supporting the sole function of creating Concept Maps.

The simple external interface of CmapTools hides significant underlying functionality that is available to increase the efficiency of Concept Map generation and enhance the effectiveness of the Concept Maps produced.

The most important reason for gaining facility with CmapTools is to know what options are available for reaching which objectives. CmapTools is a highly flexible tool, and for most desired outcomes, there are several approaches available. For example, there are a number of approaches to cluster concepts spatially. One can manually place them on the Concept Map in close proximity or in a vertical stack, or automatically align them using the style palette, or create a nested node (then arrange them within the nested node, or not), or create a box around them. Each approach can serve different purposes, e.g., visual or functional, and each comes with different follow-on requirements and options, e.g., ability to link to other concepts as a cluster.

Another important reason for gaining a deep understanding of CmapTools lies in being able to anticipate what CmapTools will do with the Concept Mapper's actions. While we cannot overstress the user friendliness of CmapTools, any tool can create surprises, particularly when a user is not highly practiced in using it. One example of a surprise we often see is when people attempt to link from one concept to another, and in the process cross over another concept. When the new concept–link–concept is created, the link seemingly is lost. In reality, however, it was created, but was placed behind the concept that was crossed over. Without a trained eye for such instances, a Concept Mapper may, at best, wind up repeating actions. At worst, the Concept Mapper may become frustrated in front of the knower, and feel helpless as the frustration spreads to the knower.

Low-risk, solitary experimentation with CmapTools is the best way to gain familiarity. One of the first discoveries that early Concept Mappers usually make is with the styles palette, which typically leads to aesthetic experimentation. Fonts, objects, lines, and Concept Maps are turned into all the colors of the rainbow. But a good Concept Map will have content-appropriate aesthetics, as a near-finished product. The most important consideration is that the entire idea of Concept Maps is to make meanings clear and explicit. Use of colors, shapes, and other features to "encode" meanings requires both a legend and a memory load for the person who is looking at the Concept Maps. As a rule of thumb, we never add any "bells and whistles" until we are certain that a Concept Map is nearly completed. Color is used very judiciously, perhaps using only a single color to make certain nodes stand out. Avoiding the temptations to introduce stylizations too early can be a time-consuming lesson to learn for the novice Concept Mapper, as color schemes that seemed to work early in the session are overtaken by considerations for meaning. Thankfully, CmapTools includes the capability to quickly change styles, and a professional Concept Mapper can rapidly turn a boring Concept Map into a work of art, though this should not be done "before its time."

Gaining a handle on quickly navigating around, then selecting, moving, and aligning the elements of the Concept Map is a finesse skill, but a highly critical one. Nothing destroys efficiency measurements more than fumbling around the Concept Map, continuously scrolling, and performing other types of place-finding. Such erratic behavior can at the very least irritate or confuse the knower. We often hear compliments following our sessions regarding the grace with which we manipulated CmapTools, and these are primarily aimed at the execution of this skill.

CmapTools includes a number of advanced tools, e.g., Autolayout, Merge Nodes, Presentation Builder, Compare to Concept Maps, that not only provide enhanced capabilities to the experienced Concept Mapper, but can be exploited for purposes beyond just building a Concept Map of a given knower's knowledge domain (cf., Harter and Moon, Chapter 7; Moon et al., 2006).

Collaboration tools in CmapTools provide a means for participants to work together while being in different locations, and possibly at different times. In cases where in-person Concept Mapping cannot be done, either synchronous or asynchronous collaboration techniques can be used to work together. Synchronous collaboration allows the Concept Mapper and the knower to view and manipulate the same Concept Map at the same time, but on different computer screens. The participants can be in the same room, or across the world. While it is possible to collaboratively develop a Concept Map from scratch using synchronous collaboration, this approach works best as a follow-on activity. For example, we have found synchronous collaboration very useful for reviewing Concept Maps that have already been developed, where the Concept Mapper is walking the knower through the Concept Map, ensuring that it captures the knower's point of view accurately.

A number of tools in CmapTools can support asynchronous collaboration. First are Annotations, which are the computer equivalent of the yellow sticky notes that adorn many computer monitors and refrigerator doors. Annotations allow others to highlight and comment on portions of a Concept Map, and have the Concept Mapper review them the next time the Concept Map is opened. Other asynchronous collaboration tools include:

1. A threaded conversation tool called Discussion Threads that attach e-mail-like conversations on particular concepts in a Concept Map.
2. Knowledge Soups, which are a way to share propositional information between Concept Mappers without sharing the entire map containing those propositions.
3. Import and Export tools that allow other programs such as text editors, outliners, and databases to be used to add or modify the Concept Map.

Skilled Concept Mappers use these capabilities where appropriate. The next skill deals with spatial considerations during Concept Mapping.

Spatial Considerations

Crandall et al. (2006) have highlighted the "shape-meaning interactions" in meaning diagrams, i.e., the shape of the diagram interacts with the semantic and syntactic features. For the Concept Mapper, finding where to place crosslinks is the most obvious skill related to the interaction. Deliberate search for crosslinks is the means through which the skill is exercised.

There are other skills that Concept Mappers attribute to the shape-meaning interaction. One is in seeking and finding a balanced structure in the Concept Map. This often means spotting opportunities for using available space within one area of the Concept Map to house other sections. Concept Maps created in CmapTools are not restricted spatially—anything *can* be placed anywhere—which is a notable departure from many other diagramming tools that restrict spatial placement of elements. Such freedom, however, can induce free-wheeling use of space in early Concept Mappers. Many tend to have concepts or groups of concepts too widely spaced, which requires lots of unnecessary scrolling. On the other hand, concepts and links also can be placed too closely and become too "scrunched." With experience comes the skill at using space, including scrunching and descrunching concepts and propositions in the Concept Map.

Good Concept Maps should also have a balanced structure, i.e., mostly proportionate spatial arrangement. The proficient Concept Mapper strives for reasonable symmetry, knowing that exact symmetry is not always possible nor even desirable, by looking for ways to shift sections of the Concept Map into areas where whitespace is available. The need for work on the symmetry of the Concept Map is suggested by the presence of many intersecting connections and multiple long connections, linking distant sections of the Concept Map. Balance in the Concept Map, whether in semihierarchical or another appropriate shape (cf., Safayeni et al., 2006, for notes on the use of cyclical Concept Maps), often requires some trial and error, guided by the Concept Mapper's efficient use of space and emergent visions of what the Concept Map will look like near completion.

Utilization of space is inextricably bound to size concerns in Concept Maps, i.e., the number of concepts and propositions. The more elements, and the bigger and longer they are, the more space is required to accommodate them. The more space required, the further away from the Concept Map one needs to be to review and engage with it. There are applications of Concept Mapping during which size does not matter in the course of a process (cf., Moon et al., 2006; Moon and Harter, Chapter 7). In most cases, though, the skilled Concept Mapper continuously seeks a "human-centered" size for the Concept Maps. In CmapTools, this can be handled by zooming, but delicately so. Our rule of thumb is to try as much as possible to avoid making Concept Maps that require scrolling, and certainly not scrolling in both the horizontal and the vertical. For most displays at most viewing distances, a "complex enough" Concept Map has about 35 and no more than 45 concepts.

Decisions about space also can include when and what to temporarily place to the side to create workable space, when to start a new Concept Map, and what elements to move into the new map. The order of the seven steps for creating Concept Maps mentioned in this chapter's introduction provides, among other things, guidance regarding spatial considerations. For example, one reason for not immediately creating links is to avoid the need to move concepts *and* links in order to make space. Once a Concept Map grows too large for viewing without scrolling, new decisions come into play regarding how to stitch together and navigate across numerous smaller Concept Maps. The graphical tricks are many, but each has tradeoffs. The skill lies in making these assessments, tracking the decisions, and advising the knower on the tradeoffs.

The next skill is about using resources.

Resourcing

Adding resources, i.e., other digital files, to Concept Maps is easy to do in CmapTools. But the marks of a skilled Concept Mapper in dealing with resources lie in:

1. Knowing when and where in the Concept Map to refer to a resource.
2. Maintaining vigilance in looking for and helping the knower think about potential resources during a Concept Mapping session.
3. Being flexible in the numerous strategies available for incorporating resources.

To demonstrate the latter point, in some cases it may be best to use the contextual menu item "Add and Edit a Link to a Resource," creating a hyperlink from the concept of reference to the desired resource. In other cases, though, it may be best to present the information, in its appropriate format, within the context of the Concept Map. Tables, figures, and lists are more often than not better shown as such.

The next skill is about working toward the big picture while Concept Mapping.

Maintaining the Big Picture

As the theme of this book implies, all Concept Mapping is conducted for a purpose. The purpose for creating a Concept Map should be the basis for all of the actions of the skilled Concept Mapper. The purpose of the Concept Map can refer to the purpose of the Concept Mapping session and/or the purpose of the Concept Mapping product. Both of these purposes can apply on the individual Concept Map level and on higher order levels, such as the purpose of the overall project in which Concept Mapping is being used.

The purpose of the Concept Mapping session plays back onto the decisions the Concept Mapper makes with regard to, for example, which knowledge domains will be addressed, how deep and detailed the Concept Map must be, how refined the Concept Map should look by the close of the session, and where and how the Concept Map might be revised after the session. We have held many Concept Mapping sessions during which we only captured the key concepts and started to spatially align them; in these cases, the purpose of the session was to spend a compressed amount of time with a knower and elicit as much information about the focus question as possible. Afterward, we completed the Concept Mapping by listening to an audio recording of the session and working with the unlinked concepts (the "parking lot") developed during the session.

Of course, there are other ways that postsession processing play out. Concept Mapping should always be regarded as an iterative process. Revisiting Concept Maps with a knower at some near-term, later date can be a valuable exercise for gaining even greater precision of meaning and identifying omissions. It also can be fruitful to have other knowers, steeped in the represented knowledge, review the Concept Maps. Some evidence exists (Hoffman, Coffey, and Ford, 2000) that the changes made by a different expert than the one from whom the Concept Map was originally elicited are relatively minor; perhaps on the order of 10% of the concepts and linking phrases might be wordsmithed. These differences can open up new doors of exploration for the organization. They may be the seeds for new innovations, or suggest changes to organizational structure or procedures.

The purpose of the individual Concept Map product involves assessing who might see or use it, and for what purpose. It may involve considering if and how the Concept Maps might integrate with other corporate products. It certainly involves assessing what elements can support different visual or search or collaboration strategies and what impacts might result. A good example of the latter assessment lies in the use of images as concepts. The mechanism for turning a concept into an image in CmapTools is simple—drag and drop the image from where it is stored onto the concept, and CmapTools does the rest. If the purpose of the Concept Map is strictly visual, for instance, to create a sales pitch or capture a manufacturing process using images of the shop floor, the work is done. If, however, the purpose of the Concept Map is to display the sales pitch on the Internet, or make the manufacturing process available on an internal Concept Map server so that new hires to the shop floor can be trained, attention must be given to the concept into which the image was dropped. Specifically, the concept can serve as a caption (made visible) or keyword list (hidden from view) for the image so that it can be *discovered by search engines.* The image itself can be synonymous with the concept label, or it can be an amplification of the concept, meant to convey the more detailed meaning possible with an image. The skilled Concept Mapper appreciates the purpose of the Concept Map, and understands the implications of the actions taken on the intended purpose.

The purpose of Concept Mapping products in the context of the overarching project and organization also influences how the Concept Mapper works. Invariably, this purpose evolves over the life cycle of the effort. While certainly not predestined, we typically see a four-phase pattern emerge when we work with clients: the picture phase, the utility phase, the extended utility phase, and the deployment phase. First is the *picture* phase: The client wants help creating Concept Maps, and thinks only of the Concept Map product. Next comes the *utility* phase. As Concept Maps are developed, the client starts to see implications for where and how the Concept Maps (as pictures) can be used. This may include augmenting training materials or as briefing slides or simply hung in the lab or pinned to the cubicle as a reference. As the client begins to appreciate that we are not only creating pictures, but also building a database of concepts, links, and propositions, the light bulbs begin to turn on and we move to the *extended utility* phase. Here the client moves from Concept Maps as pictures to Concept Maps as information resources that can be linked to other information resources that we already have and need to organize the scheme for which is already in the head of the knower and could be represented in Concept Maps and organized as a Knowledge Model. As this epiphany sets in, and hurdles are crossed (cf., Desnoyers, Chapter 16), the client moves to the *deployment* stage, launching CmapTools (clients and server) into the organization and realizing the genuine and intended purpose of broad-based, large-scale knowledge management. As Concept Maps are developed, increasing numbers of Concept Mappers search other Concept Maps, resources, and the Web for related and insightful information. Individual Concept Maps become linked to other Concept Maps, perhaps built in another department within the same organization, but for complimentary purposes. Heretofore undiscovered crosslinks are made across two Concept Maps that have been integrated into one, resulting in new and innovative product and service ideas. Importantly, the Concept Maps that are being generated across the organization do not come to be regarded as fixed artifacts. Rather, they are regarded as "living" representations rather than finished "things," to be updated and revised as the organization, its people, and its knowledge evolve.

This is a vision that the skilled Concept Mapper must foresee, and guide the knowers and clients toward. By anticipating these phases, the skilled Concept Mappers can create Concept Maps that build toward the ensuing phases. While some clients may already see it and be working toward it, the Concept Mapper can present the vision at opportune times during any given Concept Mapping session or the course of the project.

Facilitation

In addition to the skills involved in Concept Mapping, Concept Mappers who work with knowers must also be highly skilled facilitators. They must be able to forge a positive relationship with the knower, accomplished in part by fostering a sense of shared purpose in undertaking the task at hand and also by projecting a collegial disposition. They should be capable of gently drawing out a knower possessing lesser verbal acuity, or even perhaps a knower who may be less inclined to cooperate with the Concept Mapping session for one reason or another. When working with highly experienced knowers, an overarching set of unique circumstances may come into play related to their deep experience and even personalities (Moon, 2010). The experienced Concept Mapper anticipates these situations and introduces mitigation strategies while never losing sight of the big picture.

These sensitivities must be balanced with excessively leading or prompting the knower. Continuous assessment of the knower's state of mind (thinking? stumped? not understanding the purpose? tired? worried about the call that just came in on the cell phone?) must be made in order to gauge the knower's level of interest and connection with the session. Such assessments suggest to the Concept Mapper what sorts of controls on the tempo of the session need to be imposed: Should we slow it down? take a break? try to get through this Concept Map or risk losing a train of thought? let the knower talk or tell a story, leaving the Concept Map aside for a bit?

The final set of skills that mark a proficient Concept Mapper are reflected in the avoidance of novice errors.

Error Avoidance

We have already mentioned many of the novice errors we have seen new Concept Mappers make, most of which we made ourselves. Experiencing these errors a few times is a valuable learning experience, making it really possible to avoid them and introduce a level of true professionalism into Concept Mapping. The errors include:

- Rushing or skipping altogether the introduction to Concept Mapping for the knower.
- Writing sentences or verbose phrases into concepts.

- Complacency in capturing the concepts as the knower expresses them.
- Incessantly moving elements in front of the knower.
- Jumping too quickly into creating links between concepts.
- Banally repeating linking words.
- Restructuring the Concept Map outside of the view of the knower.
- Incautiously setting up links to temporary resources or resource locations.
- Neglecting to include a legend where obscure or parochial meaning was imparted on elements.
- Using acronyms.

Having defined the skills of the individual Concept Mapper, we turn now to the skills that teams of Concept Mappers must develop to work synergistically with a knower.

THE SKILLS IN TEAM CONCEPT MAPPING

Each Concept Mapping team member needs those skills described in the previous section, but the team Concept Mapping approach introduces new skill requirements. It is ideal when each team member is an accomplished individual Concept Mapper.

Roles

Team Concept Mapping is an approach to Concept Mapping during which one teammate plays the role of the "facilitator," guiding the conversation with the knower, and the other teammate plays the role of the "recorder," working with CmapTools to record what the knower says in Concept Map form. It essentially splits the duties of the individual Concept Mapper in two. The primary advantage of the arrangement lies in enabling the facilitator to more directly engage the knower. By relieving the facilitator from most of the spatial and CmapTools skills, his or her focus can be more readily maintained on articulation, facilitation, and the big picture. That said, the facilitator is not entirely relieved of the spatial and CmapTools skills. Indeed, the facilitator must also work with the recorder in such tasks as what concepts to record, where to place them, what links to make between which concepts, when to make space and move sections of the Concept Map, when to pause and reinitiate the recording, and when to start new Concept Maps and for what purpose.

The experienced recorder, meanwhile, must follow these directions while listening to the knower to capture concepts and, at many points, take direction directly from the knower. Actions may also occur to the recorder, and it is well within the bounds of the recorder role to speak up, ask questions, and make suggestions. At some points, the facilitator may also take over the reigns on CmapTools, as a vision for spatial organization may be more efficiently imposed directly by the facilitator than directed to the recorder. The well-practiced Concept Mapping team will fluidly demonstrate the ensemble nature of this relationship, each playing the proper roles while complimenting the other.

Choreography

The ensemble also must choreograph its actions in the process of creating Concept Maps. To do so, the Concept Mapping team must start with a shared sense of the Concept Mapping process, which enables them to anticipate where the session needs to go next. They must use verbal and nonverbal communications to help each other gauge and manage the pace of the session. One example of this can be observed as a facilitator, who is deeply engaged with and looking at the knower, listens to the tapping of the keyboard by the recorder, indicating that the recorder is either keeping up with the engagement or not. Neither teammate should push the other; each must show patience to allow the process to unfold while simultaneously unfolding the process for the knower. And both must be prepared to be guided by, and guide, the other.

Our discussion of skilled Concept Mapping now turns to yet another context, the skills in Concept Mapping "on-the-fly," i.e., co-creating Concept Maps with groups of people doing some sort of collaborative work.

THE SKILLS IN CONCEPT MAPPING "ON-THE-FLY"

Concept Mapping during brainstorming or in other collaborative work sessions is another skill-dependent practice. The biggest challenge lies in the fact that the Concept Mapper must work with multiple knowers simultaneously, in many cases without the benefit of a group facilitator. Sometimes, the Concept Mapper becomes the de facto group facilitator, as the artifacts being generated by the Concept Mapper are discovered to be the most useful, and sometimes only, record of the proceedings. We have created Concept Maps both in and outside of the view of the groups with whom we are working. Showing the group the Cmap that is being developed almost always leads to the Cmapper taking on some facilitation role.

The difference between individual Concept Mapping and Concept Mapping on-the-fly is one of degree, not nature. The Concept Mapper must muster and amplify all of the individual skills, often for an extended duration. While the task can be exhausting, the advantages of the output of the session are clear. Concepts expressed by one participant are directly related to another. Priority and order can be brought to unorganized thoughts. Different, even seemingly conflicting, perspectives can be integrated or merged. Differences in beliefs and meaning that had been tacitly held can emerge (cf., Hoffman et al., Chapter 9). The simultaneous viewability of all of the propositions enable otherwise hidden crosslinks to emerge into new ways of looking at problems and solutions. Previously disparate propositions can be clustered into meaningful groups. Resources that were promised to be retrieved after the session can be immediately linked during the session. It is the role of Concept Mapper to ensure that all of these potentials are realized, where they become available.

CONCLUSION

In this chapter, we have detailed the features of good, Novakian Concept Maps, and explicated the skills required to make them. In doing so, we hope to inspire others to join the growing class of professional Concept Mappers, and to encourage professionals working in applied settings to employ *skilled* Concept Mapping to solve problems.

An old adage says that when you have a hammer, everything looks like a nail. Concept Maps, in particular those developed using CmapTools, do start to feel a lot like a hammer to the incipient Concept Mapper and many topics of knowledge begin looking like nails. Each of us have seen the eyes of our colleagues roll when we have suggested (yet again) that a Concept Map might be a good way to represent or share meaning. In some cases, we have pushed forward with the Concept Map, and in the end demonstrated the value that we knew was possible all along. As skilled Concept Mappers, we also know when to restrain from Concept Mapping, and when to turn to other means of expression as the most efficient and effective way to encourage meaning making. After all, we did *write* this chapter.

REFERENCES

Cañas, A. J., M. Carvalho, M. Arguedos, et al. 2004. Mining the Web to suggest concepts during concept map construction. In *Concept Maps: Theory, Methodology, Technology, Proceedings of the First International Conference on Concept Mapping,* eds. A. J. Cañas, J. Novak, and F. González. Pamplona, Spain.

Cassata-Widera, A. 2009. *Concept mapping with young children: From representation to metacognition.* Saarbrücken, Germany: VDM Verlag.

Coffey, J. 2006. In the heat of the moment … Strategies, tactics, and lessons learned regarding interactive knowledge modeling with concept maps. In *Concept Maps: Theory, Methodology, Technology, Proceedings of the Second International Conference on Concept Mapping,* eds. A. Cañas and J. Novak. San Jose, Costa Rica.

Coffey, J. and T. Eskridge. 2008. Case studies of knowledge modeling for knowledge preservation and sharing in the U.S. nuclear power industry. *IJKM* 7 (3): 173–185.

Crandall, B., G. Klein, and R. Hoffman. 2006. *Working minds: A practitioner's guide to cognitive task analysis.* Cambridge, MA: MIT Press.

Derbentseva, N., F. Safayeni, and A. J. Cañas. 2006. Concept maps: Experiments on dynamic thinking. *Journal of Research in Science Teaching* 44 (3).

Hoffman, R. R., J. W. Coffey, and K. M. Ford. 2000. A case study in the research paradigm of human-centered computing: Local expertise in weather forecasting. Report on the Contract, Human-Centered System Prototype. Bethesda, MD: National Technology Alliance.

Hoffman, R. and B. Moon. 2010. Knowledge capture for the utilities. Paper presented at the 7th International Topical Meeting on Nuclear Plant Instrumentation, Control and Human Machine Interface Technologies, Las Vegas, NV.

Miller, N. L. and A. J. Cañas. 2008. Effect of the nature of the focus question on presence of dynamic propositions in a concept map. In *Concept Mapping: Connecting Educators. Proceedings of the Third International Conference on Concept Mapping,* eds. A. J. Cañas, P. Reiska, M. Åhlberg, and J. D. Novak. Tallinn, Estonia & Helsinki, Finland.

Moon, B. 2010. Knowgraphy[SM] and lessons learned in conducting knowledge elicitation with senior experts. Presentation to the 3rd International Summit on Knowledge Management and Organizational Learning, Bogota, Columbia.

Moon, B. and M. Kelley. 2010. Lessons learned in knowledge elicitation with nuclear experts. Paper presented at the 7th International Topical Meeting on Nuclear Plant Instrumentation, Control and Human Machine Interface Technologies, Las Vegas, NV.

Moon, B., A. Pino, and C. Hedberg. 2006. Studying transformation: The use of concept map tools in surveying the integration of intelligence and operations. In *Concept Maps: Theory, Methodology, Technology, Proceedings of the Second International Conference on Concept Mapping*, eds. A. Cañas and J. Novak. San Jose, Costa Rica.

Novak, J. 2010 *Learning, creating and using knowledge: Concept maps as facilitative tools in schools and corporations*, 2nd ed. New York: Routledge.

Novak, J. D. and A. J. Cañas. 2008. The theory underlying concept maps and how to construct them, Technical Report IHMC CmapTools 2006-01, Rev. 01-2008, Florida Institute for Human and Machine Cognition, 2008, available at: http://cmap.ihmc.us/Publications/ResearchPapers/TheoryUnderlyingConceptMaps.pdf.

Safayeni, F., N. Derbentseva, and A. J. Cañas. 2005. A Theoretical Note on Concepts and the Need for Cyclic Concept Maps. *Journal of Research in Science Teaching* 42(7), pp. 741–766.

3

Concept Mapping in the Analysis and Design of Cognitive Systems: A Historical Review

Michael D. McNeese and Phillip J. Ayoub

CONTENTS

INTRODUCTION

In this chapter, we articulate the historical progression of our approach to Concept Mapping over the past 25 years, as we have applied it to the design of cognitive systems. We also discuss key challenges that we have faced in the practical application of Concept Mapping and highlight considerations for future developments. Our overarching intent from this review is to bring attention to the rationale that grounds much of the core foundations of Concept Mapping. Understanding our past is often the best way to understand where we are now, and, more importantly, how we may best move forward into new contexts and applications.

Our review is not a comprehensive history, but is one that is specific to our strands of development in the area. This approach enables us to provide first-hand accounts and insights into the logic and contextual challenges that shaped our use, refinement, and extension of Concept Mapping over the past 25 years. To structure our review, we divide our accounts into two eras. Beginning in the 1980s, the first era reviews the emergence and early history of Concept Mapping from what were practical applications out of the exploding fields of cognitive and learning sciences. This era also spans most of the first author's work in the late 1980s and 1990s in the application of Concept Mapping to the design of cockpit and aircraft interfaces. Reaching the turn of the century, we transition to our second era, where we discuss how public and academic discourse around crisis management and terrorism led us to apply Concept Mapping to a view beyond the individual into that of complex work systems and networks of people and technology. In this second era, we bring particular attention to how we reshaped some of the founding constructs and analytics of Concept Mapping to incorporate aspects of temporality and a broader framework of organizational work factors.

PRIMORDIAL HISTORY OF CONCEPT MAPPING

Much of the first author's (McNeese) academic life and education has been concerned with cognitive psychology and cognitive science, specifically with respect to: memory–knowledge representation, acquisition, and access of that representation; use of knowledge in terms of reasoning and problem solving (both individually and in teamwork); the role context plays in situating knowledge; and how knowledge is transferred from human-to-human and human-to-intelligent agent, given specific situated context. It is from this base that we first discuss the emergence of Concept Mapping in the design and analysis of cognitive systems. Much of this research was conducted for the U.S. government, but has had broad applicability to industries involving human factors and design (e.g., transportation, aerospace, computing, health–medicine, geographic informatics, security, and multimedia).

Theoretical Formulation and Approach

Our approach to Concept Mapping has always been *cognitive-inspired* (i.e., from the perspective that knowledge is generated, acquired, and retrieved through the use of human cognitive processes), but has changed through study and experience. It has been somewhat dichotomous though because, on the one hand, knowledge can be considered very bound to language–semantic-based functions, while on the other hand, knowledge can also be based on imagery, pictures, sound, and other sensorial imprints that can be acquired. Often this is portrayed as verbal or visual function, language or imagery, or semantic or eidetic memory. This is relevant to this chapter in terms of the issue of whether Concept Mapping only captures the verbal–semantic basis of expertise, and, in turn, leaves out the perceptual–imagery component of expertise. To comprise a more holistic representation of expertise, we often had to complement Concept Mapping with other forms of knowledge representation, which we discuss below.

There were two circumstances that led to McNeese's own beginnings in Concept Mapping. First, at the U.S. Air Force Research Laboratory (AFRL) in Dayton, Ohio, in 1989, McNeese became responsible for a project—the Pilot's Associate—that was aimed at providing multiple expert systems to assist pilots in a fighter aircraft application. At that time, many experts were strongly interested in knowledge engineering (e.g., Boose, 1986; Buchanan and Shortliffe, 1984), but often took a computer-first approach (i.e., extracting rules from subject matter experts that could easily be encoded into expert systems). Second, colleagues at the Air Force Research Laboratory had also worked with Joseph Novak in completing a master's thesis using Concept Mapping in military applications (McFarren, 1987).

Because of the orientation toward cognitive science with an interest in acquiring and accessing knowledge, and given the demands inherent in the Pilot's Associate program, McNeese and colleagues conceptualized Concept Mapping from theoretical and methodological perspectives. Their 1990 government technical report (McNeese et al., 1990), entitled *An advanced knowledge and design acquisition methodology: Application for pilots associate,* was our first research product in this area. This view was different from, yet related to, the original Novakian formulation (Novak and Gowin, 1984), which we discuss below.

The main desire in developing our own formulation was to obtain and interconnect three different representations of knowledge that would prove to be useful developing pilot associate context, content, and interface elements. These representations were knowledge as functions, concepts, and sketches. The primary basis of our approach was that it was user-centered and cognitively inspired, meaning that the process for acquiring knowledge from an expert had to be such that it facilitates the representation of direct perceptual experience to be communicated back to the knowledge elicitor. Semantic memory is one known basis for how humans consolidate their experience into memories, and is used to produce language in communication processes (Anderson, 1983). We believed that if the knowledge elicitation process (i.e., Concept Maps, which are forms of semantic networks) closely aligned with knowledge representation, then (1) the elicitation of that knowledge would be easier and more natural, (2) the representations would tie into and open up spontaneous access to associated knowledge within memory (i.e., case-based reasoning), and (3) the Concept Maps of one expert could be compared with and combined with other expert maps to "search for invariance."

Along with knowledge as concepts, we also worked with experts to try to get them to draw what they mean. Because expertise is predicated in part on perceptual differentiation, another form of communicating what an expert knows is by drawing or sketching using visual imagery to inform discussion. This allows semantic understanding to fuse with perception to create more holistic elicitation of knowledge. As was similar to Novak, both semantic articulation using Concept Maps and drawing to visualize knowledge are profitable because the expert can translate experience to others with these formats.

Another form of knowledge representation we initially used was ICAM DEFinition Method zero (IDEF0) (1981) representations, which elicited functional and abstraction-level knowledge. This fulfilled the knowledge as functions expression, and thus was useful to engineers designing the software and hardware underlying the pilot's associate architecture. However, we discovered it did not facilitate very effective knowledge elicitation with the users, mainly because it corresponded with the type of knowledge that engineers use for creating their products, but did not correspond with the users' mental models of their expertise. The Concept Mapping and the drawings did correspond with the users' mental models that resulted in knowledge being effectively elicited.

Later in our work in knowledge elicitation, we returned to functional expressions—the abstraction hierarchy (Rasmussen 1986)—as a means to represent the overall contextual space that users operate and work within as part of a cognitive work analysis approaches. In the Zaff, McNeese, and Snyder (1993) paper (which is a follow-up to the McNeese et al., 1990 report), we reported that Concept Mapping produced flexible access of information, a shared communication medium, and a user-compatible knowledge acquisition procedure. Even today, as we employ these techniques, these principles still hold true.

Contrast to Novakian Approaches

At this point in our work, our Concept Maps looked similar to the traditional Novakian maps (Novak and Gowin, 1984); however, our purposing of Concept Maps as part of an overarching design process (versus an educational tool) created two noteworthy distinctions. First, our intent of Concept Mapping was to capture and transfer knowledge between the person holding the knowledge ("Cmappee") and Cmapper, whereas original Novakian approaches focus not on the explication of knowledge for transfer, but for the Cmappee's (i.e., student) learning. Procedurally, this meant we placed a lot more emphasis on the Cmapper and Cmappee sharing knowledge and feedback of the Cmappee to correct a wrong representation; in essence, the Cmappee would lead the Cmapper to the correct representation of his/her semantic memory. This also assumes the Cmappee to be the subject matter expert, while in educational uses the Cmapper (i.e., teacher) may actually be the expert who guides the Cmappee (i.e., student).

A second distinction between our work and traditional Novakian Concept Mapping was our use of Concept Maps in a broader design process. We often coupled Concept Maps with other representation and design tools, such as IDEF0 (i.e., functional information) and design storyboards (i.e., perceptual information), which meant that the procedures and structure of our Concept Maps had to be consistent and coupled with terms and processes of these other tools (Zaff et al., 1993).

Procedurally, these two distinctions lead to somewhat different processes and procedures for the generation of Concept Maps. However, many similarities still remained between our two approaches, such as the basic notions between concepts and propositions. Our focus also has always been user-centered to allow the Cmappee to guide development within a selectable target question that would begin the mapping session. In later generations of our work, we would begin to reformulate some of these other foundational points in order to adapt to the evolving challenges of the systems and people we study.

We also should note that throughout this earlier work, our Cmapping artifacts were often done in pen and paper (see Figure 3.1), but we identified a need for computer support for capture, access, categorization, storing, rearranging, combining, and coding of Cmap elements. We had a history in our own research group at AFRL in this area, and even developed two tools that we used in our early Concept Maps in the early 1990s. We developed the Concept Interpreter tool versions 1.0 and 2.0 (Snyder, McNeese, and Zaff, 1990; Snyder et al., 1992), the Concept Mapping tool 1.0 (Kottmann et al., 1991), and the TAKE tool (Spravka, Gomes, and Lind, 1994). More recently, CmapTools (Cañas et al., 2004; Novak and Cañas, 2006) has been used by many researchers, including our own group. While there are cases where we still rely on paper and pen, CmapTools has been reliable and provided a number of capabilities for standard best practices of Concept Mapping.

FIGURE 3.1
Concept Mapping session using colored pens and a large roll of white paper.

Expanding Concept Mapping for Temporality and Work Systems

In the early 2000s, we expanded our areas of study to the emerging topics of emergency crisis management and terrorism and intelligence analysis. This move brought with it new dimensions and challenges to the study and design of cognitive systems. We saw that in order for us to continue using Concept Mapping in these new domains and broader problem spaces we would need to reconsider how we elicit and represent new dimensions of cognitive activities, particularly temporality and the socio-organizational context of work.

Our expanded view of cognitive systems was not done in isolation though, but a broader and more fundamental shift occurring in the cognitive systems engineering community. Beginning in the mid-to-late 1990s, emphasis on cognition began to shift toward understanding social and organizational aspects of cognition (e.g., Hutchins, 1995; Vicente, 1999). This paradigmatic change—analyses of individuals to analyses of systems—had a strong influence on us and, in turn, the path we took in the development and application of Concept Mapping. With this underlying shift in mind, we entered into our next era of Concept Maps.

Integrating Temporality

The context of emergency crisis management can be well characterized in the preparedness and response of U.S. local, state, and federal authorities to incidents such as Hurricane Katrina in 2005. The scope of such is much broader than that of aircraft and cockpit design, involving the coordination and consideration of many more parties, social and technical systems, and events, all spread across a much wider period of time. Given the complexity that exists within these new contexts, our Concept Mapping principally changed in application in a significant way.

Our first era applications would typically produce the concept definition map (i.e., knowledge would be captured primarily as a declarative knowledge structure independent of temporal or spatial dimensionality—a hierarchy). As complexity of events increases, it becomes necessary to incorporate more temporal elements of cognition (cf., for hurricane crisis management, Brewer, 2005). Work procedures often "play out" according to time, space, and the boundary constraints that shape cognitive activity within. Our early uses of Concept Mapping were often applied to shorter duration activities and to single individuals, but crisis management requires groups of people working together over time. It therefore became more important that Concept Mapping methods enable temporality, and, in turn, the use of the procedural-based Concept Map became more prominent.

In constructing procedural Concept Maps, one of the obvious yet key constructs is the development of an intrinsic timeline from which procedures emerge. Brewer and McNeese (2004) (see Brewer, 2005, for example maps) used scenarios to develop procedural Concept Maps, both to elicit and to visually diagram the complex relationships between people, places, and artifacts as they play out over time. Other approaches to understanding decision making have also employed the use of scenarios to focus on temporal and spatial cues that lead to the development of expertise (Klein, Calderwood, and McGregor, 1989).

The methods we imposed for procedural-based Concept Mapping (e.g., Ayoub, 2005; Brewer, 2005; Brewer and McNeese, 2004; Glantz, 2006) could be thought of as developing specific knowledge clusters (miniconcept definition maps) about a given timeline of events as distilled from the script provided by the expert or team of experts. When completed, these types of maps show the specific knowledge needs surrounding a temporal progression of events.

Figure 3.2 provides an example segment of a larger procedural Concept Map created during our work with intelligence analysts (Ayoub, 2005). The map depicts clusters of activities and other elements of the domain structured around a task-based timeline. The Cmapper, depending on the intended granularity of analysis, could further probe each cluster within the larger map or a new Cmap that is later reintegrated into the timeline. To aggregate to higher levels of analysis and to integrate maps, a Cmapper may use the timeline as the common denominator for comparing maps (across individuals or whatever the unit of analysis is per map).

In many cases, procedural-based Concept Maps then can be used as a basis to begin design storyboards, which also were laid out according to the scripted event sequence. This allowed full development of the "knowledge as design" initiatives (Perkins, 1986). When experts would think about a script in time, it was often the case that they also would generate and construct spatial dimensions. (They would think about a scene with geospatial properties, and a context wherein a specific case/event occurred.) This helped to consider additional boundary constraints of work.

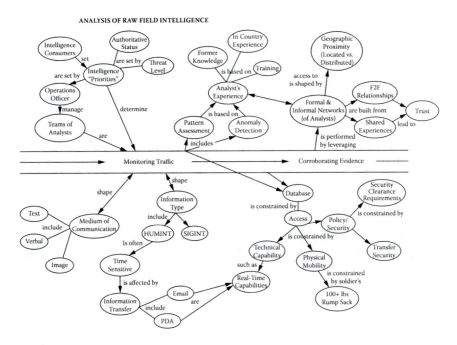

FIGURE 3.2
Segment of a procedural Concept Map from work with U.S. intelligence analysts.

One thing we discovered in using the procedure-based Concept Mapping method for complex emerging systems is that time is not necessarily a linear progression, as it may be that different time sequences layer across and emerge from other time sequences in particular patterns. One problem with the procedure-based Concept Map was that it tended to be rigid, inflexible, and only framed time as a linear sequence (Brewer and McNeese, 2004). In real work situations, temporality can be recursive, extensible, and is often disrupted or even suspended according to the nature of work and boundary constraints. The more recent applications involving emergency crisis management and disasters produce timelines that are larger time scales (e.g., work is often thought of as days rather than hours or even minutes), hence, producing more of these nonlinear patterns. Often these patterns of work-in-progress show cyclic or temporal events that underlie important specifications of how work comes to pass. Therein, time can be nonlinear, even chaotic as it appears to unfold. This is especially true in teamwork wherein one member may be dependent on receiving another worker's output before beginning his/her input or process. The unexpected nature of work also makes temporality full of iterations, deadlines, and necessary temporal ordering (see Hamilton et al., in press).

To address these components, we first classified the type of temporal events that workers were involved with in their particular examples as being: linear, cyclical, metered, or regulated, opportunistic, or iterative/ recursive. Next, we use these temporal categories to overlay traditional Concept Maps to help identify the types of timing that are present within the overall script so the reader can understand how the concepts with the map develop or emerge on a temporal basis (see Brewer, 2005, for examples). This approach supports the shift in understanding not just *what* but *when* certain tasks occur, particular information is required, and key decisions are made. Together, these provided new insight into how ordering and temporality shapes an emergent crisis and how we may better design the system—people, technology, and events—to manage such a crisis. Most of the situations we have used for procedure- or temporal-based Concept Mapping are highly knitted to specific stories, cases, or real world examples with which experts are intimately familiar.

Feedback from experts reviewing these kinds of Cmaps suggested they really appreciated the outputs and the timing element and, thus, show what is salient at a given time point. This allowed the expert to connect more with the Cmap as it becomes a bridge with their expertise. Because procedures represent what they actually do in a situation, these kinds of Cmaps were perceived to be more valuable as they moved the expert's thinking more toward the practical real world concerns and issues that can make or break a solution path. In contrast, the concept definition (i.e., traditional Novakian Cmaps) is good at facilitating what the expert knows, which may be constructed with more abstract knowledge without temporal elements.

Another example of procedural Concept Mapping was developed for our work in intelligence analysis (Connors et al., 2004). We started our methods by having analysts work together on a representative scenario prior to any of the mapping sessions. In this case, it was a scenario involving hypothetical situations underlying a "dirty bomb" in a heavily populated area of the United States. The Cmapper—using the scenario—worked with the analysts to distill six distinct progressive, temporal stages from the overall scenario, as follows:

1. Activities prior to threat escalation
2. Receipt of a golden nugget of information

3. Bomb detonation
4. Immediate response of the intelligent analyst community
5. Credit for detonation claimed by a terrorist organization
6. Confirmation of bomb composition and severity of damage (Connors et al., 2004)

Concept Maps were then constructed with each individual analyst within each of these stages to see what knowledge is necessitated over time as each stage developed.

Expanding to Work Systems

While temporality proved a critical addition to understanding complex cognitive activities of emergency management, studies of cognitive systems were also challenged to address socio-organizational factors of cognition. Our application of Concept Maps, therefore, would require another shift in structure and procedure in order to incorporate these broader aspects of cognitive *work* systems. Nowhere was this more evident than in the cognitive work of intelligence analysts. Following the September 11, 2001, terrorist attacks in the United States, significant attention was turned toward better understanding the cognitive nature and tasks of analysts and the U.S. intelligence community as a whole.

Under traditional views of analysis, the work of the intelligence analyst can be characterized as the ability to arduously search through enormous volumes of data and to band together scattered and seemingly unrelated events into a calculated estimation of a complex, dynamic situation. However, the story does not end there. Missing in this depiction is how assessments are often distributed across networks of analysts, where the cross-organizational sharing of information is required to validate the authenticity and completeness of the story. Intelligence work thus requires a networked view of cognitive activity that is distributed across multiple analysts, organizations, and situated conditions. Temporality seemed a natural aspect of intelligence work (McNeese et al., 2004; Elm et al., 2005), but Concept Mapping also needed to take on new analytic structures in order to incorporate organizational and contextual factors into a more holistic assessment of the work system.

We approached the work of the intelligence analysts as a distributed cognitive work system (Hutchins, 1995) and searched for techniques to incorporate this broader view. We found existing cognitive task analyses (CTA) and cognitive work analyses (CWA) to be strong starting points, but equipped to examine more structured engineering-like environments. Thus, we integrated Zaff et al.'s (1993) basic Concept Mapping techniques and Brewer and McNeese's (2004) spatio-temporality approaches with the theoretical backdrop of Vicente's (1999) five-stage CWA framework (Ayoub, 2005; Ayoub, Petrick, and McNeese, 2008). Vicente's framework incorporated (1) *work domain* analyses, (2) constraint-based *task* analyses, (3) analyses of affective *strategies*, (4) analyses of *social and organizational factors*, and (5) identified demands of *worker competencies*, which provides a model for capturing and analyzing broader aspects of cognition and work in an integrated and holistic fashion. While Vicente and others offer specific analyses for each of the five stages, we elected to use Concept Maps as the primary means for elicitation and representation because they provided a more flexible means for mapping the links between stages and for representing the networked structure of the intelligence community domain.

Procedurally, our methods followed the spatio-temporal techniques and role of scenarios similar to that of Brewer and McNeese (2004). During elicitation sessions, Cmappees also were asked a range of probing questions throughout the session to ensure all five stages of Vicente's framework were captured. Maps were initially created on large roles of white paper using colored markers. Finalized versions that incorporated a detailed review of session audio recordings were later drawn electronically. Each concept was later color-coded according to the categories described in Vicente's CWA framework. Figure 3.3 depicts the color-coded Concept Map (compare to an uncoded map depicted in Figure 3.2).

The approach allowed us to map the temporal nature of the intelligence work while also identifying and linking the relationships between work domain, tasks, strategies, socio-organizational factors, and knowledge competencies. In reviewing the final Concept Maps, a third-party analyst (one not involved in the initial elicitations) validated the accuracy of our analyses, and specifically commented that the technique provided a detailed yet clear and well-organized depiction of an analyst and the larger cognitive work system in which the analyst was embedded. Based on our analyses using this form of Concept Maps, we were also able to create specific design recommendations where there was a clear transparency between the cognitive demands of the analyst, the relationship to the broader work system, and the recommended system design (Ayoub, 2005).

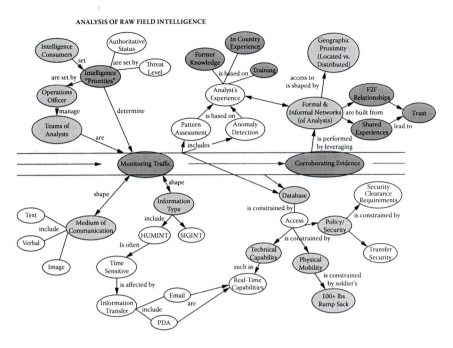

FIGURE 3.3
Procedural Concept Map color-coded according to Vicente's (1999) five-stage CWA framework.

CHALLENGES IN CONCEPT MAPPING

Over the past 20 years, we have seen many issues and challenges arise in our application of Concept Mapping in the analysis and design of cognitive systems. We first addressed these issues at a panel McNeese chaired as part of the Second Conference on Naturalistic Decision Making, Dayton, Ohio, 1994 (see Zsambok and Klein, 1997). Many still remain. While we cannot address all of these challenges, we bring attention to four of the more prominent issues:

1. Level of expertise
2. Pacing
3. Integrating Cmaps
4. Visualization complexity

Before moving on to these particular challenges, we first remind the reader that Concept Mapping is subject to the broader methodological constraints of qualitative and interpretive research. Concept Mapping is a time-intensive activity, but with time comes the increased depth of understanding, and this tradeoff should be understood. Concept Mapping within real world settings is also flexible and open to interpretation, and it is good practice during design to triangulate the Concept Mapping method with observation of human behaviors, performance data (if available), survey data, and other methodological means of capturing expertise. To the extent Concept Mapping outputs can be holistically situated, a better picture can emerge that informs design.

Level of Expertise

One challenge to consider is the expertise of the Cmapper and the Cmappee. Expertise of the Cmapper can be defined as: (1) skills related to conducting the Cmapping methods (see Moon et al., Chapter 2), and (2) knowledge about the subject domain the Cmapping session is designed to elicit. A Cmapper can be a novice or expert in either area, with ensuing consequences. In contrast, the Cmappee also can be a novice or expert, but typically a designer is only interested in knowledge about a given subject domain, and in our work, we typically work with Cmappees who are experts. Novices can be Cmapped as well to show differences with experts in a given domain. Considering these issues, one of the biggest challenges in Concept Mapping is how to train the Cmapper, given the specific method called for. Like most skill acquisition tasks, the Cmapper will get much better practice in actually performing the methods if they receive immediate and direct feedback. In workshops we have conducted to train our approaches to Cmapping, we try to act as mentors to point out some of the typical problems when novices begin Cmapping.

It also is possible to have Cmappers, who are domain experts themselves, stall out in the process as the Cmapper's own knowledge conflicts with his/her own sense of rightness in contrast to what he/she is depicting. One example of this happened during our early days when the Cmapper team was well-versed in human factors and were Concept Mapping pilots. Even though the pilots had great knowledge about flying, some of the ideas they had about controls and displays were counter-intuitive to human factors guidelines. One of the ways to overcome this is to try to get a variety of experts mapped (e.g., avionics specialists, usability experts, and fighter pilots) so that different Cmaps can be compared. This represents situations wherein different experts do have differing mental models regarding an area or topic they all work in. We trained our Cmappers to authentically represent the expert's knowledge to the extent possible. If a given Cmapper begins to get hung up on the mapping owing to conflicts in their own knowledge and the expert's knowledge, having other mappers as part of the process can help.

Generally, we begin training Cmapping novices through (1) observation, (2) test cases with familiar topics so they become experienced, and (3) iterative mentoring with more expert Cmappers. One of the difficult components of Cmapping is translating the auditory language they are hearing into a visual representation format in real time. We always ask the Cmappee to correct the Cmapper if the Cmapper gets it wrong, but sometimes experts may feel this is awkward to do. In general, our form of Concept Mapping is picked up fairly easily, but again, Cmapping is inherently a qualitative research method that requires skills beyond just that of mapping.

Pacing

Every variant technique of Concept Mapping exists as a given procedure or process that has to be implemented with some degree of fluency. Often these types of challenges are indigenous to a particular research methodology and the natural constraints that surround implementing it in a field of practice. One issue in particular that we have repeatedly encountered is trying to capture everything (i.e., formulating the Cmap) in a set amount of time available. Often this creates overloading problems and results in a highly scattered, loosely connected Cmap that is difficult to follow and interpret. We have learned it is better to slow the process down and try to capture information and knowledge over two, possibly three interviews (roughly one to two hours per interview) to allow Cmaps to naturally develop, and, in turn, to delve deeper into progressions in a focused topic over time. This pacing allows the Cmappers to go back over the Cmaps after the session, and add in additional notes (whether sticky notes or color-coded notations if using paper, or additional nodes if using CmapTools) with clarifications and questions that can be used to revise the Cmap with the Cmappee in a follow-up session. This in turn creates a more comprehensive and comprehensible map.

Integrating Maps

Another challenge lies in how to integrate data points (i.e., multiple Concept Maps) across experts. Integration across Cmaps comes with practice, and there are numerous approaches for achieving this end (cf., Harter and Moon, Chapter 7). We have manually integrated Cmaps together by binding various unique sections of each Cmap, which basically forms a union. Another method is to look for intersections across Cmaps wherein knowledge is invariant. Obviously, when trying to form unions of multiple Cmaps, this becomes unmanageable, and this is a specific area where the use of computer-support (e.g., CmapTools) is particularly helpful. Other approaches can include:

- Searching Cmaps for clusters defined according to key words or phrases.
- Categorizing Cmaps according to set themes.
- If it is a procedural-based Cmap, parsing Cmaps according to set time lines and looking for common clusters within a time unit.
- Color-coding different types or levels of knowledge so they are easily identified across Cmaps.

If there is time, it can be useful to have a group of experts integrate the Cmaps as well. One way to do this is by manually clustering similar elements of different Cmaps together to focalize knowledge that seems to naturally fall together. In many cases, different experts raise unique aspects of the same kernels of knowledge, so integration is often straightforward at key concept levels, i.e., by adding additional details around the key concepts. Cmaps also can be looked at as a function of the level of expertise of the Cmappee (i.e., novice versus expert Cmaps), and then compared and contrasted along these lines. As we have mentioned, if different experts are Cmapped on the same query or topic, then their area of expertise also can be a construct by which Cmaps can be compared. Looking for invariance shows common, shared viewpoints across constructs.

Visualization Complexity

As a method reliant on visualization, Concept Mappers will find an upper boundary in the level of complexity that can be represented and interpreted in any single Cmap or even group of Cmaps. This boundary is determined by the medium and structure used to represent a system (e.g., pen and paper versus computer supported tool, color coding, 2D versus 3D, temporality). For example, pen and paper methods allow for more free-flowing interaction and co-construction of maps between Cmapper and Cmappee, whereas CmapTools is a more flexible means for later rework and coding (as well as being more portable and easier to share with others). However, both methods are constrained in their ability to readily integrate between Cmaps. While the Cmapper can embed Cmaps using CmapTools, there is no easy overarching visualization capability for shifting between Cmaps or providing 3D views, though some practitioners have sought innovative means to move the boundaries even higher (cf., Moon and Hoffman, 2008; Chapter 15).

There is also a maximum level of complexity that any one Cmap can represent. For example, when Cmapping spatio-temporal dimensions along with the broader work system factors (as presented in our work with intelligence analysts), we found that only so much could be represented in a single Cmap. The complexity by which we Cmap a system directly correlates to its representation, and there comes a point when too much complexity becomes so visually overwhelming that the observer cannot extract any useful information. This issue goes along with the constraints of pacing and integrating maps. While we suggest slowing down and creating multiple Cmaps in order to capture more complex systems, the issue of linking Cmaps becomes more apparent. While we have not found a single point where a Concept Map reaches that point of over-saturation, we believe that future advancements in visualization techniques in Concept Mapping tools may alleviate some of these issues.

FUTURE DIRECTIONS FOR CONCEPT MAPPING

Our approach for this chapter has been to trace the developments and refinements in our approaches to Concept Mapping that have occurred over the past 25 years. Our applications in aircraft design, emergency crisis management, and intelligence analysis have demonstrated the value and versatility of Concept Mapping in the analysis and design of cognitive systems. We believe the challenges we see, while not comprehensive, extend to many contexts and applications of Concept Mapping. We hope both theorists and practitioners of Concept Mapping find our history, evolution of key aspects, and challenges useful in furthering the field into new industrial contexts and applications.

REFERENCES

Anderson, J. R. 1983. *The architecture of cognition*. Cambridge, MA: Harvard University Press.

Ayoub, P. J. 2005. *Cognitive work analysis: Identification of problem solving tasks and work constraints of intelligence analysts*. Master's thesis (unpublished), The Pennsylvania State University, University Park, PA.

Ayoub, P. J., I. J. Petrick, and McNeese, M. D. 2008. Weather systems: A new metaphor for intelligence analysis. Paper presented at the Human Factors and Ergonomics Society 51st Annual Meeting, Baltimore, MD.

Boose, J. H. 1986. *Expertise transfer for expert systems design*. Amsterdam, The Netherlands: Elsevier Science Publications.

Brewer, I. 2005. Understanding work with geospatial information in emergency management: A cognitive systems engineering approach in GISscience. PhD disser. (unpublished), The Pennsylvania State University, University Park, PA.

Brewer, I. and M. D. McNeese. 2004. *Expanding concept mapping to address spatio-temporal dimensionality*. In *Concept Maps: Theory, Methodology, Technology, Proceedings of the First International Conference on Concept Mapping*, eds. A. Cañas, J. Novak, and F. González. Pamplona, Spain.

Buchanan, B. and E. Shortliffe. 1984. *Rule-based expert systems*, Reading, MA: Addison Wesley.

Canas, A. J., G. Hill, and R. Cariff, et al. 2004. CmapTools: A knowledge modeling and sharing environment. In *Concept Maps: Theory, Methodology, Technology, Proceedings of the First International Conference on Concept Mapping*, eds. A. Cañas, J. Novak, and F. González. Pamplona, Spain.

Connors, E. S., P. L. Craven, and M. D. McNeese, et al. 2004. An application of the AKADAM approach to intelligence analyst work. Paper presented at the Proceedings of the 48th Annual Meeting of the Human Factors and Ergonomics Society (pp. 627–630). Santa Monica CA: Human Factors and Ergonomics Society.

Elm, W., S Potter, and J. Tittle, et al. 2005. Finding decision support requirements for effective intelligence analysis tools. Paper presented at the International Conference on Intelligence Analysis, Washington, D.C.

Glantz, E. J. 2006. *Challenges supporting cognitive activities in dynamic work environments: Application to police domain*. PhD disser. (unpublished), The Pennsylvania State University. University Park, PA.

Hamilton, K., Mancuso, V., Minotra, D., Hoult, R., Mohammed, S., McNeese, M., Parr, A., Dubey, G., & MacMillan, E. (September, 2010). Using the NeoCITIES 3.1 simulation to study and measure team cognition. *Proceedings of the Human Factors and Ergonomics Society 54th Annual Meeting* (27Sept–1Oct). Human Factors and Ergonomics Society: Santa Monica, CA.

Hutchins, E. 1995. *Cognition in the Wild*. Cambridge, MA: MIT Press.

ICAM Architecture Part II-Volume IV—Function Modeling Manual (IDEF0), AFWAL-TR-81-4023, Materials Laboratory, Air Force Wright Aeronautical Laboratories, Air Force Systems Command, Wright-Patterson Air Force Base, OH, June 1981.

Klein, G. A., E. Calderwood, and D. McGregor. 1989. Critical decision method for eliciting knowledge. *IEEE Transactions on Systems, Man, and Cybernetics,* 19 (3): 462–472.

Kottmann, B., B. Porter, B. S. Zaff, and M. D. McNeese. 1991. Producing concept maps: The concept mapping tool 1.0 [Computer program]. Wright-Patterson Air Force Base, OH: Armstrong Laboratory, Human Engineering Division.

McFarren, M. R. 1987. Using concept mapping to define problems and identify key kernels during the development of a decision support system. Master's thesis. AFIT/GST/ENS/87J-12. School of Engineering, Air Force Institute of Technology, Wright-Patterson AFB, OH.

McNeese, M. D. 1994. A summarization of concept mapping as cognitive task analysis. In *Cognitive Task Analysis,* Chair S. Gordon. Panel presentation at the 2nd Conference on Naturalistic Decision Making, Dayton, OH.

McNeese, M. D., B. S. Zaff, and K. J. Peio, et al. 1990. An advanced knowledge and design acquisition methodology: Application for the pilots associate. AAMRL-TR-90-060. Armstrong Aerospace Medical Research Laboratory, Wright-Patterson Air Force Base, OH.

McNeese, M. D., E. Connors, and T. Jefferson, et al. 2004. An assessment of image analyst work using the living laboratory framework (Tech. Rep. No. 0017). University Park, PA: Pennsylvania State University, School of Information Sciences and Technologies. Report to the National Geospatial-Intelligence Agency (NGA), Washington, D.C.

Moon, B. and R. Hoffman. 2008. Rapid and accurate idea transfer: Presenting ideas with concept maps. Scientific and Technical Final Report. Contract No. W31P4Q-08-C-0229. Washington, D.C.: Defense Technical Information Center.

Novak, J. D. and D. B. Gowin. 1984. *Learning how to learn*. New York: Cambridge University Press.

Novak, J. D. and A. J. Cañas. 2006. The origins of the concept mapping tool and the continuing evolution of the tool. *Information Visualization,* 5: 175–184.

Perkins, D. N. 1986. *Knowledge as design*. Hillsdale, NJ: Lawrence Erlbaum.

Rasmussen, J. 1986. *Information processing and human-machine interaction: An approach to cognitive engineering*. New York: North-Holland.

Snyder, D. E., M. Gomes, and S. Lind, et al. 1992. Integrating cognitive maps: The concept interpreter 2.0 [Computer program].

Snyder, D. E., M. D. McNeese, and B. S. Zaff. 1990. Integrating cognitive maps: The concept interpreter 1.0 [Computer program]. Wright-Patterson Air Force Base, OH: Armstrong Laboratory, Human Engineering Division.

Spravka, J. J., M. E. Gomes, and S. Lind. 1994. Tools for automated knowledge engineering (TAKE) system evaluation methodology. No. AL/CF-TR-1994-0113. Ohio: Armstrong Laboratory, Write-Patterson Airforce Base.

Vicente, K. J. 1999. *Cognitive work analysis: Toward a safe, productive, and healthy computer-based work*. Mahwah, NJ: Lawrence Erlbaum.

Zaff, B. S., M. D. McNeese, and D. E. Snyder. 1993. Capturing multiple perspectives: A user-centered approach to knowledge and design acquisition. *Knowledge Acquisition,* 5 (1): 79–116.

Zsambok, C. and G. Klein. 1996. *Naturalistic decision making*. London: Psychology Press.

4

Concept Maps: Tools to Enhance Executive and Team Effectiveness

Barbara L. Bowen

CONTENTS

INTRODUCTION

Effective executives, teams, and individuals focus on contribution: "To focus on contribution is to focus on effectiveness" (Drucker, 1967). Effective contributions assist an organization to fulfill its mission, to achieve its strategic goals, and to build its capacity to continue to do both. Effective contributions require strategic alignment. While there are many executive and management functions, fostering the alignment of people's work so that it contributes to the organization's purpose and goals is arguably the most important. In the absence of such alignment, money and human effort are wasted, productivity suffers, morale tends to suffer because people lack a clear sense of purpose, and it is difficult to move forward with potential innovations because they lack a context. W. Edwards Deming argued that "it is necessary for people to understand the purpose of the organization and how their jobs relate to the purpose of the organization" (Deming, 2000, p. 202), and that a key job of management is to ensure that this is the case.

STRATEGIC ALIGNMENT FAILURES: EXECUTIVE UNDERPERFORMANCE IN A KEY EXECUTIVE FUNCTION

The High-Performance Workforce Study 2004 (Blakely et al., 2004) reports the findings of a survey Accenture conducted with 264 executives of leading companies in 15 industry groups. (Accenture is a global management consulting, technology services, and outsourcing company headquartered in Chicago.) A notable finding was that "just 20 percent of executives ...

said that three-quarters or more of their employees understand the company's strategic goals, while 41 percent said fewer than half have such an understanding. Furthermore, only 22 percent of executives ... said that at least three-quarters of their employees understand how their jobs contribute to the company's ability to achieve its strategic goals, while 40 percent said fewer than half have such an understanding" (p. 6).

A study by Microsoft* in the same year found that 67 percent of employees surveyed reported only three productive days a week at work; the biggest time-waster was "unclear objectives" (Microsoft, 2004).

Concept Maps of an organization's goals and objectives—and those of its divisions, departments, and key functions—can be used to enhance executive and team effectiveness. Concept Maps of strategic objectives function as cognitive scaffolds that foster shared mental models and that can activate the knowledge, know-how, and skills an individual or team needs to make effective contributions.

Concept Maps used in this way enable people at all levels in the organization to "see the big picture," to understand where their work fits in, and how it can contribute to making a difference to the organization, as a whole. Deming argues that such executive and management support for sense-making is essential. Nevertheless, as the Accenture and Microsoft surveys make clear, executives and managers too often fail to fulfill this responsibility, even in world-class organizations and businesses that are regarded as leaders.

This paper presents four case studies that describe how executives and teams in small business, government, and a not-for-profit organization used Concept Maps and Concept Map-based knowledge elicitation to enhance their own effectiveness and that of key teams by fostering strategic alignment, shared vision, and capacity building.

CASE STUDY 1: FOSTERING EFFECTIVE CONTRIBUTION AND CAPACITY BUILDING FOR A DISTRIBUTED TEAM

Distributed teams have become commonplace not only in multinational companies, but in many other kinds of organizations as well. For distributed teams, the challenges of focusing on strategic goals and maintaining alignment within the team are increased because the integument of conversations and professional interactions that take place in shared physical space—the proverbial "water cooler" conversations—are missing. To be consistently effective, distributed teams require tools and processes that foster their alignment and that help them focus on making contributions that aid their organization in achieving its goals.

The Challenge

The Center for Strengthening the Teaching Profession, an independent, nonprofit organization in Washington State funded by the Paul G. Allen Family Foundation and the Bill and Melinda Gates Foundation. The mission of the Center is to foster student achievement by improving the quality of teaching. One of its initiatives is the New Teacher Alliance, whose purpose is to build school district capacity to retain new teachers for the crucial first five years of teaching. The New Teacher Alliance consists of teams from seven partner districts and two educational service districts, as well as the Center's staff responsible for project leadership and management. A key goal for the New Teacher Alliance is to focus the work of the partner districts on developing their capacity to implement the five standards of effective induction: hiring, orientation, mentoring, professional development, and assessment for learning.

The geographic distance between partners, the relatively infrequent face-to-face meetings, and the press of everyday work are challenges for partners in their efforts keep these standards at the center of their attention and work. These same factors also made it challenging for Center staff to assess the growing capacity of the New Teacher Alliance and to identify capacity gaps in a timely fashion. As a distributed, multistakeholder organization, the New Teacher Alliance faces many of the same challenges as companies that utilize distributed and virtual teams. Jeanne Harmon, executive director of the Center for Strengthening the Teacher Profession, put it this way: "Managing a multifaceted, complex statewide project … is a huge challenge, and sharing lessons learned amongst the many partners is absolutely critical to our success" (Harmon, personal communication).

The Method

To address this management challenge, the Center for Strengthening the Teaching Profession contracted Sound Knowledge Strategies to create a

Concept Map of the five essential standards for successful teacher induction, and related subelements. These standards had been identified by a group of master teachers, district administrators, mentors, and other education experts and are the basis for a handbook, *Effective Support for New Teachers in Washington State* (Center for Strengthening the Teaching Profession, 2006). The Concept Map embodies the key elements of this 36-page document in one knowledge representation and makes visible key interrelationships among the standards and elements. It serves three key purposes. First, it fosters strategic alignment and effectiveness by making the strategic goals visible so that they can guide the daily work of teachers and administrators. Second, it facilitates capacity building by providing a knowledge-building infrastructure (Scardamalia and Bereiter, 1993; 2006), which is continuously improved by partners' contributions. Third, it fosters rapid knowledge transfer and development of expert cognitive structure for New Teacher Alliance partners. Reporting on the contribution the Concept Map makes, Mindy Meyer, New Teacher Alliance Project Director, noted:

> The concept map gives a visual representation of our standards that helps many of our team members see the work from a holistic viewpoint and allows them to make connections between the standards and elements and their impact on each other (Meyer, personal communication).

Figure 4.1 shows the Concept Map: What Are the Essential Requirements for Successful Support of New Teachers in Washington State? The dotted lines represent crosslinks and propositions New Teacher Alliance partners have contributed to extend the original Concept Map. The small icons on the concept nodes represent knowledge resources developed by the partners and contributed to the Concept Map. A quick scan of the Concept Map reveals which "essential requirements" for which New Teacher Alliance partners have developed resources. Thus, the Concept Map can be used as a management tool to identify areas of strength as well as gaps in capabilities or performance. It is a tool that is transparent; the same information is available to the partners as to the project executives.

The progressive differentiation and integration of the Concept Map by New Teacher Alliance Partners is an example of "collective cognitive responsibility" (Scardamalia, 2002) and the application at an organizational level (Bowen and Meyer, 2008) of the New Model of Education,

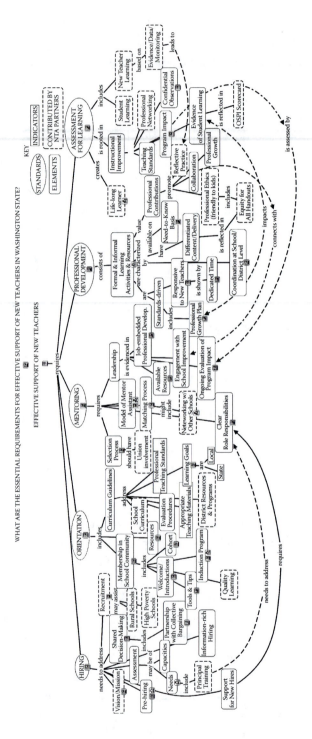

FIGURE 4.1

What are the essential requirements for successful support of new teachers in Washington State?

originally proposed by Novak and Cañas (2004) as a way to help students build powerful, expert-like cognitive structure by extending and enhancing "skeleton expert Concept Maps."

The Concept Map was introduced to 21 New Teacher Alliance teachers, mentors, and administrators during a professional development workshop in November 2006. The project director and author had worked closely together for over a month to design the introduction of the Concept Map and meaningful activities to engage partners with it. Three versions of the Concept Map were used in the workshop:

1. The Cmap version was projected onto a screen and was used by the author to introduce Concept Maps and the role of this particular one.
2. Concept Maps on 11 × 14-in. paper were distributed to the attendees together with Post-it™ notes. The New Teacher Alliance project director facilitated district teams to attach Post-it notes with the titles of their work products to the Concept Map next to the standard or element that each one addressed.
3. A 4 × 3-ft Concept Map printed on vinyl was displayed in the front of the room and as a culminating activity, each team added Post-It notes with the titles of documents and work products to this map. These Post-it notes were a way to easily and quickly see the standards where partners had done the most work and the standards they had not yet addressed. The Concept Map with these Post-It notes represented the current collective capacity of the Alliance. A Board member used the Concept Map with all the Post-it notes to review what had been accomplished and to preview the work ahead.

The Concept Map was used to help the participants see the conceptual landscape for successful teacher induction, identify the standards and elements their own work-to-date addressed, and identify the standards and elements that represented areas of collective strength (hiring, orientation, mentoring) and those where work had not yet been done (professional development, assessment of learning). In addition, during an interactive session, participants contributed to further refinement and application of the Concept Map. The new links and propositions contributed by the participants are represented as dotted lines in the Concept Map. These extensions and refinements of the Concept Map are what Ausubel (1963) calls progressive differentiation and integrative reconciliation.

During the 2006–2007 school year, the author developed formatting guidelines and a six-item, five-point scale, assessment: Rubric to Assess Partner Contributions to the New Teacher Alliance Concept Map. The assessment items included:

- Alignment: Document's content aligns with standard and element to which it is contributed.
- Effectiveness/Impact: Document conveys systemic impact on the whole school district.
- Meaningful Learning: Document provides evidence that the team has incorporated new information to improve existing knowledge and practice related to this Element.
- Self-Assessment/Reflective Practice: Document includes techniques, guidelines, or goals the team is using for self-assessment of progress.
- Professional Contribution: Contributed work advances the knowledge and practice of NTA.
- Continuous Improvement: Document provides evidence for continuous improvement of knowledge and practice.

This rubric was used by the author to evaluate each document and the contribution it made to help the New Teacher Alliance achieve its goals.

In Spring 2007, the Web page version of the Cmap was linked to the New Teacher Alliance Web site, making it and all of the attached knowledge resources readily accessible to all New Teacher Alliance participants as well as other educators involved in improving teacher induction.

Results and Impact

Results and impacts that were found for executive effectiveness and team effectiveness are presented below.

Executive Effectiveness

The executive director of the Center for Strengthening the Teaching Profession and the project director of the New Teacher Alliance used the Concept Map to help the people in their organization function "… to understand the purpose of the organization and how their jobs relate to the purpose of the organization" (Deming 2000, p. 202).

The director of the New Teacher Alliance has effectively used the Concept Map as a tool to clarify the "big picture" of successful teacher induction, and to foster alignment of partners' work with the strategic goals of the project: the implementation of the five standards, and associated elements, of successful teacher induction. At the time of this writing, partners have contributed 84 documents. Each of these has been vetted for the quality and scope of the work it represents in alignment with the standard to which it is contributed. The collective knowledge resources attached to the Cmap represent enhanced capacity for partners and others to effectively implement these standards.

The project director reported that the Concept Map "… allows districts to see the standards in a visual way that shows the interconnectedness of the work. It also creates an opportunity for the Alliance partners to build from each other's work" (Meyer, personal communication). New Teacher Alliance partners made effective contributions and enhanced organizational capacity by adding new elements and identifying new crosslinks to the Concept Map, and by contributing their work products to "flesh out" a knowledge model.

The Concept Map also supported another executive function: preserving the assets of the organization, including its knowledge assets. It reduces the "lost knowledge" phenomenon that is a problem for so many organizations as baby boomers retire (DeLong, 2004).

Partners have fleshed out the Concept Map by contributing knowledge resources and by adding new links and propositions. These contributions, based in real-world practice, have become the living tissue for the Concept Map. The contribution of documents and insights builds capacity by enabling the work of each partner to be shared both within the New Teacher Alliance as well as with the wider education community interested in teacher induction. Each contribution to the standards and elements Concept Map builds the capacity of the New Teacher Alliance and its partner districts to successfully induct new teachers.

Team Effectiveness

Project Director Mindy Meyer reported:

> At the start having the map was helpful because it allowed the participants to demonstrate their understanding of the standards and add to the

learning of the group. It also gave them a place to house their documents. The simplified version of the concept map helps visual learners to see the big picture and connections between the standards (Meyer, personal communication).

This assessment was echoed by workshop participants who reported that the Concept Map enhanced their "… ability to collect the broad picture with details that can clarify issues," and to "…. think more clearly about the wide range of initiatives implied by the standard." The project director also reported that some partners experienced challenges in using the Concept Map in the course of their work. "For some educators, the detailed map was too busy and harder for them to sort through than the standards" (Meyer, personal communication). She also reported that some partners did not use the Cmap to access the work of other partners because it took a long time for the Cmap to download on the computer equipment in their schools. NTA partners used the rubric as a self-assessment tool to guide the revision and upgrading of their work products.

The availability of the Concept Map in its Web version enables the leading edge work the New Teacher Alliance is doing to be easily accessed not only by educators in Washington State, but also by any educator involved in improving teacher induction.

CASE STUDY 2: FOSTERING EFFECTIVENESS VIA KNOWLEDGE-SHARING TO CREATE SHARED VISION

This case study describes a Concept Map-based knowledge elicitation project that took place in the offices of a county public health agency. The agency is divided into two divisions: community health and environmental health. Staff includes community health nurses, a physician who is the county medical officer, environmental health specialists, and administrators.

Agency staff members are specialists in a broad range of public health functions including: maternal and child health, epidemiology, water quality, septic system compliance, watershed health, storm water management, and solid waste education. At the time the project started, the average length of employment had been 12 years for the community health nurses and 6 years for environmental health staff. The agency director is an experienced public health nurse who had held her position as agency director for 10 years.

The current culture of the agency is rich with knowledge-sharing that takes place both in staff meetings and "on-the-fly" in the course of daily work. While this sharing has enormous value, it is informal and does not create permanent organizational resources that increase capacity and effectiveness.

The Challenge

Due to the long-standing history of community health in the United States, the work of community health nurses is strongly rooted in community health concepts, i.e., prevention and the value of building and maintaining relationships with clients and colleagues. Because the background and training of environmental health staff are more varied, these community health concepts do not occupy the same core status in guiding their daily work.

The two goals of the agency director who sponsored the project were to (1) foster a common vision of public health that is rooted in core community health concepts, and (2) reduce the time and cost of integrating new staff, both community health and environmental health, into the agency. She saw the Concept Map-based team knowledge elicitation as a way to advance both goals by enhancing the shared knowledge and shared vision for both the community health and environmental health staff.

The value of team knowledge elicitation as a tool for enhancing the effectiveness of teams was first described by Novak (1998):

> ... in seminars with research directors at a very large consumer products company, we used concept maps ... to help groups design new products and to pinpoint gaps in knowledge available that needed to be filled through new, targeted research. The manager of the program remarked, "You led the team to see better the nature of the new product and research that needs to be done in four hours than usually occurs in four months" (p. 97).

Perez and Bowen (2008) described the use of Concept Maps to facilitate feedback from all stakeholders to evaluate and improve a national environmental monitoring program. Fourie and van der Westhuizen (2008) explored the use of Concept Maps to facilitate alignment of strategic intent between executives and employees in South African wine cooperatives.

The Method

The focus question identified by the agency director to guide knowledge elicitation and development of the top Concept Map was: "What are the core knowledge and capabilities needed by a public health agency in order to protect and improve community health?" The agency director invited five experienced and respected community health nurses, three environmental health staff, the chief medical officer, and the finance manager to participate in the Concept Map-based knowledge elicitation sessions. One of the community health nurses was a national leader in the field of maternal and infant health and another was a statewide leader in epidemiology. In general, their colleagues regarded the community health nurses as "wise elders."

Eleven Concept Map-based team knowledge elicitation sessions were conducted. Four of these sessions were with groups of 7 to 13, four were with groups of 3 to 4 staff involved in developing a key subConcept Map, and three sessions were with the agency director to review and format the emerging Concept Maps. The sessions with the larger groups were four hours in length, the small group sessions were two hours, and the sessions with the director typically lasted an hour or less. As a result, in some sessions the focus shifted as different staff contributed their knowledge and perspectives.

The knowledge elicitation sessions were conducted by one Cmapper, following the process developed by Novak (1998, pp. 101-111). Novak's method involves developing a focus question to define the knowledge domain, eliciting concepts related to the focus question, and gathering them in a "parking lot." When 15 to 25 concepts are gathered, participants are asked review them to identify the most general, top-level concept, in relation to the focus question. Then the relationships between concepts are defined. The Concept Map is differentiated until the knowledge represented in the Concept Map is regarded by the client as an adequate knowledge representation to provide a full answer to the focus question.

Overall, Novak's method was used as a guide, but the actual process was a bit more improvisational. The team was quite diverse and the responses and conversation tended to veer in different directions reflecting the interests, insights, and experience of the participants. The results of the initial session, in which community health nurses focused on the importance of their capacity to build and maintain relationships as a core capability, were three or four subConcept Maps, rather than one main Concept Map. Later these were organized under the concept "building and maintaining effective relationships."

In the second large-group session, a Concept Map, The Decision to File a Child Protective Services Report, was developed as an example of a "tough decision" faced by community health nurses. What became clear during the creation of this Concept Map was how the core values and concepts of public health—prevention and value for relationships—guided the work of community health nurses. One highly respected veteran community health nurse spoke to the "pain of seeing" and the need to have the "courage to see." The commitment to relationships (with the family involved and with fellow nurses) is a core value that makes it possible "to do this hard work." Environmental health staff commented to the agency director after this session, "It's the same for us, but we haven't viewed it in this way before."

During the third large group knowledge elicitation session, the environmental health staff identified the job of responding to citizen complaints as a problematic area due to the absence of a shared set of principles or guidelines for decision making. Responsibility for responding to citizen complaint calls rotated and each staff member made decisions based on his or her perspective, values, and skills. As a result, it was difficult for other staff to respond to questions from citizens about how or why a decision was made, or why their complaint had not been addressed. The focus question, "What is the process for prioritizing citizen complaint responses?" was used to guide knowledge elicitation to develop a Concept Map that could be used as a decision-support tool. The remaining knowledge elicitation sessions were devoted to the development of the Concept Map: Environmental Health Complaint Response Prioritization Process, shown in Figure 4.2.

Following each knowledge elicitation session, the author formatted the Cmaps that had been created, generated clarifying questions, e.g., about concept hierarchy, linking phrases, and knowledge gaps, and sent picture files of the Concept Maps to those involved with a request for feedback. The agency director was the primary, but not the sole, source of feedback. The finance manager made important contributions to and provided important insights about the organization of the Concept Map used to prioritize responses to citizen environmental health complaints.

Focus Question: How does [ABC public health agency] prioritize complaint investigations & client intakes
to insure the most effective use of limited resources?

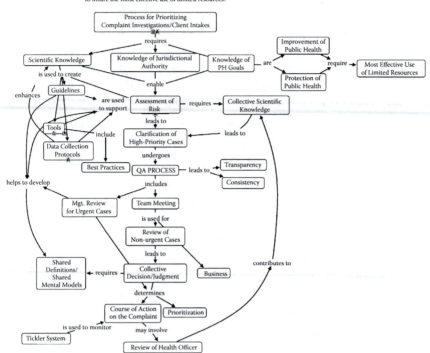

FIGURE 4.2
Process to prioritize citizen complaints.

Results and Impact

Results and impacts were found for executive and management effectiveness and team effectiveness.

Executive and Management Effectiveness

The agency director reported that the Concept Map-based knowledge elicitation sessions and the resulting Concept Maps advanced her goals, i.e., enhancing strategic alignment through expert knowledge sharing and creating a shared vision to unite the community health and environmental health departments:

> [The] processes of tacit knowledge elicitation and creation of concept maps of our collective knowledge and insights leave us with training procedures

and tools for prioritization and planning. Everyone finally has a common language that helps us orient ourselves in the context of core principles of community and public health (Baldwin, personal communication).

W. E. Deming (2000, p. 473) wrote that the aim of an organization "is to make best use of all knowledge and skill in the [organization] to improve its quality, productivity, and competition." As a result of her participation in the knowledge elicitation sessions, the finance manager who made major contributions to the Concept Map Environmental Health Process for Prioritizing Complaint Investigations expanded her role to serving as de facto operations manager for environmental health response to citizen complaints. This expanded role enabled her knowledge and capabilities in organizing and managing operations to be mobilized for the benefit of the agency. She and the environmental health team have used the Concept Map as tool to foster consistency, transparency, and quality control for dealing with citizen complaints.

The agency director reported using the top level Concept Map, Core Knowledge and Capabilities Needed for a Public Health Agency to Protect and Improve Public Health, as an orientation tool for new staff.

Team Effectiveness

Enhanced effectiveness for the environmental health team, and the agency as a whole, was signaled by the director's statement of greater alignment and shared vision between community and environmental health. The development and use of a Concept Map that was used as a facilitative decision support tool for the environmental health team is de facto evidence of enhanced effectiveness due to enhanced alignment of the environment health team.

A questionnaire was e-mailed to each participant, 13 in all, and 6 staff and the director responded. This was a consultative engagement, and not a research project. Staff are overloaded and a better than 50 percent return rate was appreciated under the circumstances. Staff responses addressed the value of being able to "look at the big picture," the importance of shared vision and common language, and the value of a tool that helps keep agency and department goals in focus in the course of daily work. Specific comments included:

- It's not that often that we get a chance to look at the bigger picture of public health, even at the local level. ... The process helps strengthen my resolve to continue in the work.
- [I have] a clearer understanding of what my colleagues face day to day in their jobs and how they frame important questions about how [our agency] serves the needs of the public and environment.
- I had anticipated parallels between caring for the community and for our piece of the planet, but the mapping clearly demonstrated how we are dealing with two sides of the same coin. I'd like to see the language and approaches to human and environmental health become increasingly consistent over time.
- As I deal with projects ... I will refer back to the mapping exercises to envision how my work interfaces with the larger [context of our agency] and department goals.

While these comments are admittedly anecdotal evidence, they do point to the Concept Map-based knowledge elicitation as a vehicle for more effectively mobilizing the knowledge and skills of agency staff to more effectively fulfill the agency's mission.

Challenges and Suggestions for Improvement

Suggestions for improvement in the Concept Map-based knowledge elicitation sessions included having more staff participate. A couple of staff members found the sessions frustrating and commented during the sessions, "This is not the way I think." One staff member who initially voiced this objection became the lead person for the development of the Concept Map to prioritize responses to citizen environmental health complaints. A grounding in the cognitive research and theory of meaningful learning on the part of the facilitator/knowledge-elicitor, as well as skill in group facilitation, is necessary to address this and other objections.

The agency director attempted to use the top-level Concept Map during discussions with public health policy analysts from the state, but reported difficulty in engaging people to extend the Concept Map and use the core concepts in the formulation of public health policy. It seems likely that orientation to Concept Maps and Novak and Ausubel's theories is an essential element to include in any effort to introduce and use Concept Maps.

CASE STUDY #3: REDUCING RAMP-UP TIME FOR CUSTOMER SERVICE SPECIALIST

Thinking of You is a home-based business specializing in the sale of high-quality, high-performance vitamins and nutritional supplements designed to be maximally bio-assimilable and hypoallergenic. Thinking of You's customers include a high percentage of people with autoimmune issues, allergies, and who are cancer survivors or undergoing treatments for cancer. Its customers tend to be highly knowledgeable about their health condition and about physiology and nutrition. While Thinking of You does not provide medical advice, the quality of its products and its highly knowledgeable customers require that its customer service representatives answer high-level questions about the products in order to provide customers with the high-quality customer service they have come to expect. The owner has been in business for over 10 years and is related to the physician and biochemist who develops the products. As a result, she has substantial knowledge in the above areas and has learned from years of experience what her customers want and expect from their conversations and contact with the company.

The Challenge

As a result of the high quality and effectiveness of the products and the high quality of customer service, the business has grown rapidly, requiring the hiring of customer service representatives. The owner has found getting new customer service representatives "up to speed" to be a time-consuming process that is a drain on her own time and that results in a period when responses to customers may not meet customer, and her own, expectations:

> I realize I keep so many details in my head when I assist a customer that it is impossible to get a back-up, front desk person trained in short order (or at all). I recently needed to train a replacement, as I'll be traveling, and I tried the best way I could, through repetition and some helpful notes. We worked for nearly six weeks and nothing was "sticking." I had to start over (Jaffe, personal communication).

The Method

Thinking of You's owner hired the author to conduct Concept Map-based expert knowledge elicitation. The purpose was to create a suite of Concept

Maps representing her knowledge and perspective of outstanding customer service that could be used as a performance support tool to help new customer service representatives get up-to-speed and respond effectively to customer phone calls. A suite of five Concept Maps was created:

1. The "root map": Thinking of You: Quality Customer Service for Quality Customers
2. Thinking of You's Positive Customer Experience
3. Thinking of You's Order Process
4. Qualifying Orders
5. Responding to Unqualified Orders—No Healthcare Practitioner

Interestingly, the Concept Map that became the "top map" was the last to be constructed. After eliciting the owner's knowledge of the processes and documents involved in responding to customers and fulfilling orders, the author had a feeling that these process diagrams, while extremely useful, did not fully capture the owner's vision for her business. The author asked the owner, "What do you know about your customers that the new customer service representative does not know, and needs to know if she is going to do the job the way you want her to do it?" The owner immediately started to explain that her customers were highly knowledgeable and had typically tried other products to address their health challenges. This was the essential context that the customer service representative needed to have, in addition to the knowledge of the processes, in order to respond to customers in the way that has become a core part of Thinking of You's brand (Figure 4.3).

Results and Impact

Results and impacts that were found for executive and management effectiveness and team effectiveness are reviewed below.

Executive and Team Effectiveness

The author received a letter from Thinking of You's owner shortly after the conclusion of the project. It provided a summary statement of the results her business realized from the Concept Map-based knowledge elicitation.

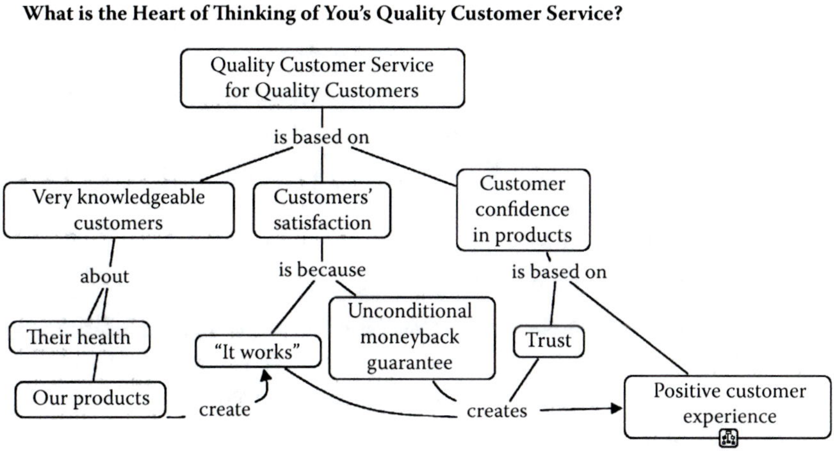

What is the Heart of Thinking of You's Quality Customer Service?

FIGURE 4.3

Thinking of You's quality customer service.

… in less than six hours, we refined a new vision for the company. We were able to link resources to the Cmap that were otherwise in various electronic files or lost in a shuffle. You helped me reframe the important role of our key customer service contact. Once training of [the] new customer service expert was underway, in less than a week our new trainee was taking phone calls. By week two, she is handling complex calls with ease. [The] CMaps gave her a context and references to understand her new role and ways to answer a variety of situations that she is called to respond to. The reduced ramp-up time was a huge success for us. [The] CMap tool can be updated easily and allows us to add resources and documents as those evolve with the organization. Call us, you will be quite impressed with our new team member (Jaffe, personal communication).

CASE STUDY 4: CONCEPT MAPS AS TOOLS FOR EFFECTIVE EXECUTIVE PRESENTATIONS

S2KM is a boutique consulting firm specializing in legal and financial services for the structured settlement industry. A structured settlement is a financial or insurance arrangement, including periodic payments, that is developed as part of the legal settlement of a personal injury claim. The structured settlement industry is highly regulated and is impacted by both state and federal laws, including Internal Revenue Service codes, Medicare, and Medicaid. S2KM's mission is to "Use Knowledge Management to Improve Performance in the Structured Settlement Industry." S2KM Managing Director Patrick Hindert is an attorney, experienced business executive, and an innovative entrepreneur. He is a co-author of the leading textbook in the field of structured settlements, *Structured Settlements and Periodic Payment Judgments* (Hindert et al., 1986) and is a recognized expert in the field, especially in the area of federal law and regulations and their impact on the industry. Hindert has served as president of major professional organizations in the field and is a featured speaker at national and regional conferences.

S2KM's business strategy combines Hindert's knowledge of, and interest in, current and emerging interactive capabilities of the World Wide Web, and his expert knowledge of the law and regulatory environment to develop and deliver new structured settlement products and services. Examples of such products and services might include: interactive, collaborative knowledge-bases that can be used as performance support by special needs and elder law attorneys and financial planners; a Web-based marketplace for buying and selling structured settlements in the secondary marketplace; and a Web-based marketplace for targeted expert consulting services.

The Challenge

The legal and regulatory landscape of structured settlements is complex and dynamic, with almost continuous changes in regulations and codes. The impact of the Web 2.0—the "interactive Web"—and of social media are also complex and not well understood. S2KM's business strategy involves both of these domains.

S2KM's managing director understands the power of what he calls "visual thinking," and commissioned Sound Knowledge Strategies to develop a suite of Concept Maps over a period of two and a half years. The suite includes Concept Maps of online social media, e.g., podcasting; the impact of Web 2.0 on lawyers; the structure of the primary and secondary structured settlement markets; new business opportunities created by the intersection of the capabilities offered by the Internet; and opportunities for new financial and structured settlement products and services created by changes in federal laws and Internal Revenue Service Codes. An example is shown in Figure 4.4.*

The Method

The Concept Map-based knowledge elicitation for S2KM utilized Web-based collaboration tools, e.g., e-mail, Skype, and CmapTools. The process typically began with a three- to five-page memo created by Hindert outlining the key issues and concepts related to the focus question. The author transformed this outline into a draft Concept Map using CmapTools, and after studying it, returned a picture file of the draft map together with a list of clarifying questions to the managing director. The questions focused on clarifying the linking phrases describing the relationships between concepts, probing to determine that the "top concept" in the draft Cmap was the correct one in light of the focus question, and identifying apparent knowledge gaps in the Concept Map(s). The suite of Concept Maps was revised via online meetings using the Cmap as a shared desktop and Skype and e-mails for communication. Typically, the complete refinement of a suite of Concept Maps was accomplished over a period of weeks, sometimes revising and tweaking the Concept Maps continued for months.

Since the new business ventures Hindert was developing were to be Web-based, optimizing Google Rank and increasing traffic to S2KM's blog and wikis was a critical element of S2KM's business strategy. Flickr*, a Web application for photo sharing, is known to be "Google friendly," so picture files of several Concept Maps, including, "What is Podcasting," were posted to Flickr.

Results and Impact

Results and impacts that were found for executive effectiveness are discussed below.

---

* Many of the Concept Maps developed for S2KM can be accessed in this wiki: http://soundknowledgestrategies.wikispaces.com/Structured++Settlement+Concept+Maps; in various posts on the S2Km blog, http://s2kmblog.typepad.com/; or the Portfolio page of the Sound Knowledge Strategies Web site, www.soundknowledgestrategies.com.

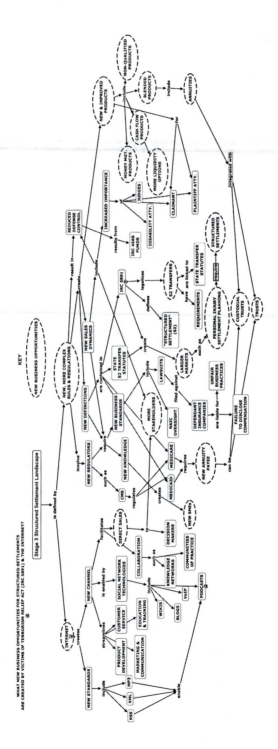

FIGURE 4.4

New business opportunities created by the Internet and the Victims of Terrorism Relief Act (IRC 5891).

Executive Effectiveness

S2KM's managing director has used Concept Maps consistently to communicate his knowledge and perspectives on regulatory changes and to communicate the potential of new business ventures in this conceptually complex industry. Hindert has used the Concept Maps as executive presentation tools on S2KM's blog, in presentations to key industry associations, in presentations to potential business partners and investors, and in wikis, a Web-based publishing and collaboration tool. He has used Concept Maps to increase the Web presence of S2KM's blog and wikis, to build an audience able to understand the business potential created by the intersecting trends in structured settlements and the Web.

Hindert and a business partner also launched a joint venture to develop a Web-based product and service that will provide expert knowledge to five different client groups. They commissioned the author to create of a suite of Concept Maps for a key presentation to the National Association of Special Needs Attorneys and potential investors.

A client's repeat business is a signal of success. Another measurable success has been the high Google Page Rank achieved by the Web version of the suite of Concept Maps, "Web 2.0 and Lawyers." Sometime after the Web-based version of the Concept Maps that make up "Web 2.0 and Lawyers" was introduced on the S2KM blog, Hindert called the author and said, "Barbara, we're #1 on Google!" A Google search using the terms "lawyers" and "Web 2.0" delivers about 2,700,000 hits. For the past four years, "Web 2.0 and Lawyers" has consistently appeared on the first page of this search report. For S2KM, this achievement is a high-impact result that is a consequence of the combined effectiveness of Concept Maps to represent expert knowledge and the expert knowledge of S2KM's managing director that is represented in the suite of Concept Maps.

SUMMARY

Peter Drucker, founder of modern management theory, proposed the concept of effectiveness as the core function of management in knowledge-based organizations (Drucker 1967). The essential requirement for effectiveness, in Drucker's view, is to focus on contributions; in particular, contributions that assist the organization to fulfill its purpose, to achieve its strategic goals, and to build its capacity to continue to do both in the future. Executives who foster effectiveness help people to see "the big picture," to understand the organization's goals, and to align their work so that it contributes to achieving them.

The executives of the organizations discussed in the previous case studies used Concept Maps to address these essential requirements of effectiveness. The results, while they cannot be reported with statistical significance, are promising. The executives of the Center for Strengthening the Teaching Profession and the New Teacher Alliance used Concept Maps as tools to ensure every participant in the project understood the strategic goals and aligned their work to achieving them. The Concept Map of Standards and Elements for Successful Teacher Induction and the almost 100 vetted documents and work products that its partners have contributed constitute a valuable organizational knowledge asset. In light of the low levels of executive effectiveness reported in Accenture's The High Performance Workforce study, the executives of this not-for-profit would have ranked at the top.

A public health agency has a new Concept Map-based decision support tool and a new staff-developed process for prioritizing citizen environmental complaints. The agency director reports her goal of creating a shared vision and common language for community health and environmental health has been advanced.

A small business that sells high-quality vitamins and supplements has used Concept Maps to substantially reduce the ramp-up time needed for new customer service representatives to successfully respond to a range of customer inquiries.

The managing director of S2KM has used Concept Maps to advance his goals of developing new Web-based businesses that develop and market new structured settlement and financial services and products. The ability of the Concept Map "Web 2.0 and Lawyers" to maintain a First Page Google Rank has increased the number of hits on the S2KM Web site, which is essential for the success of a Web-based marketing business.

While nothing can replace the need for highly knowledgeable, experienced, and skilled executives and managers in today's business climate, even the already effective manager can use all the help he or she can get to "to make the best use of all the knowledge and skill in the organization to improve its quality, productivity and competitive advantage" (Deming, 2000, p. 473). Concept Maps and Concept Map-based expert knowledge elicitation have a place among the tools that executives and teams can use to meet the challenges that face not only businesses, but all organizations that need to make the best use of their people's knowledge and know-how.

REFERENCES

Ausubel, D. 1963. *The psychology of meaningful verbal learning*. Grune & Stratton: New York.

Bowen, B. and M. Meyer. 2008. Applying Novak's new model of education to facilitate organizational effectiveness, professional development and capacity building for the New Teacher Alliance. In *Proceedings of the Third International Conference of Concept Mapping*, eds. A. Cañas, P. Reiska, M. Ahlberg, and J. D. Novak. Tallinn, Estonia and Helsinki, Finland Helsinki, 310–315.

Brakely, H., P. Cheese, and D. Clinton. 2004. *The high performance workforce study*. Accenture. Accessed online at: hp_study_2004_exec.pdf/ p. 5.

Center for Strengthening the Teaching Profession. 2006. *Effective support for new teachers in Washington State: Standards for beginning teacher induction*. Silverdale, Washington.

DeLong, D. 2004. *Lost knowledge: Confronting the threat of an aging workforce*. New York: Oxford University Press.

Deming, W. E. 2000. *Out of the crisis*. Cambridge, MA: MIT Press.

Drucker, P. 1967. *The effective executive*. New York: Harper Business, p. 70.

Fourie, L.C.H. and T. van der Westhuizen. 2008. The value and use of concept maps in the alignment of strategic intent. In *Concept Mapping: Connecting Educators: Proceedings of the Third International Conference on Concept Mapping*, eds. A. Cañas, P. Reiska, M. Åhlberg, and J. Novak. Tallinn, Estonia and Helsinki, Finland.

Hindert, D., J. Dehner, and P. Hindert. 1986. *Structured Settlements and Periodic Payment Judgments*. New York: Law Journal Press.

Microsoft®. 2004. Survey finds workers average only three productive days per week. http://www.microsoft.com/presspass/press/2005/mar05/03-15threeproductivedayspr.mspx (accessed January 2010).

Novak, J. D. 1998. *Learning, creating and using knowledge: Concept maps as facilitative tools in schools and corporations*. Mahwah, NJ: Lawrence Erlbaum Associates, p. 97.

Novak, J.D. and R. Gowin. 1984. *Learning how to learn*. New York: Cambridge University Press.

Novak, J. and A. Cañas. 2004. Building on New Constructivist Ideas and CmapTools to Create a New Model of Education. *Concept Maps: Theory, Methodology, Technology: Proceedings of the First International Conference on Concept Mapping*, eds. A. Cañas, D. Novak and F. M. Gonzales Pamplona, Spain.

Perez, R. and B. Bowen. 2008. Cmaps: A useful tool for improving a national environment monitoring system design. In *Concept Mapping: Connecting Educators: Proceedings of the Third International Conference on Concept Mapping*, eds. A. Cañas, P. Reiska, M. Åhlberg, and J. Novak. Tallinn, Estonia and Helsinki, Finland.

Scardamalia, M. and C. Bereiter. 1993. Technologies for knowledge-building discourse. *Communications of the ACM*, 36 (5): 37–41.

Scardamalia, M. 2002. Collective cognitive responsibility for the advancement of knowledge. In *Liberal Education in a Knowledge Society*, ed. B. Smith. Chicago: Open Court.

Scardamalia, M. and C. Bereiter. 2006. Knowledge building: Theory, pedagogy, and technology. In *The Cambridge Handbook of the Learning Sciences*, ed. R. Sawyer. Cambridge, MA: Cambridge University Press.

5

Concept Mapping on the Road: Applied Business Concept Mapping in Software Implementation and Training Consulting

Bennet Larson

CONTENTS

INTRODUCTION

When consulting with clients in person or online during projects, meaningfully clear communication is obviously desired. My work involves remote software installation, onsite implementation, and training for higher education administrative personnel. I need an effective method to explain the architecture and operation of my company's and its partners' products. In addition, the client and I must collaborate during onsite needs analysis sessions to appropriately tailor the software to fit into the school's administrative processes.

I have found that employing Concept Mapping ("Cmapping") using CmapTools in standard and hybrid ways is key to obtaining a well-documented, shared understanding and, ultimately, a successful project. My aim in this chapter is to explain the usefulness of Concept Mapping and show Cmap layout techniques that have worked well while traveling on both real and virtual roads, for internal company and future uses. The Concept Map in Figure 5.1 outlines the foci of the chapter.

I chose Cmapping using CmapTools over other modeling methods and software tools for simplicity, expressiveness, and readability. The diagramming conventions I have seen used in 25 years of working with information

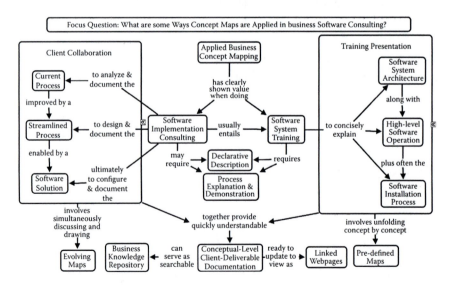

FIGURE 5.1
Chapter organization.

technology (IT), typically require significant expertise to create and need inconvenient legends for laypersons. Using the simple CmapTools interface to draw expressive Concept Maps, I can create plainly readable diagrams while simultaneously talking with a client. In addition, other types of diagrams can be expressed with hybrid Concept Maps—maps that mix the standard declarative hierarchy along with other forms, such as processes. Because I also can easily make and navigate linked diagrams with CmapTools, it is simple to break a discussion into chunks and not worry about fitting it all onto one screen. The fact that I can publish the linked Concept Maps as Web pages on a private or public password-protected CmapServer for viewing with a browser is valuable for communicating with a wider audience. Considering that my clients and colleagues are a mix of managers, software users, and IT staff members, these features make it ideal for a common and meaningful method of communicating among all project stakeholders.

CASE STUDIES

Using the framework shown in Figure 5.1, the following four brief case studies demonstrate how I have used Concept Mapping: (1) with corporate students for "document imaging software" collaboration and training, (2) to provide classroom software training, (3) for Web form requirements and design, and (4) to facilitate online collaboration. In each of these areas, the focus is on a project I created or a class I taught that received positive feedback from the clients. All of the Concept Maps have been modified to remove specific product and client identification information.

Case Study #1: Collaboration and Training in Document Imaging Software

The main goal for a client implementing document imaging software is to scan documents and index (file) them electronically so they can be searched, routed, reviewed, and archived, thereby eliminating the paper and the associated physical filing cabinets. The implementation effort requires both business process collaboration and software training. Specifically, this means doing remote software installation, onsite

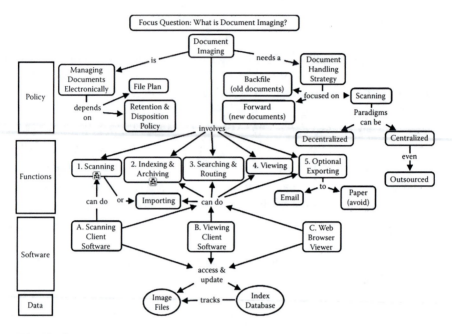

FIGURE 5.2
Document imaging overview.

requirements discussions, software configuration, and, finally, user training. Because most new clients are unfamiliar with document imaging, I first show the overview using Figure 5.2. With CmapTools' presentation mode, I display one concept at a time to explain the big picture. This hybrid Concept Map is organized in four general architectural layers (usually in different colors). Five of the concepts are numbered to show a process. This structure helps clarify the meaning of the concepts and gives a general context useful for the follow-on collaborative discussions. Links to more detailed scanning and indexing maps help in organization and reduce the temptation to make overly busy diagrams.

After discussing the basics of document imaging, the clients and I start analyzing their current business documents and processes one office at a time, usually evaluating two offices during a three-day period. Interface points with other offices are also considered. This collaborative process is shown on the left side of Figure 5.1. Once their current documents and processes are identified and drawn, I suggest a streamlined document-handling process based on what the new software can do for them and then either modify the Concept Map or create a new one to show the suggested approach. Because my job is to enable them to make their own subsequent changes to the solution, I highly recommend they use the developed Concept Maps as the starting point for future requirements discussions. Once they see how easy CmapTools is to use and that it is freely available, they usually agree to try it.

Capturing the configuration details, such as index values, file cabinet names, and user roles, is also done jointly with Concept Maps. Later, the IT staff and I use these technical details to set up the software. Once configured, the users rejoin us to try out the software to make sure the system works as expected. Adjustments to the Concept Maps and configurations are made as necessary.

At the end our collaboration, clients have a set of diagrams they can use to explain to others how they are implementing the software to eliminate paper files and automate office processes. More than once I have heard someone exclaim, "Now I can show what I do so my boss can understand it!" These comments appear to agree with the sentiment expressed by Novak (2010), "… most administrators and managers have a surprisingly poor conceptual understanding of their organizations" (pp. 141–142). In this kind of work, Cmaps proved very useful in solidifying understanding of new processes and capturing implementation details. They also can help both office workers and administrators better understand how their organization functions.

Case Study #2: Software Training for Corporate Students

For training classes, I use Concept Maps to explain software architecture, installation, and operation as outlined on the right side of Figure 5.1. Depending on the client's needs, topics can include system administration, report writing, and document imaging. Concept Maps are useful in the classroom and for curriculum review.

When organizing training materials, I find it helpful to consider what's being taught in terms of either declarative or procedural knowledge (cf., Anderson, 1983). In *Telling Ain't Training* (Stolovitch and Keeps, 2002), the authors apply this distinction to corporate training and explain how we typically explain our knowledge declaratively while learners need to translate it into procedures. Although I agree with Novak (2010) that "knowledge is fundamentally concept-propositional in nature" (p. 113), I still find the declarative–procedural distinction useful in organizing hands-on software system administration training material. It guides me to think about what to explain and then how to translate that into the exercises the students can do to help apply and remember the key concepts.

As is common when teaching corporate-level students in the same class with different knowledge levels, I set the agenda and present material both synchronously and sequentially. While keeping the students' unique backgrounds in mind, I unfold prepared Concept Maps in presentations, explaining each concept. Scripted practice exercises pertaining to various computer system administration tasks are intermingled and self-paced. To minimize the chance of the exercises becoming rote learning experiences, I encourage the learners to keep the Concept Maps handy for review while doing the exercises to keep the objective in context. Although during class we do not have time to create Concept Maps from scratch, I do encourage students to make their own back in their offices as they learn new topics. As a practitioner of what I teach, using Concept Maps this way has helped me, especially for tasks done infrequently. I encourage my students to consider a similar approach. In this way, meaningful learning is being reinforced even in a "time is money" corporate training environment.

One Concept Map I use in class is shown in Figure 5.3. It depicts the database backup subject covered in our basic system administration course. Considering server configuration and budget, class discussion

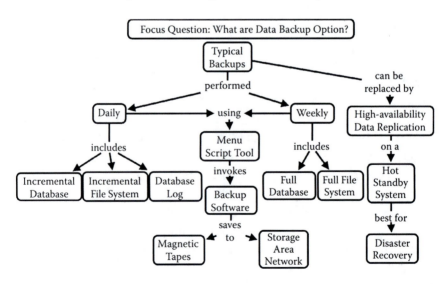

FIGURE 5.3
Data backup options.

focuses on the pros and cons of different backup techniques. Although the exercise involved is partially simulated due to resource limitations, we are able to investigate the delivered menu script tool used for the basic backups. Feedback has been generally positive with this presentation approach. It is usually after doing this kind of Cmap "unfolding" that I get requests for diagram copies.

As the trainer for the course, I am also responsible for improving it. When planning for class learning guide updates, Concept Maps can help to show the current and proposed structure of a curriculum to those who assist in making and approving changes (cf., McDaniel, Roth, and Miller, 2005). Following McDaniel et al., I used Concept Maps to show the current curriculum organization to subject matter experts to get ideas for improvements. It was easy to get them quickly oriented to the course content before we focused on their input. Several topics are often quickly identified as obsolete or missing. Though the quantitative benefit is hard to determine, I have often received positive comments about how the Cmaps clearly showed the courses' organization.

Case Study #3: Web Form Requirements and Design

Another aspect of my work is estimating, designing, and implementing Web forms for the document imaging system. I was motivated to use Concept Maps for a form estimation project after reading about Web design communication techniques in *Communicating Design: Developing Web Site Documentation for Design and Planning* (Brown, 2007).

Brown mentions Cmapping as an inspiration, but uses the terminology *concept modeling* instead to describe a variation to document Web site plans and designs for clients. I extended Brown's approach to the next level of detail to depict form data elements on a Web page. Figure 5.4 shows a prototype design of a four-page form plus a login page for a student academic plan. This diagram started as a requirements document during an online needs analysis meeting with the client, and eventually became an effort estimation tool and design document.

One important recipient of this diagram was a database programmer who was designated to integrate the form with the student database and help with estimating the development time. When we discussed this Cmap, he was impressed with how well it worked communicating what he needed to know for estimating implementation time. Even though the form was only

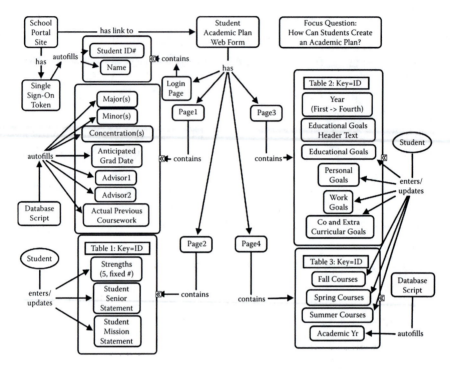

FIGURE 5.4
Student academic plan Web form.

prototyped, the Concept Map proved to be an efficient method of estimating the effort and clearly communicating among all of the geographically separated parties: the client, database programmer, account representative, my supervisor, and myself. This project proved to me the flexibility of creating meaningful Cmaps for a nontraditional, hybrid use case.

Case Study #4: Online Collaboration

I have described online collaboration with Concept Mapping with Web page design among distributed stakeholders. Other experiences I have had include supporting sales presentations for products that clients do not fully understand. They usually want to figure out what a product exactly does and how it would fit in their IT architecture. In one case with a vendor partner, I was actually learning about the new product myself while the salesperson explained it to the client. To be useful, I requested permission to show my desktop for all to see on the Web conference link and, with

CmapTools, proceeded to build a Concept Map during our discussion. I figured this would be beneficial because I have often been on Web or phone conferences where diagrams were not used and the whole discussion seemed confusing because nobody was really sure they understood one another.

After the session was over, everyone quickly asked for a copy of the Concept Map. I also sent a copy to the account manager, who could not attend the discussion, and she was amazed at how easily she could understand the result of the meeting. After this experience, I encourage using Concept Mapping for online meetings as often as possible.

Feedback

On nearly every project, clients have told me how intuitive they have found the Concept Maps created together or used for training. Although the following numbers are drawn from anecdotal evidence, I believe they give some insight into how favorably Concept Maps have been received by people from 15 states in the United States, all in higher education administration. During a 22-month period, I traveled a total of 42 times to 28 different colleges and universities, spending three to five workdays conducting training or for consulting purposes. Of those 42 trips, 17 were for my training and 25 were consultations with approximately 200 people in all. In addition, from my office, I was involved in at least 20 client or colleague Web-based discussions related to demonstrations, sales, and training or software installations. In the 17 cases in which I was the learner, I used CmapTools to outline concepts for my own knowledge and for potential use with future clients. For each of the 45 onsite or online consultations, I created or used at least one Concept Map to facilitate and document joint discussions.

In most cases, when people saw a Concept Map being used, they made positive comments. Practically everyone asked for copies of the diagrams after our sessions and some inquired about CmapTools. The only negative reaction I recall was when I rushed through the presentation of a Concept Map, displaying the entire diagram at once instead of stepping through its development. Not surprisingly, most of my clients had never seen Concept Maps before our sessions together. Even so, reaction to their use was overwhelmingly encouraging. I believe these experiences can be considered additional support for research indicating that Concept Maps are a useful and easy-to-use communications tool (cf., Freeman, 2004; cf., Moon et al., 2008).

OTHER BUSINESS USES

In addition to the client case studies, I have found Concept Maps useful for several other purposes. They are a concrete and flexible way to communicate with colleagues when discussing internal organizational structure, new initiatives, conference presentations, and, hopefully in the future, as a part of a knowledge repository. These uses often help support the externally client-focused consulting and training sessions and so are included to highlight their significance.

Meaningful Organizational Charts

One use has been explaining our organization to newly hired associates. My supervisor asked me several times to help orient new associates and I used Concept Maps to show them how the company was structured, beyond the standard organizational chart and briefing slides. Discussing the diagrams while viewing them as Web pages from a CmapTools server proved convenient and allowed for easy review at a later time. These enhanced diagrams showed company personnel their office functions, product lines, and administrative systems in an interconnected, layered, and multilinked set of maps. During a significant reorganization, I revised the Cmaps to illustrate for myself how the textual announcement translated into a new graphical structure. I am convinced that augmenting traditional organizational charts with expressive Concept Maps makes the traditional chart more meaningful and useful for training and future reference.

Clarifying New Initiatives

Another internal use for Concept Maps has been for clarifying initiatives that appear somewhat confusing at first glance. From our company's periodic employee retreat came an effort to improve internal processes.

E-mailed to everyone as text, matters regarding who-was-supposed-to-do-what-and-when sounded complicated to a relative newcomer like me. Representing the information in a Concept Map format clarified the process and players. I shared it with my supervisor and the lead of the project to help verify that I understood the effort correctly and to encourage communication about its progress. They confirmed I clearly understood the initiative.

Conference Presentations and Reuse

Annually, our company hosts a large customer conference where consultants (and clients) are encouraged to give presentations explaining how our products and partner products are being successfully implemented. I used Concept Maps in this context to outline my thoughts and also used them as diagrams within my slides to explain the product I was promoting. Because my talk was done jointly with a client and with a vendor partner, the Concept Maps were useful during collaboration in preparation for the talk. I had hoped to use the CmapTools presentation feature, however, I was not able to do so because it was a requirement to present slides using a specific template that was also used for the online proceedings. Still, the Cmaps created for the presentation were useful later at client sites to explain product features. This kind of Concept Map reuse has been a frequent occurrence in my experience.

Future Internal Knowledge Repository

Our company may form a comprehensive knowledge repository for use internally and include a CmapServer for Concept Maps. Already there is a good set of well-organized intranets and wiki sites supporting administration and certain product lines. But when I was new to the company, I had that common feeling of being lost without a map to find my way through a maze. A way-finding set of Cmaps could be the top-level gateway to these other resources for newcomers and even not-so-newcomers. On many occasions, I have talked with long-time associates who were still not aware of certain sites or the proper use of multiple product sites that looked the same, but were intended for different purposes. Because company associates are scattered among several offices and in many remote locations, it seems even more important to consolidate organizational knowledge and make it readily accessible. Connecting all of the internal resources together in the form of a linked set of readable "Way-finding Cmaps" may help overcome this conundrum.

Prospects for Additional Applications

For new associates, being able to navigate a set of Concept Maps guiding them through company resources and their position responsibilities would be beneficial and enable them to grasp at least some of the explicit knowledge (otherwise left tacit) of colleagues or those whom they are replacing. It would be ideal if the people who are departing the company would leave a set of continuity Concept Maps that explain, and link to their work, documents and resources they found useful. I was able to do this when I left my previous two positions. Although I do not know if the Cmaps I left behind were fully used, it was personally satisfying to know that I had shared what I had learned. I think any organization would greatly appreciate and value knowledge left behind so others could pick it up and build upon it.

CLOSING THOUGHTS

My work is project-oriented and I spend only days or a few intermittent weeks on any one project with any particular client. Most projects involve introducing clients to new technology and often I have little interaction with them afterwards. Even though I solicit feedback, I rarely capture it formally, so I rely mostly on the verbal comments given during my consulting or training to get an indication of Concept Mapping's usefulness. Because of this, it is difficult to assess the lasting impact of Cmapping as a result of my work. Even though many clients have indicated they are likely to expand on the Concept Maps used during our sessions, I can only verify a few who have followed through. In my line of work, not hearing complaints often indicates all is well. Even without formal feedback, my own project successes give me confidence that choosing to use Concept

Mapping in business consulting and training is a decision that helps me work with clients in a meaningful and lasting way.

REFERENCES

Anderson, J. A. 1983. *The architecture of cognition*. Cambridge, MA: Harvard University Press.

Brown, D. 2007. *Communicating design: Developing Web site documentation for design and planning*. London: New Riders Press.

Freeman, L. 2004. The power and benefits of concept mapping: Measuring use, usefulness, ease of use, and satisfaction. In *Concept Maps: Theory, Methodology, Technology, Proceedings of the First International Conference on Concept Mapping*, eds. A. Cañas, J. Novak, and F. González. Pamplona, Spain.

McDaniel, E., B. Roth, and M. Miller. 2005. Concept mapping as a tool for curriculum design. Paper presented at the *Informing Science + Information Technology Education Conference Proceedings*. Flagstaff, Arizona.

Moon, B., R. Hoffman, and L. Shattuck, et al. 2008. Rapid and accurate idea transfer: Evaluating concept maps against other formats for the transfer of complex information. In *Concept Mapping: Connecting Educators, Proceedings of the Third International Conference on Concept Mapping*, eds. A. Cañas, P. Reiska, M. Åhlberg, and J. Novak. Tallinn, Estonia and Helsinki, Finland.

Novak, J. 2010. *Learning, creating, and using knowledge: Concept maps as facilitative tools in schools and corporations*. New York: Routledge.

Stolovitch, H. D. and E. J. Keeps. 2002. *Telling ain't training*. Alexandria, VA: American Society for Training and Development.

Section II

Recent Case Studies and Results

6

Using Concept Maps to Improve the Practice and Organization of Intelligence in Canada

Natalia Derbentseva and David R. Mandel

CONTENTS

INTRODUCTION

Intelligence production is a vital state function that supports military and policy decision making (Davis, 2006; Herman, 1996; Jervis, 1991). The underlying process of intelligence analysis is inherently challenging. It involves a great deal of uncertainty (Davis, 1992; Heuer, 1999; Lefebvre, 2004) and, with today's "information tsunami" only gaining strength, it is increasingly likely to prompt cognitive overload (Johnson, 2007; Treverton, 2001; Woods, Patterson, and Roth, 2002).

While the intelligence function goes largely unnoticed by the public eye, intelligence failures that significantly impact human lives or international relations bring it acutely into the spotlight. Intelligence failures, such as those associated with the 9/11 terrorist attacks on the United States and misjudgment of Iraqi weapons of mass destruction (WMD) capability, drew considerable public attention to the U.S. intelligence community and triggered a number of commissions of inquiry tasked with recommending reformative measures (Butler et al., 2004; National Commission on Terrorism Attacks upon the United States, 2004).

Although intelligence misjudgments are inevitable due to the uncertainty of events and inherent low predictability of human behavior (Brady, 1993; Heuer, 1999), the tendency to form poor judgments may be affected by several factors, including:

- Poor leadership, lack of interorganizational coordination, and information sharing (Hulnick, 2008).
- Low quality of available information (Pritchard and Goodman, 2009).
- Misinterpretation of available information due to cognitive biases and mindsets (Butterfield, 1993; Heuer, 1999).
- The necessity "to rely on fallible assumptions and inconclusive evidence" as a consequence of substantive uncertainty (Davis, 2008).
- "Lack of analytical imagination," i.e., an inability to generate unlikely hypotheses, which may subsequently impede proper collection requirements from being developed (Bruce, 2008).
- Too much emphasis on current reporting and quantity of production (Johnston, 2005), organizational culture, and incentive structure (Davis, 2008; Johnston, 2005).
- Dynamics of the decision maker–analyst relationship that could result in politicization of intelligence or failures of decision makers to heed accurate intelligence assessments and failure to dismiss inaccurate ones (Steinberg, 2008; Treverton, 2008).

Not surprisingly, due to recent intelligence failures, intelligence organizations in many countries are under significant pressure to review and improve their processes in order to overcome the aforementioned challenges. In an effort to address these issues and explore potential contributions of cognitive and behavioral sciences to intelligence analysis, the Global Futures Forum's Community of Interest on the Practice and Organization of Intelligence (now under the direction of the U.S. Department of State), in collaboration with Defense R&D Canada (DRDC) and Canada's Privy Council Office, hosted a workshop in February, 2009 (Campbell and Mandel 2010). Among the workshop's recommendations was the importance of developing visualization techniques to support analysis and communication of analytic products. (We report in this chapter on the Concept Mapping exercise that represents one of our early attempts to address this issue through research and development.)

Concept Mapping (Novak, 1998; Novak and Cañas, 2008) is a knowledge representation and diagramming method that is suitable as a tool to support various forms of intelligence analysis activity (Heuer and Pherson, 2010; Moore and Hoffman, 2010). Unlike some other knowledge representation techniques (cf., Moon and Hoffman, 2005), Novakian Concept Mapping is rooted in learning theory (Ausube, 1963; Novak and Cañas, 2008). It has over a three-decade history of diverse application within an international community of practice, and is supported by a substantial body of research and practitioner literature (Cañas and Novak, 2006; Cañas, Novak, and González, 2004; Cañas et al., 2008; Coffey et al., 2003; Hoffman, 2008). The development of Concept Maps and Concept Map knowledge models has been greatly facilitated by the creation of CmapTools (Cañas, Hill, and Lott, 2003).

As Moon et al. noted in the Introduction, Concept Mapping and knowledge modeling has attracted the attention of some defense and security agencies of Canada's allies. For example, Hoffman (2008) described current applications of Concept Mapping within the U.S. Department of Defense, including the evaluation of expertise in social network analysis, mapping the "true work" of intelligence analysts and revealing leverage points for aiding analytic work, and improving methods for capturing and sharing a commander's intent.

One of our goals was to introduce Concept Mapping to the Canadian defense and security community and examine its applications. In this chapter, we report on our efforts and preliminary findings. Our efforts consisted of two main activities. First, we developed a Concept Map knowledge model of intelligence analysis as a comprehensive resource on the topic, which is freely available to Canadian stakeholders. Second, we hosted a workshop in February 2010 for Canadian intelligence professionals to introduce them to Concept Mapping and the specific knowledge model we had developed, and to elicit their feedback on the model and on Concept Mapping in general.

The remainder of the chapter is organized as follows: The chapter begins with an explanation of how our current Concept Mapping efforts developed out of prior intelligence-related research activities at DRDC. This explanation is followed by a report on the organization and preliminary findings of the aforementioned workshop, especially the participants' feedback. The chapter concludes by outlining directions for future research on, and future applications of, Concept Mapping in support of rigorous intelligence analysis.

MODEL DEVELOPMENT

In 2008, we conducted an exploratory interview study with a small sample of managers from two Canadian intelligence organizations, the results of which are summarized in a technical report (Derbentseva, McLellan, and Mandel, forthcoming). Derbentseva began developing a Concept Map knowledge model of intelligence analysis that would be a supplement to the report. The initial aim of the model was to help us organize our own conceptual understanding of various issues involved in intelligence analysis. Another aim was to organize the key contents of the report in an interactive and visual manner for potential stakeholders.

Although it is not our aim here to review the model itself, we show in Figure 6.1 the top map of the knowledge model in order to provide the reader with some sense of the model's scope. As of this writing the model consists of 23 Concept Maps, which contain 490 concepts, over 700 propositions, and 290 links to various resources, including text files, images, audio, Web addresses, and Concept Maps. The model is not nearly a finished product in terms of depth or breadth of coverage, although such knowledge models should never be thought of as "finished" (Hoffman and Lintern, 2006). The model is expanding and is subject to reorganization based on new information and feedback we receive.

As the knowledge model was developed, it became evident to us that input from members of the Canadian intelligence community would be beneficial in order to better understand how such a model might be used

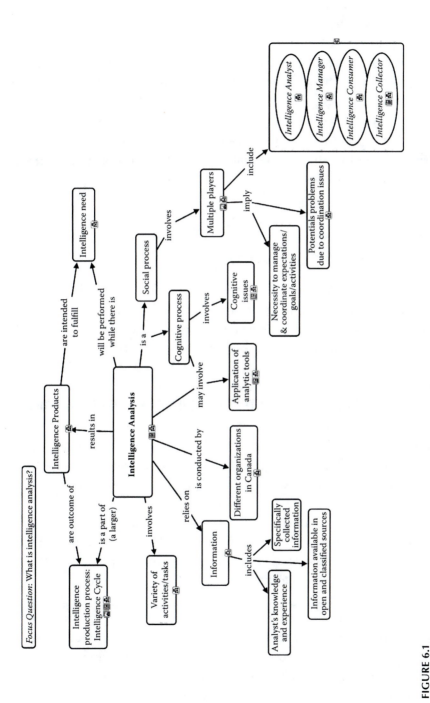

FIGURE 6.1

The top map of the Concept Map knowledge model of intelligence analysis.

by intelligence personnel and, more generally, what uses Concept Mapping might have for the intelligence community. For instance, we saw potential in the model not only as a means of knowledge capture, but also as a medium within which to promote dialog among members of the intelligence community on key issues germane to the practice and organization of intelligence, much as the Global Futures Forum Web site does (GFF, 2010) with its reference, forums, and blogs sections. Thus, the expansion of the model, and our realization of its potential uses beyond simply capturing our technical reports' main points, provided the impetus for organizing the recent workshop.

WORKSHOP ORGANIZATION

We solicited participation in the workshop by contacting members of the Canadian intelligence community with whom we had an established relationship. Of the 12 individuals invited, 9 participated, and, in one case, invited another participant. The 10 intelligence experts were from both civilian and military intelligence organizations, to include Campbell Intel Services, Canada Border Services Agency, Canadian Forces School of Military Intelligence, Chief of Defense Intelligence, the International Assessment Staff of Canada's Privy Council Office, and the Library of Parliament. Most of the workshop participants had over 10 years of experience in the intelligence domain and were senior members of the intelligence community. In addition, most participants held positions as directors and educators.

None of the participants had prior exposure to Concept Mapping as a potential tool in support of intelligence, although some had seen various forms of visual–textual diagrams (e.g., mind maps). The half-day workshop began with introductory remarks by Mandel and an introduction to Concept Mapping. Derbentseva provided a demonstration of the scope and usability of our Concept Map knowledge model of intelligence analysis. Most of the workshop time was reserved for two small-group discussion sessions, for which workshop participants were divided into three groups. Each of the discussion sessions was followed by reports in plenary sessions by rapporteurs from the three groups.

The first session had two objectives. The first was to identify and prioritize potential uses of the Concept Map knowledge model and Concept Mapping, more generally, within the intelligence community. The second objective was to identify anticipated benefits and drawbacks of using Concept Mapping for the identified purposes.

The second session involved a collaborative exercise in which participants were asked to construct a Concept Map that answered the focus question: "What is analytic integrity?" For that activity, we provided participants with IHMC's Concept Map: Steps in Building a Concept Map (Crandall, Klein, and Hoffman, 2006; IHMC, 2010).

WORKSHOP RESULTS

Our observations and participants' insights and comments during the workshop, are discussed in the following sections. We begin by summarizing perceived applications of Concept Mapping within the intelligence community, followed by a discussion of anticipated benefits and drawbacks of Concept Mapping. We conclude this section with the report on the collaborative Concept Map construction exercise in which participants engaged during the second part of the workshop.

Perceived Applications

To minimize leading participants toward certain answers that might cast the utility of Concept Mapping in a positive light, the workshop organizers did not share with participants their own vision of how Concept Mapping or the knowledge model could be applied within the intelligence community. Each of the three discussion groups identified a number of potential applications of Concept Mapping within the intelligence community. These were grouped into six categories listed below. All three groups noted the first four uses in the list below, while the last two functions were discussed by two of the three groups

1. Tool for system analysis and management, i.e., to analyze and manage a topic or an issue that is comprised of various interrelated components
2. Tool to conduct analysis

3. Tool to assist with validation of analytic judgments and quality control
4. Collaboration tool to develop shared understanding
5. Training and knowledge transfer tool
6. Communication tool

The identified potential applications are distinct, yet interdependent, and arise from specific properties of Concept Mapping as a process and Concept Maps as products. We discuss these properties in the context of each of the applications below.

System Analysis and Management Tool.

Participants noticed that a Concept Map may be a useful tool to analyze a system of interdependent issues by decomposing the system into its components and showing their interrelationships. Participants in all three groups noted that Concept Mapping may be a more appropriate method for intelligence collection planning than the existing methods, such as spreadsheets and lists. Intelligence analysts heavily rely on information and need to be able to identify what information needs to be collected to advance their analysis (Bruce, 2008; Treverton, 2001). In collection planning, the analyst surveys the known information about the problem at hand and identifies what currently remains unknown. A Concept Map was seen as a model that has the capability of structuring the "system of information" relevant to a problem. One of the groups also offered another example of potential system analysis application of Concept Mapping, namely, the analysis and management of military force development. In addition, some participants proposed that any analytic issue needs to be treated as a part of a system (i.e., in the context of other relevant and interdependent issues), and that Concept Mapping thus could be used for analyzing intelligence problems from a systems perspective.

Analytic Tool

The group discussion focused mainly on the application of Concept Mapping as a structured analytic technique. All three groups recognized the potential of applying Concept Mapping during the process of analysis as an imagination-promoting, structured, analytic technique. Participants noted that constructing a Concept Map as a component of the analytic process could help structure an intelligence problem, organize and discipline analysts' thinking processes, and help analysts detect links between concepts and identify gaps.

In line with participants' observations, we believe that Concept Mapping has several properties, both as a process and as a product, that may be advantageous for analysis. As a process, Concept Mapping (1) requires analysts to externalize their thinking, (2) requires analysts to decompose a problem into its core conceptual elements, (3) requires analysts to establish relationships among those elements by forming propositions, and (4) promotes synthesis through the requirement that the entire map provide a comprehensive answer to the focus question. All of these properties have been recognized as requirements for rigorous analysis (Heuer, 1999; Heuer and Pherson, 2010).

As a product, a Concept Map serves as a record of one's thinking process, and it provides a "transparent" representation that allows analysts to "smoke out" unwarranted assumptions, identify gaps in analysis and logic, and promote dialog with other analysts. In general, participants recognized these various benefits for promoting rigorous analysis.

As noted earlier, intelligence analysts deal with problems that are characterized by a great deal of uncertainty. The future that analysts endeavor to anticipate and describe is uncertain, as is the accuracy and completeness of information available to the analyst. The process of intelligence analysis has been characterized as the process of putting together a jigsaw puzzle with many missing pieces and an unknown final picture (Johnson, 2007). A Concept Map may be instrumental in structuring and providing a representation of the current state of such a "puzzle" in an analyst's mind. That representation, in turn, may serve as a basis for discussion with the analyst's manager and peers.

Validation Mechanism and Quality Control

Concept Maps have a proven record of application (and their widest use) in the educational setting to promote meaningful learning and capture changes in students' understanding of the subject (Cañas et al., 2008; Novak, 1998; Novak and Musonda, 1991). Concept Maps capture the creator's understanding of a topic and represent it in an explicit form, which allows teachers to easily identify students' misconceptions and to evaluate the quality of their learning (Hay, 2007; Hay and Kinchin, 2008; Kinchin, 2000; Novak,

1998). Although it may be impossible in the intelligence domain to compare an analyst's Concept Map against a correct answer, except in hindsight, Concept Maps may help to reveal differences in current understanding of the topic among analysts. In addition, adult learners have reported that constructing a Concept Map allows them to identify gaps in their own understanding and leads to a much more thorough processing of information (Derbentseva and Safayeni, 2008). All three groups at our workshop noted the property of Concept Maps to make a map creator's understanding explicit and considered it to be valuable for intelligence analysis.

Participants outlined a number of advantages in having an explicit representation of an analyst's thinking. First, it would allow analysts to review their Concept Maps and identify gaps in their logic or information that might have been overlooked during the analytic process. Some participants commented that identifying gaps in logic from a Concept Map might be easier and more efficient than from a standard written intelligence assessment because, as one group member stated, "The gaps in logic will jump in your face." One group suggested using Concept Mapping at the end of the analytic process as a "sanity check," by which an analyst would transform his or her written report into a Concept Map to see whether everything that the analyst wanted to say actually got said and made sense.

Second, a Concept Map might also be instrumental in the process of evaluating the quality of intelligence assessments because it provides a transparent record of an analyst's thinking and allows identification of gaps and assumptions. Similarly, one group discussed how a Concept Map could be used as a defensible record of an analyst's thinking in the audit process, if the product is challenged at a later date.

Finally, a Concept Map might serve as a means of sharing an analyst's way of thinking about a problem with other analysts in order to promote a collaborative discussion. We focus more on this aspect in the following section.

Collaboration Tool to Develop Shared Understanding

The groups discussed two different aspects of collaboration that may be prompted through Concept Mapping in the intelligence context. First, as we noted earlier, participants regarded Concept Maps as having the capacity to promote discussion in the context of the analysis process. Second,

Concept Mapping also was seen as a collaborative tool to discuss general topics related to intelligence analysis within the entire community.

The first application may facilitate the process of analysis of a particular issue, while the second application may promote dialog within the community and may help develop shared understanding. However, it is the same property of Concept Maps—the explicit representation that they provide—that may lead to collaboration in the two contexts. A Concept Map presents a set of propositions that can be evaluated. Identifying logic gaps, finding missing crosslinks, and finding divergent propositions could be beneficial in stimulating collaborative discussions. Such collaboration in the context of analyzing an intelligence issue may help to uncover hidden assumptions and verify an analyst's logical thinking.

In the broader context of discussion within the intelligence community about how to improve the practice and organization of intelligence, collaborative Concept Mapping could facilitate the development of common understanding and help the community arrive at consensus on key concepts and standards.

Training and Knowledge Transfer

Two of the groups discussed the potential utility of Concept Mapping for training and knowledge transfer, and their discussions revolved around slightly different ideas. One group proposed that Concept Mapping may be a good way of training intelligence analysts to avoid linear thinking patterns and to visualize more complex relationships among concepts. This group also suggested that implementing Concept Mapping in the training context might serve as a test bed for validating the utility of the tool.

The other group proposed that Concept Maps could be used to transfer knowledge from an experienced desk analyst to his or her replacement in order to accelerate the newcomer's learning about important issues. Accordingly, an experienced desk analyst would develop and maintain a Concept Map knowledge model of the important issues in his or her area. The incoming analyst would then use that model to get up to speed when taking over the desk, and later, as he or she gains more knowledge, would be able to update and maintain the model. Although the group did not explicitly discuss technical requirements to support this activity, it seems that a Concept Map knowledge modeling environment, such as

CmapTools, would be required to provide the necessary information management flexibility and support.

One potential challenge with this application of Concept Mapping may be in the time and effort required to develop the initial model and its subsequent maintenance. The application of Concept Mapping to knowledge capture and transfer in the domain of intelligence analysis could, however, draw upon a growing body of literature on the application of Concept Mapping to knowledge preservation and sharing in various areas (Coffey et al., 2003a; Hoffman, 2008; Moon, Hoffman, and Ziebell, 2009). Moreover, the intelligence community could develop partnerships with the research and development community in order to capitalize on expertise and reduce the burden on intelligence personnel (Mandel, 2009).

Communicative Function

Two of the three groups discussed a possibility of using the Concept Map as an aid for communicating with intelligence consumers. Intelligence consumers often do not have time to read lengthy intelligence reports, and effective communication of intelligence judgments to consumers has been an important issue in the community (Hulnick, 2006). Some participants suggested that providing a Concept Map of alternative possibilities to intelligence consumers might allow them to expand their horizons by exposing them to novel representations of information. It was noted, however, that Concept Maps will appeal only to "visually inclined" individuals and may not be suitable for everybody, and that such Concept Maps could not replace written reports. Yet, as Moon et al. (2008) demonstrated, Concept Maps hold more potential than PowerPoint for rapidly and accurately conveying complex information—an important finding given the vast amount of Microsoft® PowerPoint® presentations that regularly circulate throughout the intelligence community.

Another challenge in the relationship between consumers and producers of intelligence is that consumers often have limited understanding of capabilities and processes involved in the intelligence production (Davis, 2006; Gardiner, 2009). Some participants recognized that a Concept Map knowledge model of intelligence analysis may be an appropriate tool to educate consumers about the issues involved in analysis and to demonstrate the breadth and complexity of various activities and issues involved.

According to some of the workshop participants, this may help with the "sales" angle of intelligence to the consumers and also could help with securing resources for intelligence agencies.

To summarize, workshop participants perceived the greatest value of Concept Mapping in:

- Providing an external, visual, and transparent representation of the thinking process
- Exposing gaps in logic and information
- Supporting and encouraging collaboration
- Allowing representing complex problems and thinking about broader ideas
- Prompting thinking about relationships

Our workshop participants independently arrived at conclusions regarding utility of Concept Mapping in the intelligence context that are similar to applications envisioned and discussed by other researchers (Hoffman, 2010). Our study thus provides an independent confirmation of the perceived utility of Concept Mapping in the intelligence domain and ensures face validity of the findings given that the applications were envisioned by the intelligence professionals themselves.

Advantages and Drawbacks of Concept Mapping

Some of the properties of Concept Mapping that are advantageous in one situation may be a hindrance in another situation. For instance, the ability to produce a visual and nonlinear representation of the thinking process with a Concept Map was identified as one of the tool's main advantages. However, participants also noted that such a representation may be unsuitable for those who are more comfortable with a linear or nondiagrammatic representation.

Also, the fact that Concept Maps allow representation of complex problems and thinking about broader ideas was seen as an advantage, which may broaden one's view and be a useful way to explain a subject matter to someone. However, participants commented that a Concept Map does not seem to provide a single, specific answer or "bottom line" to the focus question, which may be necessary in some situations. Thus, some participants viewed it as an inappropriate means to represent answers to some intelligence questions, such as those required in tactical intelligence. Tactical intelligence is short-term and deals with specific questions that are of interest to a commander. Some participants commented that linear presentation methods that follow a more typical linear thread, such as textual summaries, may be more appropriate for tactical intelligence briefs.

Some participants said that Concept Maps may be more appropriate to answer focus questions, such as "what is …," or to describe "things that are," whereas they might be less useful for describing the world of "might be;" in other words, to represent forecasts of future events and their potential impact. It is an interesting observation that Concept Maps may be more appropriate for some questions and less so for other questions, and one that could be tested empirically. For example, there is empirical evidence that (unguided) Concept Mapping tends to facilitate representation of static relationships and that such Concept Maps tend to answer "what is …" type of questions (Safayeni, Derbentseva, and Cañas, 2005). This concurs with our participants' observation.

Nevertheless, research also suggests that it is possible to increase expressive variety in Concept Maps through strategies, such as adjusting a map's structure and posing explicit focus questions (Derbentseva, Safayeni, and Cañas, 2007). At least in principle, Concept Mapping morphology and semantics do not preclude the expression of probabilistic or hypothetical propositions. Thus, Concept Mapping ought to be able to support the construction of diagrams that explore hypothetical or even counterfactual events. Developments in this area have been explored at IHMC (Hoffman, 2010).

The representation of probabilistic relationships in Concept Maps would have to rely on verbal expressions of uncertainty, which are inherently vague, but this is no different than current practices involving written reports. Moreover, just as reports *could* be supplemented with numeric probabilities, so too could Concept Maps. In a related vein, some workshop participants noted that it would be useful to be able to show the importance or centrality of propositions in a map, such as one might do in some influence diagrams of varying degrees of computability (Fischhoff, 2009) or social network models (Bavelas, 1950; Knoke and Yang, 2008), respectively.

Two of the groups expressed a concern regarding the lack of existing mechanisms to determine whether the application of Concept Mapping or any other tool would yield a better outcome than status quo practices. Participants noted that it would be helpful if Concept Mapping was validated with respect to specific requirements of the intelligence domain, to identify the most appropriate and beneficial areas of application and to assess whether the benefits associated with implementing the tool would outweigh the costs. Participants, however, also recognized that validation of analytic techniques, although desirable, is not yet a common practice in the intelligence community. In general, there is a lack of a scientific base of research concerning the validity and usability of structured analytical techniques, with some exceptions (e.g., see Cheikes et al., 2004; Folker, 2000; Pirolli, 2006). Application of analytic techniques greatly relies on the intuitions and preferences of experienced analysts (Heuer and Pherson, 2010).

A more general concern was raised regarding the fact that intelligence analysts operate under a significant "pressure to get their products out the door." Thus, some participants believed that analysts simply would not have the time to apply any analytic tools, even the simplest and quickest ones. Also, such issues as analysts' learning and reasoning styles play a role in acceptance of analytic tools, as some analysts may prefer not use any tools at all.

Some participants also thought that analysts could get too bogged down with structured analytic tool use, and that it remained an empirical question as to whether a particular tool would yield the anticipated benefits. As one participant noted, overemphasis on tools could have the deleterious effect of having analysts lose their focus on solving the pertinent analytic problem. We suggest that the prospect for this type of unwanted outcome would be more likely early on in the tool use phase, as analysts acquire their tool use skill. As that skill is developed, however, fewer cognitive resources would need to be applied to using the tool itself. Thus, the cost–benefit ratio would be expected to become more favorable over time.

To complement participants' understanding of Concept Mapping and enrich it with practical experience, the second session of the workshop was devoted to hands-on Concept Mapping, the results of which are discussed in the next section.

Collaborative Map Construction

The second session of the workshop was devoted to a collaborative Concept Map construction exercise. Workshop participants spent 40 minutes in their groups constructing a Concept Map to answer the focus question:

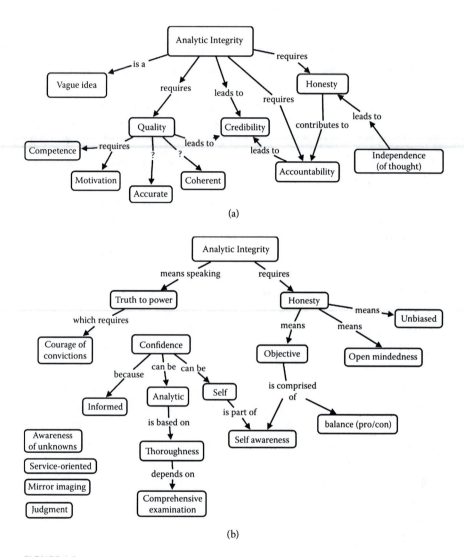

FIGURE 6.2a–c

Concept Maps constructed by the three groups to answer the focus question "What is analytic integrity?" (a) Group 1, (b) Group 2, (c) Group 3.

"What is analytic integrity?" Although the available time was insufficient for groups to fully complete their Concept Maps, the groups nevertheless had an opportunity to immerse themselves in the Concept Map construction process and acquire some first-hand experience with Concept Mapping. Figure 6.2a–c shows the "in progress" Concept Maps produced by the three groups at the end of the session.

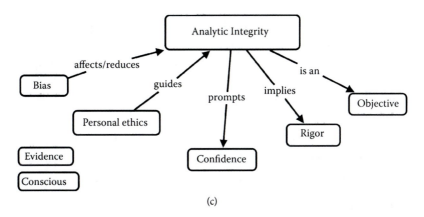

(c)

FIGURE 6.2a–c (continued).

As one might expect, the groups experienced some difficulty in constructing their Concept Maps. This was certainly due, at least in part, to the fact that the Concept Mapping process was unfamiliar to participants. However, it was also partly due to the fact that the answer to the question posed was more elusive than participants had initially thought it would be. Group 1 expressed this idea in their map with a proposition: "Analytic integrity is a vague idea" (see Figure 6.2a). The variability in ideas associated with the concept of analytic integrity is also represented in the range of concepts that different groups generated for their Concept Maps. Only one concept—namely, *honesty*—was used by two groups (see Figure 6.2a and Figure 6.2b). In other words, the remaining concepts were unique in each group.

All three groups concluded that Concept Mapping was a difficult process that required much thinking and clarity in the terms used. Participants experienced their greatest difficulty with defining linking terms, which was not surprising as it is a common challenge in Concept Map construction (Derbentseva and Safayeni, 2008; Novak and Cañas, 2008).

Participants observed that the collaborative map construction process allowed them to uncover differences in individuals' understanding of various concepts. These differences became evident during the process of linking concepts and defining the relationships. Also, participants pointed out that Concept Map construction allowed them to reach conclusions that would not have been possible with conventional presentation means, such as a written definition or a bulleted list. In particular, while constructing relationships in their Concept Map, group 1 reached a conclusion that *quality* is a central concept in defining *analytic integrity* and that the two concepts have very similar meaning in this context.

Participants generally enjoyed the hands-on Concept Mapping activity, which clearly demonstrated to them some of the benefits of Concept Mapping that they anticipated. It is also worth noting that some workshop participants who were skeptical toward Concept Mapping at the beginning became much more favorable to the method after acquiring first-hand experience with the Concept Mapping process.

FUTURE DIRECTIONS

Our workshop generated considerable interest in Concept Mapping from the intelligence professionals who took part. As a result, Concept Mapping is finding its way into Canadian intelligence analyst training. For instance, the authors received a request to develop a "one-pager" on Concept Mapping as an "imagination" structured analytic technique for the Canadian "Aide Memoire on Intelligence Analysis Tradecraft," which is used in training intelligence analysts in the Canadian Forces (Thompson, 2009). Currently, the memoire contains 29 structured analytic techniques recommended for intelligence analysis. We expect that a description of Concept Mapping will complement this collection in the near future.

The authors were requested as well to develop a Concept Map knowledge model of one of the sections in the Aide Memoire that discusses analytic rigor for potential application in intelligence analyst training. The development of the Concept Map model of analytic rigor contributed to further development of the concept of rigor by identifying areas that required expansion.

In upcoming intelligence analysis courses, we will be working in conjunction with the Canadian Forces School of Military Intelligence to pilot a collaborative Concept Mapping approach to solving analytic problems. Using Concept Mapping in the analyst training environment will expose cohorts of analyst trainees to the tool and will allow us to assess the effectiveness of the tool in an analytic environment where any potential detrimental consequences would not have an impact on real intelligence products. Exposure to Concept Mapping during training also may contribute to its future application in actual analytical activities and reporting.

Plans are also underway for one of us (Derbentseva) to facilitate a workshop session on Concept Mapping as part of an upcoming Global Futures Forum's Community of Interest on the Practice and Organization of Intelligence (COI POI) roundtable. COI POI is an international community of intelligence professionals interested in multidisciplinary collaboration on various intelligence issues. The idea is to use Concept Mapping as a medium to launch an experiment on virtual international collaboration (cf., Moon et al., Chapter 15).

In summary, our interactions with Canadian intelligence experts demonstrated that Concept Mapping has a potential to contribute to the community in various ways, realizing, of course, that no tool is a panacea. In implementing structured analytic techniques, care should be taken to match the capabilities of the tool or technique with the task requirements. Our nascent research program on Concept Mapping is aimed at validating the use of this technique with respect to specific requirements of the intelligence domain, and we will continue to provide support to the Canadian intelligence community and its allies in further Concept Map research and development.

REFERENCES

Ausubel, D. P. 1963. *The psychology of meaningful verbal learning.* New York: Grune and Stratton.

Bavelas, A. 1950. Communication patterns in task-oriented groups. *Journal of the Acoustical Society of America* 22 (6): 725-730.

Brady, C. 1993. Intelligence failures: Plus Ca change. *Intelligence and National Security* 8 (4): 86–96.

Bruce, J. B. 2008. The missing link: The analyst-collector relationship. In *Analyzing intelligence: Origins, obstacles, and innovations* (pp. 191–210), eds. R. Z. George and J. B. Bruce. Washington, D.C.: Georgetown University Press.

Butler, R., J. Chilcot, and P. Inge, et al. 2004. *Review of intelligence on weapons of mass destruction.* HC898. London: House of Commons.

Butterfield, A. P. 1993. *The accuracy of intelligence assessment: Bias, perception, and judgment in analysis and decision.* Newport, R.I.: Naval War College.

Campbell, A. and D. R. Mandel. 2010. Summary record of the GFF community of interest on the practice and organization of Intelligence Ottawa Roundtable: What can the cognitive and behavioural sciences contribute to intelligence analysis? Towards a collaborative agenda for the future (No. CR 2010-012). Toronto: DRDC Toronto.

Cañas, A. J., G. Hill, and J. Lott. 2003. Support for constructing knowledge models in CmapTools (No. 93-02). Pensacola FL: IHMC.

Cañas, A. and J. Novak. 2006. Concept maps: Theory, methodology, technology. Paper presented at the Proceedings of the Second International Conference on Concept Mapping. San Jose, Costa Rica.

Cañas, A., J. Novak, and F. González. 2004. Concept maps: Theory, methodology, technology. Paper presented at the Proceedings of the First International Conference on Concept Mapping. Pamplona, Spain.

Cañas, A., P. Reiska, M. Åhlberg, and J. Novak. 2008. Concept mapping: Connecting educators. Paper presented at the Proceedings of the Third International Conference on Concept Mapping. Tallinn, Estonia and Helsinki, Finland.

Cheikes, B. A., M. J. Brown, P. E. Lehner, and L. Adelman. 2004. *Confirmation bias in complex analyses.* Bedford, MA: MITRE Center for Integrated Intelligence Systems.

Coffey, J. W., A. J. Cañas, and G. Hill, et al. 2003. Knowledge modeling and the creation of El-Tech: A performance support and training system for electronic technicians. *Expert Systems with Applications* 25 (4): 483–492.

Coffey, J. W., M. J. Carnot, and P. J. Feltovich, et al. 2003. A summary of literature pertaining to the use of concept mapping techniques and technologies for education and performance support. No. technical report submitted to the Chief of Naval Education and Training. Pensacola, FL: IHMC.

Crandall, B., G. Klein, and R. Hoffman. 2006. *Working minds: A practitioner's guide to cognitive task analysis.* Cambridge, MA: MIT Press.

Davis, J. 1992. Combating mindset. *Studies in Intelligence* 36 (5): 33–38.

Davis, J. 2006. Intelligence analysts and policymakers: Benefits and dangers of tensions in the relationship. *Intelligence and National Security* 21 (6): 999–1021.

Davis, J. 2008. Why bad things happen to good analysts. In *Analyzing intelligence: Origins, obstacles, and innovations* (pp. 157–170), eds. R. Z. George and J. B. Bruce. Washington, D.C.: Georgetown University Press.

Derbentseva, N., L. McLellan, and D. R. Mandel. Forthcoming. Issues in intelligence production: Summary of interviews with Canadian managers of intelligence analysts. DRDC Toronto, Ontario, Canada.

Derbentseva, N. and F. Safayeni. 2008. CMap construction: Challenges for the first time users and perceptions of CMap's value: A qualitative study. In *Concept mapping: Connecting educators,* eds. A. Cañas, P. Reiska, M. Åhlberg, and J. Novak. Proceedings of the Third International Conference on Concept Mapping. Tallinn, Estonia and Helsinki, Finland.

Derbentseva, N., F. Safayeni, and A. J. Cañas. 2007. Concept maps: Experiments on dynamic thinking. *Journal of Research in Science Teaching* 44 (3): 448–465.

Fischhoff, B. 2009. Integrating formal and narrative analysis. Paper presented at the Global Futures Forum Community of Interest for the Practice and Organization of Intelligence Ottawa Roundtable: "What can the cognitive and behavioural sciences contribute to intelligence analysis? Towards a collaborative agenda for the future." Meech Lake, Quebec, Canada.

Folker, R. D. 2000. *Intelligence analysis in theater joint intelligence centers: An experiment in applying structured methods.* Washington D.C.: Joint Military Intelligence College.

Gardiner, K. L. 2009. Squaring the circle: Dealing with intelligence-policy breakdowns. In *Secret intelligence* (pp. 129–139), eds. C. Andrew, R. J. Aldrich and W. K. Wark. New York: Routledge.

GFF. 2010. Global Futures Forum Web site (requires login): https://www.globalfuturesforum. org/Home.php (accessed March 31, 2010).

Hay, D. B. 2007. Using concept maps to measure deep, surface and non-learning outcomes. *Studies in Higher Education* 32 (1): 39–57.

Hay, D. B. and I. M. Kinchin. 2008. Using concept mapping to measure learning quality. *Education and Training* 50 (2): 167–182.

Herman, M. 1996. *Intelligence power in peace and war.* Cambridge, U.K.: The Royal Institute of International Affairs, Cambridge University Press.

Heuer, R. J. 1999. *Psychology of intelligence analysis.* Washington, D.C.: Center for the Study of Intelligence, Central Intelligence Agency.

Heuer, R. J. and R. H. Pherson. 2010. *Structured analytic techniques for intelligence analysis.* Washington, D.C.: CQ Press.

Hoffman, R. 2008. Concept mapping and its applications. Report to the QinetiQ Ltd on the Project "Critiquing in IO, EBA and Intelligence Analysis No. QINETIQ/CON/DSP/ TR0801549/1.0)." Oxford, U.K.: QinetiQ.

Hoffman, R. and G. Lintern. 2006. Eliciting and representing the knowledge of experts. In *Cambridge handbook of expertise and expert performance* (pp. 203–222), eds. K. A. Ericsson, N. Charness, J. Feltovich, and R. Hoffman. New York: Cambridge University Press.

Hulnick, A. S. 2006. What's wrong with the intelligence cycle. *Intelligence and National Security* 21, 959–979.

Hulnick, A. S. 2008. Intelligence reform 2008: Where to from here? *International Journal of Intelligence and CounterIntelligence* 21 (4): 621–634.

IHMC. 2010. Constructing good concept maps: http://cmapskm.ihmc.us/servlet/ SBReadResourceServlet?rid=1064009710027_279131382_27088andpartName= htmltext (accessed March 31, 2010).

Jervis, R. 1991. Strategic intelligence and effective policy. In *Security and intelligence in a changing world: New perspectives for the 1990s* (pp. 165–181), eds. A. S. Farson, D. Stafford, and W. K. Wark. London: Frank Cass.

Johnson, L. K. 2007. Introduction. In *Handbook of intelligence studies* (pp. 1–14), ed. L. K. Johnson. London, U.K.: Routledge/Taylor and Francis Group.

Johnston, R. 2005. *Analytic culture in the U.S. intelligence community: An ethnographic study.* Washington, D.C.: Central Intelligence Agency.

Kinchin, I. M. 2000. Using concept maps to reveal understanding: A two-tier analysis. *School Science Review* 81, 41–46.

Knoke, D. and S. Yang. 2008. *Social network analysis.* Thousand Oaks, CA: Sage Publications.

Lefebvre, S. P. 2004. A look at intelligence analysis. *International Journal of Intelligence and CounterIntelligence* 17 (2): 231–264.

Mandel, D. R. 2009. Applied behavioural science in support of intelligence: Experiences in building a Canadian capability. Commissioned report to the Committee on Field Evaluation of Behavioral and Cognitive Sciences-Based Methods and Tools for Intelligence and Counter-Intelligence, Division of Behavioral and Social Sciences and Education. Washington, D.C.: The National Academies.

Moon, B. and R. Hoffman. 2005. How might "transformational" technologies and concepts be barriers to sensemaking in intelligence analysis? Paper presented at the Seventh International Naturalistic Decision Making Conference. Amsterdam, The Netherlands.

Moon, B., R. Hoffman, and L. Shattuck et al. 2008. Rapid and accurate idea transfer: Evaluating concept maps against other formats for the transfer of complex information. In *Concept mapping: Connecting educators*, eds. A. Cañas, P. Reiska, M. Åhlberg, and J. Novak. Proceedings of the Third International Conference on Concept Mapping. Tallinn, Estonia and Helsinki, Finland.

Moon, B., R. Hoffman, and D. Ziebell. 2009. How did you do that? *Electric Perspectives* 34 (1): 20–29.

Moore, D. T. and R. Hoffman. 2010. A practice of understanding. In *A structure of an intelligence revolution*, ed. D. T. Moore. Washington, D.C.: National Defense Intelligence College Press.

National Commission on Terrorist Attacks upon the United States. 2004. The 9/11 commission report: Final report of the National Commission on Terrorist Attacks upon the United States, Washington, D.C.

Novak, J. D. 1998. *Learning, creating, and using knowledge: Concept maps as facilitative tools in schools and corporations*. Mahwah, NJ: Erlbaum.

Novak, J. D. and A. J. Cañas. 2008. *The theory underlying concept maps and how to construct them*. Pensacola, FL: IHMC.

Novak, J. D. and D. Musonda. 1991. A twelve-year longitudinal study of science concept learning. *American Educational Research Journal* 28 (1): 117–153.

Pirolli, P. 2006. *Assisting people to become independent learners in the analysis of intelligence* (No. CDRL A002). Arlington, CA: Palo Alto Research Center, Inc.

Pritchard, M. C. and M. S. Goodman. 2009. Intelligence: The loss of innocence. *International Journal of Intelligence and CounterIntelligence* 22 (1): 147–164.

Safayeni, F., N. Derbentseva, and A. J. Cañas. 2005. A theoretical note on concepts and the need for cyclic concept maps. *Journal of Research in Science Teaching* 42 (7): 741–766.

Steinberg, J. B. 2008. The policymaker's perspective: Transparency and partnership. In *Analyzing intelligence: Origins, obstacles, and innovations* (pp. 82–90), eds. R. Z. George and J. B. Bruce. Washington, D.C.: Georgetown University Press.

Thompson, G. 2009. *Aide memoire on intelligence analysis tradecraft*: Ottawa, ON: Chief of Defence Intelligence.

Treverton, G. F. 2001. *Reshaping national intelligence for an age of information*. Cambridge, MA: Cambridge University Press.

Treverton, G. F. 2008. Intelligence analysis: Between "politicization" and irrelevance. In *Analyzing intelligence: Origins, obstacles, and innovations* (pp. 91–104), eds. R. Z. George and J. B. Bruce. Washington, D.C.: Georgetown University Press.

Woods, D. D., E. S. Patterson, and E. M. Roth. 2002. Can we ever escape from data overload? A cognitive systems diagnosis. *Cognition, Technology, and Work* 4, 22–36.

7

Common Lexicon Initiative: A Concept Mapping Approach to Semiautomated Definition Integration

Andrew G. Harter and Brian M. Moon

CONTENTS

INTRODUCTION

A presenter speaks to U.S. Department of Defense (DOD) officials, his efforts derailed by a discrepancy on the use of the words *risk* and *vulnerability* on slide 2. A U.S. Department of Homeland Security (DHS) analyst pulls his hair out at his desk, two dozen studies from different states before him, each assessing terrorist threat to the electricity sector, but unable to be compared. A police officer in a state terrorism fusion center pores through a database interpreting each report's use of the term *threat*. All across the U.S. government, disparate terminology causes difficulties in the transfer of information: errors in translation and time wasted. The language is all the same, but the concepts they represent differ enough to cause dissent.

After the terrorist attacks of September 11, 2001, practitioners flocked to the security risk management career field both out of necessity and opportunity. Best practices were adopted from virtually every government agency and from the fields of security analysis, risk management, information assurance, operational security, actuarial science, military theory, law enforcement, and others. Like the workers of the Tower of Babel, meanings were confounded, and over the years since, parochial pockets have become attached to certain terms and interpretations.

In 2006, the Security Analysis and Risk Management Association (SARMA) established itself as a nonprofit professional association dedicated to bringing together these practitioners to share knowledge at a community level. Following their first annual conference in 2007, they expressed that "without a doubt, the most commonly voiced obstacle to progress in the field of security analysis and risk management is the lack of a common vocabulary, used consistently, even by a simple majority of practitioners" (Harter, 2007).

Professionalization of a career field requires common terminology, shared methodology, and a baseline of generally accepted principles that can train, inform, and guide the profession's work. These are the initiatives that SARMA undertook as its initial mission, with terminology being one of the first to be addressed. Rising from the frustrations expressed at the first annual conference in 2007, the discrepancies in concepts being utilized in the profession required action.

Bringing together terminology appears, at first, to be deceptively simple. Many attempts had previously been made within different pockets, agencies, and fields of study, and different lexicons were already identified as authoritative within subgroups and contributing disciplines. The confusion arose, however, when they interacted. The need was not to have a greater authority that could dictate a correct definition, but to elicit and deal with the underlying problem, i.e., that the concepts at the heart of the profession were what really required standardization. Addressing terminology in terms of glossaries and definitions invites a focus on "wordsmithing" to shape sentences and phases.

Investment in the shape of the phrase versus the concept that it represents created just the kinds of arguments that practitioners desired to end.

An ontological approach overcomes this problem by addressing the root concepts rather than the phrasing of the statements about them. Originating in philosophy with the discussion of the nature of reality, ontology has become more commonly known as a practice for mapping the concepts, entities, and relationships for practitioners in computer science and knowledge management.

The SARMA Common Lexicon initiative developed and tested a method for integrating parochial definitions using Concept Mapping. The method brought together concepts from all fields contributing to the current study of security and risk management to find commonalities and advance the state of the profession in ways that were not previously envisioned. This use of Concept Mapping for ontological development of common terminology within a domain provided beneficial results based on the project's intentions as well as unforeseen benefits. The methodology and benefits are described in this case study.

METHODOLOGY

The project was based on the principles of voluntary consensus standards put forth by the U.S. National Institute of Standards and Technology (www.standards.gov). The purpose of the effort was to bring all sectors of the security risk management community to common concepts, allowing work within the community to be understood, communicated, and comparable based on a common lexicon. This standardization of concepts, not methods, then, allows education, training, and certification efforts to grow and the community to move forward into new areas of development based on common understandings.

The project proceeded across seven steps as shown in Figure 7.1.

Step 1. Gathering existing definitions: All past efforts to develop and standardize concepts, terminology, or lexicons were solicited and incorporated in an open wiki format, casting as wide a net as possible to bring current terminology usage into the process.

FIGURE 7.1
Seven steps.

Steps 2 through 5. Integration: Concept Maps for each definition were integrated following a semiautomated process into one overall Concept Map representing an integrated definition.

Step 7. Consensus Process: The overall Concept Map was then brought in front of a working group of subject matter professionals in the security risk management field, giving them the opportunity to use the Concept Maps as a starting point for arriving at a consensus model and definition.

Each of these steps is described in detail below.

Step 1. Gathering Existing Definitions

The most important aspect of collecting the existing definitions is casting a wide enough net that all members of the professional community are included. If this breadth of initial research is neglected, impacts can be felt across the subsequent phases. A practitioner whose conceptual model is not contained within the whole will have more difficulty finding his "starting point" when looking at the integrated definition, and therefore have difficulty in adding the additional concepts of the other disciplines to his or her understanding. Moreover, by missing important past efforts, people may feel excluded from the process and therefore not buy into the results, causing rejection of the consensus.

The collection effort consisted of both passive and active components. A call was put out to the community to contribute definitions to the common lexicon effort, allowing the wiki social collaboration tools to serve as a passive recipient of everyone's efforts. Some individuals added definitions directly, while others provided doctrinal lexicons to the project team, who entered the definitions on their behalf. More actively, the project team also searched out common definitions from known disciplines and government authorities to add to the lexicon until enough definitions were added to be reasonably deemed ready as a starting point.

Definitions were gathered for 202 terms, and posted on the SARMA Common Knowledge Base in an open wiki format (SARMA, 2008). Definitions for each term ranged from one per term to as many as 13 per term.

The first term submitted to subsequent steps was *asset*, for which seven definitions were collected. The definitions collected for the term *asset* provided below show the variance in initial phrasing and terminology (and include other sources):

1. In business and accounting as asset is any economic resource controlled by an entity as a result of past transactions or events and from which future economic benefits may be obtained. Examples include cash, equipment, buildings, and land. [Common definition. Wikipedia.]

2. Any person, facility, material, information, or activity that has positive value and requires protection. The asset may also have value to an adversary, although the nature and magnitude of the values may differ. [Analytical Risk Management (ARM) definition. Central Intelligence Agency (CIA).]

3. Any person, facility, material, information, or activity that has positive value to its owner. The asset may also have a given level of value to an adversary as well as its owner, although the nature and magnitude of the values may differ dramatically. [Analytical Risk Management (ARM) definition. Independent.]

4. Any people, facility, physical system, cyber system, material, information, activity or intangible attribute that has positive value to an owner or to society as a whole and requires protection. General organizational context: An asset whose absence or unavailability would significantly degrade the ability of an organization to carry out its mission. Functional context for asset owner: An asset whose absence or unavailability would represent an unacceptable business consequence, i.e., for which the sum of the consequences of its loss represents an unacceptable financial or political impact on the owner. [Risk Analysis and Management for Critical Asset Protection (RAMCAP). ASME Innovative Technologies Institute (ASME-ITI).]

5. Contracts, facilities, property, electronic and nonelectronic records and documents, unobligated or unexpended balances of appropriations, and other funds or resources (other than personnel). [National Infrastructure Protection Plan (NIPP). U.S. Department of Homeland Security (DHS).]

6. A distinguishable network entity that provides a service or capability. Assets are people, physical entities, or information located either within or outside the United States and owned or operated by domestic, foreign, public or private sector organizations. [Defense Critical

Infrastructure Program (DCIP) Guidelines. U.S. Department of Defense (DOD).]

7. Any potential target of terrorist attack, most commonly people, equipment, a building, or an outdoor venue (in whole or in part). [U.S. Air Force. DOD.]

We demonstrate the subsequent steps by walking through the example of *asset*.

Steps 2 through 6. Integration

The basis for the integration phase was Concept Maps; specifically, Concept Maps created using CmapTools. Concept Maps were chosen for their capacity to specify relationships between concepts, the *sine qua non* for any ontology integration effort. CmapTools was selected for its automated support for merging concepts, automatic layout support, and flexibility in manipulation of the elements of the Concept Map and large-scale Concept Maps. CmapTools provided leverage for doing the mental work of integration, which remains a human analytic task.

Step 2: Decomposition

Individual definitions were first decomposed into Concept Maps. This was a manual and highly cognitive step, requiring deep proficiency in Concept Mapping. Specifically, the step requires the skills noted by Moon et al. in Chapter 2. Figure 7.2 demonstrates one definition of *asset*, gathered from Wikipedia, and the resulting Concept Map. In this example, the concept of "Control" was pulled from its prose form "controlled by." In so doing, the concept of Control could then be related to other concepts. The adjective "past" and its corresponding noun "transaction" became "Transactions -> happen in the -> Past," as this enabled the concept of "Transactions" to stand alone. The prepositional phrase "(i)n business and accounting" does not appear in the Concept Map, as it only serves the purpose of specifying the use of the definition and thus was deemed irrelevant.

All identified concepts were then linked with the linking phrase "is inherent in" to the entire definition, which was in turn linked to its source. This initiated an audit trail that ran through the subsequent steps and tied all concepts back to their original definitions.

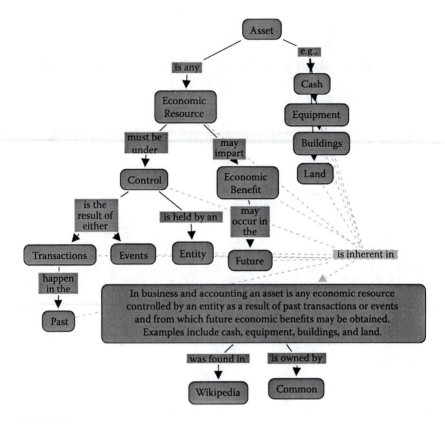

FIGURE 7.2
One asset definition in Concept Map form.

The Concept Maps were then color coded such that each concept and link were the same color.* The links and linking phrase to the original definition were dashed and greyed out so that they did not visually overwhelm the Concept Map. Subsequent definitions repeated the process, and a new color scheme was applied to each Concept Map. Importantly, all Concept Map definitions were created in one Concept Map, as shown in Figure 7.3.

---

* The Concept Maps published here are not color-coded. The grey scales, however, suggest the color schemes. Also, it is not intended that the larger Concept Maps be fully readable, indeed, they are very large Concept Maps. They are provided here to illustrate the process.

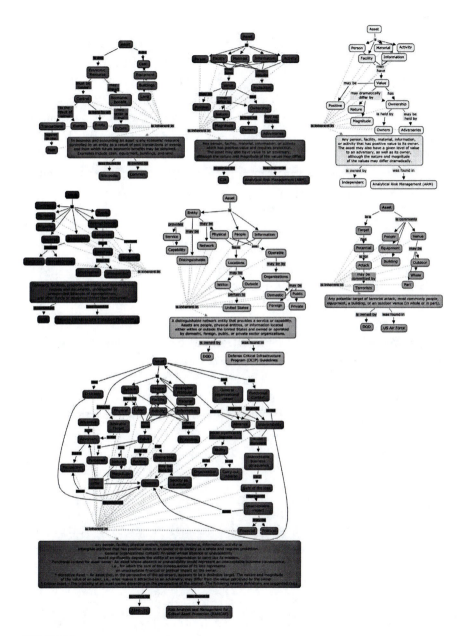

FIGURE 7.3
All asset definitions in Concept Map format.

Step 3: AutoMerge

Next, concepts that were alike across the Concept Mapped definitions were merged. This is an automated step, supported by CmapTools' Merge Nodes tool. Importantly, only Concepts were selected for merge, not Linking Phrases. Also, "Only merge if node labels match" was selected to ensure that only exact matching terms would be merged. The resulting Concept Map is shown in Figure 7.4. Strikingly, the overlap of concepts becomes clear, as multiple instances are merged into one, and yet the connection to their corresponding linking phrases remains intact, resulting in the emergence of an array of long links.

Step 4: Autolayout

In another automated step, the now AutoMerged Concept Map was arranged using CmapTools Autolayout format, shown in Figure 7.5. This view brought into high relief the commonalities across the definitions, and showed at a glance the parochial parts of each definition. The different shades of grey in Figure 7.6 demonstrate the overlaps. Concepts linked to linking phrases, but having different colors, were the result of Step 3, and represented a direct overlap of concepts.

Importantly, the concepts containing the full definitions were turned "invisible" in this step in order to declutter the Concept Map. They are not deleted, however. All color was taken out of the font, objects, and lines. The audit trail remained, but was now in the background.

Step 5: ManualMerge

Next, the Concept Map was subjected to manual merging. As in Step 2, this was a highly cognitive activity involving some judgment. First, concepts and propositions unique to one definition were extracted, i.e., spatially set aside, from the rest of the Concept Map. Categories were then developed for groups of concepts where appropriate. In this case, many amplifying examples of *asset* were provided in the definition. They were clustered into "Types" and extracted from the Concept Map. Next, alias resolution was performed. All like, but not matching, concepts were *manually* merged. This involved merging singular and plural instances, and commonly understood synonyms. In the latter cases, the default approach was to not

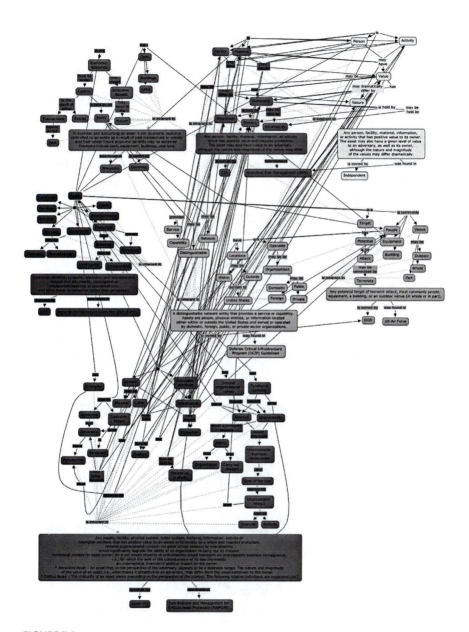

FIGURE 7.4
AutoMerged Concept Map.

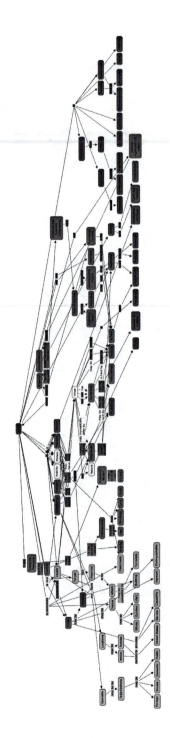

FIGURE 7.5
Autolayout.

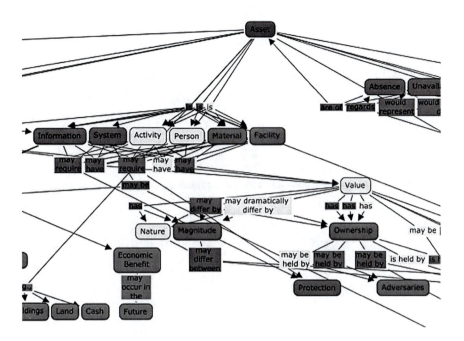

FIGURE 7.6
Autolayout (zoom view).

merge if the synonyms could take on different meaning in different contexts. Next, all like linking phrases that linked previously merged concepts were manually merged if, and only if, the linking phrases were linked to the same concept. In Figure 7.6, examples of such linking phrases can be seen, for example, in the multiple instances of "is" linking *asset* to multiple previously merged concepts, and in the linking phrase "has" linking "Value" and "Ownership." A final sweep through the remaining propositions was conducted for minor wordsmithing (taking care not to change meaning), bringing the core propositions into high relief with thick linking lines, and formatting to decrease the overall size of the Concept Map. Figure 7.7 shows the resulting manually merged Concept Map, with the extracted elements.

Step 6: CleanUp

In this step, all color was removed from all concepts. The font and all lines in the primary Concept Map were colored black, leaving a clean appearance. The Concept Map demonstrated the hallmark features of a

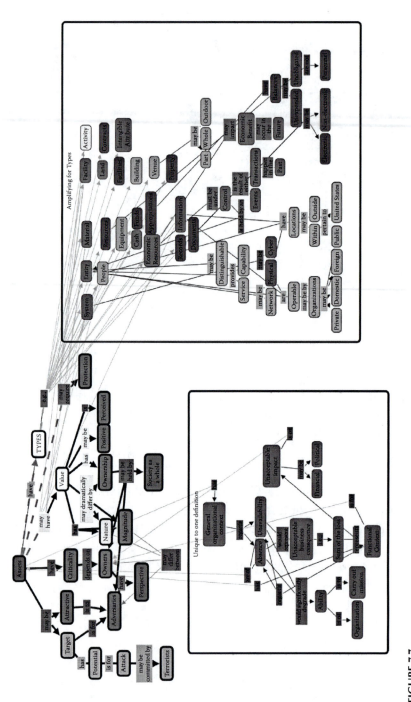

FIGURE 7.7
Manually merged Concept Map.

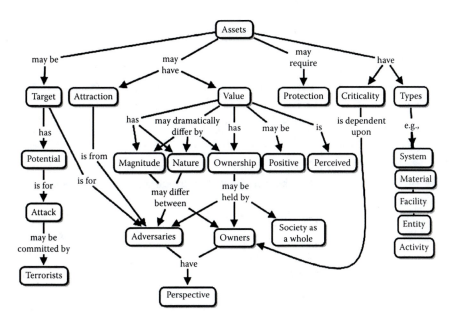

FIGURE 7.8
CleanUp Concept Map.

"Novakian" Concept Map, i.e., semihierarchical morphology, and propositional coherence, and represented the integration of all definitions into one Concept Map representation (Figure 7.8).

Step 7: Consensus Process

The integrated definition formulated through the five preceding steps served as a basis for a consensus process and the development of text-based versions of the definition. The consensus process selected was a facilitated working group discussion amongst subject matter professionals from the security risk management profession. The professionals convened to review the map with the goal of arriving at a common definition derived from the set of the definition's core concepts. The goal of the group was, initially, definition-focused, and the group set about reviewing the integrated Concept Map with the intention of writing a new definition.

The power of the Concept Maps quickly became apparent, however, in allowing explicit consideration of the underlying concepts behind the definitions. The group realized in short order that the concepts that were underlying the definitions were, in fact, out-dated. The security and risk management communities had moved forward in their thinking, adopting an all-hazards approach to risk management in the post-9/11 paradigm. This approach considers all sources of harm, be they environmental or adversarial, and the current terminology was based on the ideas of intentional actors. It is likely that the definitions would have raised disagreement if read and considered individually, but none did so when integrated. Thus, the group recommended changes to the Concept Map, which were captured "on-the-fly" by a Concept Map recorder. The map was reorganized to capture the current state of the profession and the concepts that were inherent in the new paradigm being used for risk management.

Rather than a simple effort in wordsmithing, the effort resulted in an advance in the state of thinking for the profession. The consensus definition resulting from the discussion was: *"An asset is something of value that may be subject to harm or hazard."* Even more important than that definition were the context discussions that were elicited from the working group, as they centered the discussion on the Concept Map. These were captured during the statement, and later written in prose. Some examples of these context statements included:

Targeting: Almost all definitions of asset currently include explicitly or implicitly the concept that assets are targeted by adversaries. While this makes sense in a traditional security risk management context, it was thought that this concept was too limiting in the current context where natural hazards, interdependencies, and incidental effects are also taken into account. It is important that assets not only be considered from the viewpoint of red team targeting, but also in an "all-hazards" context where they can generate consequences due to nonhuman factors, or where they are affected by secondary effects when another asset is actually the target.

Protection: The idea that assets may require protection also is a common concept in past definitions. The decision to protect an asset, however, is for the decision maker as a result of the risk analysis—a component of the risk management process, not part of the core definition when determining what an asset is. Security risk management has evolved beyond the idea of protection-focused countermeasures to also consider thresholds of acceptable risk and asset recovery as options in addition to protection, so this concept was left out of the core definition of term asset.

Intangibility: Another course of discussion was tangible versus intangible assets. Security risk management definitions and methodologies now frequently consider the consequence arising from effects upon intangible factors such as business good will, intellectual property, proprietary information, public confidence, or morale. This translates into the core definition by consideration of value. Whether tangible or intangible, something can be considered an asset if it has a value, whether or not it can be accurately measured, and thus relevant to the security risk management process. If it is not possible to at least estimate the value of something, then it is not considered to be an asset in the risk equation (SARMA, 2008).

LESSONS LEARNED

In reviewing the methodology, we identified key lessons learned. First, while Step 2: Decomposition and Step 5: Manual Merge were conducted by one of the authors (Moon), we agreed that it is ultimately desirable to have at least a second set of eyes on these steps. This can be accomplished by simply sharing the results of each step before moving forward, to get a check on the validity of the Concept Maps. A more stringent approach could be to have multiple Concept Mappers working at these steps, either in a group setting or individually. The latter approach may result in the need to conduct additional steps to merge the multiple variations, but it would ensure the reliability of the steps.

Related to this point, the author conducting the Integration steps was not steeped in the field of security and risk management. The trade-off here lies between the benefit of having no "dog in the fight" and thus not being burdened with the socio-historico-politico baggage that the definitions may carry, and the disadvantage of not knowing the finer nuances of concepts. We, and the group of professionals, agreed that the Integration is best done by an outsider, who may be aided, where necessary, by an insider.

Our second lessons learned arose from the consensus process. It is important to note that a facilitated working group discussion amongst subject matter professionals is only one approach to reaching consensus. Having the definition in Concept Map form opens up numerous other approaches, to include having interested parties revise the Concept Map independently or even in collaborative mode via CmapServer. Whatever the approach, it is clear that the Concept Map resulting from Step 6 will most likely not be the final statement. We view this as a benefit of the overall approach. The Concept Map should be viewed as a setup for consensus—a reflection of the current, known state of affairs.

We were a bit surprised at how terse the final definition was—14 words boiled down from 7 definitions comprised of over 350 words, or 161 propositions in the original Concept Maps. But, we should not have been. One of the key benefits of Concept Maps is their capacity for boiling down key elements of information into an easily digestible yet meaning-rich representation. We believe providing the Step 6 Concept Map enabled the group to efficiently reach the final definition because the boiling work had already been accomplished.

Our final lesson regarded efficiency. Our rule of thumb for time to completion of the Integration steps was approximately 2.5 hours. We regard this as a major advantage of the approach, particularly in light of the fact that the Integration effort can be managed by one person. This can allow other interested parties to focus on the other steps, e.g., gathering and consensus building. Such a federated approach can allow the approach to scale to large volume efforts (cf., Moon, Pino, and Hedberg, 2006).

OTHER TERMS AND FUTURE DIRECTION

The results of the *asset* effort were published on the SARMA Common Knowledge Base. Following the success of this effort, the SARMA Board of Directors elected to continue the effort into six additional, high visibility terms in the SARMA Common Knowledge Base: Consequence, Risk, Risk Assessment, Risk Management, Threat, and Vulnerability. The resulting Concept Maps were used to facilitate a working group discussion, this time with a larger group of security and risk management professionals. Here, the Concept Maps served a similar function in driving the discussion. Revisions to the Concept Maps were captured and posted to the SARMA Common Knowledge Base, which is available in full color at http://sarma-wiki.org/index.php?title=Category:Definitions.

The long-term proposition for the effort is to provide the results of working group sessions, and make them available to the entire professional community for comment and consensus. This plan will be pursued when the community is considered large and representative enough to have the results stand as a valid voluntary consensus standard for government agency consideration. In the interim, they are available for teaching efforts across the profession as the state of knowledge is moved forward.

The underlying difficulty of the security and risk management field's efforts to converge as a community is that so many different disciplines and modes of thought are represented, each with their own originating concepts and ways of processing challenges in the field. By acknowledging the legacy of Joseph Novak and executing our methodology, this problem can be addressed. Each field of study can identify its own originations within the concepts represented in the ontology, and use that as the educational stepping off point for understanding and integrating the new concepts of other disciplines into their own way of thinking. Rather than focusing on individual words and definitions, they are able to concentrate on concepts and propositions, and come to an understanding of their fellow practitioners' ways and methods, without having to relinquish their own. Through this effort, education, rather than authoritative definition, provides the greatest benefit to the community. The context and evolution of the community through working groups that utilize our methodology have the potential to do far more than any authoritative lexicon could accomplish.

REFERENCES

Cañas, A., G. Hill, and R. Carff, et al. 2004. Concept maptools: A knowledge modeling and sharing environment. In *Concept maps: Theory, methodology, technology.* Proceedings of the First International Conference on Concept Mapping, eds. A. Cañas, J. Novak, and F. González. Pamplona, Spain.

Harter, A. G. 2007. Same words, different meanings: The need for uniformity of language and lexicon in security analysis and risk management. Paper delivered at Critical Infrastructure Protection: Elements of Risk. Critical Infrastructure Protection Program (CIPP), Fairfax, VA: George Mason University School of Law.

Moon, B., A. Pino, and C. Hedberg. 2006. Studying transformation: The use of concept maptools in surveying the integration of intelligence and operations. In *Concept maps: Theory, methodology, technology,* eds. A. Cañas and J. Novak. Proceedings of the Second International Conference on Concept Mapping. San Jose, Costa Rica.

SARMA. 2008. SARMA Common Knowledge Base Project: http://sarma-wiki.org/index. php?title=Category:Definitions

8

The Use of Concept Mapping in Ecological Management: A Case Study Involving Grassland Ecosystems in Victoria, Australia

Andrea White

CONTENTS

INTRODUCTION

This chapter details a pilot program that was undertaken for the development of conceptual models for the broad ecosystem groups that occur across Victoria, in southeastern Australia. This project was carried out in conjunction with Parks Victoria (PV), the organization responsible for managing parks and reserves in Victoria. The aim of this program is to develop conceptual models for each ecosystem type that will identify the values, threats, processes, and drivers for ecosystem health, and to provide decision support for park management. The case study presented here (the pilot program) concentrates on grassland ecosystems.

Natural systems are complex, with many interacting components and many potential responses to management actions. It is difficult for individuals to conceptualize these systems and, therefore, to make decisions regarding their management. In addition, the information required to make informed decisions about ecosystem management is commonly fragmented and diffuse. Currently, the information required to manage Victorian parks resides in PV branch and regional offices: internal reports, peer-reviewed literature, unpublished data, and the knowledge of experts and other external stakeholders. Ecosystem models have the potential to bring this information and knowledge together as an integrated whole, identifying threats to the biological values of the parks, the causal structure of ecosystems, and the likely outcomes of specific management interventions. They also will promote understanding and support communication within PV and with external stakeholders, by providing a transparent way to communicate the rationale behind management actions. The aim is to be able to make clear, knowledgeable, and explainable management decisions (McNay et al., 2006).

OBJECTIVES

Parks Victoria has two programs that could benefit from the development of ecosystem conceptual models: (1) Levels of Protection, which aims to identify priorities for management, and (2) the Signs of Healthy Parks program, which aims to assess performance of that management. Both programs need ways of identifying what the main values, threats, and emerging issues are in these systems and determining the efficacy of management activities, while ensuring that different programs are consistent with one another. Conceptual models have the potential to fulfill this role, and contribute to the selection of variables for monitoring.

Addressing objectives associated with the management of natural systems cannot be restricted by incomplete or biased empirical information (McNay et al., 2006). Decisions about management need to be made by managers even when faced with uncertainty. The aim of this work is to investigate methods for using the information available (from all sources) to make clear, explainable management decisions, and identify areas for further research.

The pilot program explored three alternative modeling methods, using Grasslands as a case study. An ideal modeling approach would be one that (1) effectively captures knowledge of ecological interactions, (2) is simple enough for operational use, (3) communicates causal understanding effectively to managers and stakeholders, and (4) is not prohibitively expensive in the time and resources required for model construction.

The modeling method also needed to deliver a product that would present contemporary understanding to managers and stakeholders in a transparent and explicit manner, as a means of communication and decision support. Transparency in information sources and assumptions allows the interrogation of the ideas, logic, and reasoning behind the models; the assessment of relative differences among alternative perspectives in causal understanding; and the relative merit of different management approaches (McNay et al., 2006).

The development of these models will assist PV with key management questions, i.e., what to manage (prioritizing threats), what to monitor, and what research to do. The conceptual models will provide a transparent means with which to communicate the values, threats, and drivers in the ecosystem types; make explicit what it is we aim to protect; and what we measure in order to gauge our effectiveness. It is a method that can be used to convey to staff and other stakeholders how monitoring is targeting various ecosystem processes, threats, and the impacts of management actions. We expect that these models will be useful for corporate and business plans (funding cases) and also to inform policy, especially in a strategic sense.

Thus, the objectives of the pilot program were:

- To gather information necessary to describe Victorian grassland ecosystems, including the values to be protected, threatening processes, and potential management interventions
- To use causal maps, Bayesian networks, and state transition models to model these systems
- To document the strengths and weaknesses of each modeling method for use in the management of Victorian parks by PV

The next sections provide background in the domains of grasslands and ecological modeling. Following this background, the method and results of the pilot program are presented.

BACKGROUND: GRASSLANDS

Lowland grasslands in southeastern Australia have been greatly depleted in area and condition throughout their original range, including in Victoria; drivers of change have been the clearing, livestock grazing, and cultivation. Australian ecosystems evolved with low grazing pressure from native herbivores and, because of this, the large herds of sheep and cattle that were introduced postsettlement had immediate and severe impacts on soils, landscape processes, and flora and fauna (Mack and Thompson, 1982; Lunt et al., 2007).

Grazing influences grassland condition via a number of pathways: floristic changes related to differences in palatability and defoliation tolerance, soil compaction and disturbance, weed invasion, and modifications to nutrient cycling and a loss of structural diversity (Dorrough et al., 2004; Lunt et al., 2007). Grazing also has resulted in an increase in bare ground, especially at the end of summer when soil moisture is low. Widespread clearing and loss of deep-rooted perennial grasses leads to disruption of physical processes, changes that can lead to salinization and threaten remaining flora and fauna (Prober and Thiele, 2005). Grazing may be a useful management tool as well if it controls the biomass of existing potentially dominant, grazing-sensitive plants (native or exotic); maintains habitat structure; and enhances diversity of species and vegetation structures (Lunt et al., 2007).

Themeda triandra is the dominant species of native grasslands on volcanic soils in western Victoria (Morgan and Lunt, 1999). *Themeda* is most productive in the first three to four years after fire, after which productivity declines. Before European settlement and the clearing and cultivation of grassland habitat, fire was a regular source of disturbance for these grasslands. It is estimated by Morgan and Lunt (1999) that intervals of less than five years are necessary to maintain the health of these *Themeda*-dominated systems.

Burning is also important for intertussock native flora that can be rapidly eliminated from grasslands due to severe competition from *Themeda* in the absence of disturbance. Faunal species, such as the Earless Dragon and Plains Wanderer, also rely on the creation of intertussock spaces. The native faunal assemblages of grasslands have been very much depleted and simplified since settlement of the medium-sized, ground-dwelling mammals that once inhabited these areas, are mostly now extinct (Prober and Thiele, 2005).

Grasslands are dynamic systems that require regular disturbance to maintain natural processes and a diversity of species; this disturbance is now mainly provided by land managers. Potential management activities in grasslands include manipulations of grazing pressure (native and introduced) and fire regimes, mowing or slashing, selective use of herbicides, and the reintroduction of native species. A particular management intervention will target specific issues in a grassland (or a section of grassland). For example, it may focus on weed control, biomass management, maintaining habitat requirements for specific species, improvement of soil structure, or nutrient balance. Any one management action may have multiple benefits.

BACKGROUND: ECOLOGICAL MODELING

Ecological models are used to examine, compare, and contrast hypotheses that can explain observed patterns in natural systems. An individual model that is coherent and consistent with observations can be thought of as a formal hypothesis of system dynamics (Neuhauser, 2001). Statistical modeling tools in ecology have traditionally been based on frequentist methods (Pollino, White, and Hart, 2007). These have been used to explain patterns in ecological systems where causes are single and separable, and discrimination can be provided using pair-wise hypotheses and a simple yes or no answer (Holling and Allen, 2002). However, causes in ecological systems are likely to be multiple and overlapping (Holling and Allen, 2002), and data are usually sparse.

Predicting ecosystem behavior is inherently uncertain, and knowledge of these systems will always be incomplete. In addition, the system itself is dynamic and evolving due to management interventions and other anthropogenic impacts (Walters and Holling, 1990). Levins (1966) proposed an approach whereby models are used to simplify in a way that "preserves the essential features of the problem." He pointed out that all models leave out a lot of information and that they are false, incomplete, and inadequate. Levins suggested precision could be sacrificed for realism and generality using flexible (often graphical) models.

The preceding section's description of Grassland dynamics (a summary of a more comprehensive document that appeared in the pilot program report) represents a written synthesis of the research literature, together with commentary on ecological values, threats, and possible management options. Literature reviews are by far the most common approach used in evidence-based decision making in ecological systems. However, it is unlikely to be the best approach. The complexity of interactions, the varying scale involved in individual studies, and the speculative narratives of cause and effect linking management actions to outcomes all conspire against the reader's ability to form a coherent understanding.

Graphical models provide a more effective approach. Axelrod (1976) contended that "when a cognitive map is pictured in graph form, it is then relatively easy to see how each of the concepts and causal relationships relate to each other and to see the overall structure of the whole set of portrayed assertions." de Bruin et al. (2009) tested understanding of medical risks among study participants who were provided communication materials based on written scenarios or graphical models. Graphic representations substantially outperformed scenarios in improving people's understanding of risks.

The current study explored three alternative approaches to the graphical capture of our understanding of Grassland dynamics: causal maps, i.e., an adopted form of Concept Maps using CmapTools (IHMC, 2008); Bayesian networks using Netica (Norsys, 2005); and state transition models.

Causal Maps

Casual maps (also known as influence diagrams) are a type of network-based model that is used to represent the domain knowledge of experts (Nadkarni and Shenoy, 2001). They express the judgment that certain events or actions will lead to particular outcomes. Individuals reason by accumulating possibly significant pieces of information and organizing them in relation to each other and combining them in order to make conclusions. We use such processes to put together cause-and-effect events into series to predict the future course of events (Nadkarni and Shenoy, 2001). Larger frameworks are created when smaller sets of causal relationships are brought together (cf., Klein, Moon, and Hoffman, 2006). The components of a causal map are the factors that influence the system being modeled (nodes) and the causal relationships between the nodes (arcs or arrows). The direction of the arrows implies causality. These same features are hallmarks of Concept Maps, which require explanatory text to be included as part of the arrow and help to describe the nature of the relationship.

Bayesian Networks

Bayesian networks (BNs) are a type of graphical probabilistic model, the basis of which is an influence diagram (as described above) conceptualizing the system to be managed (Cain, 2001). BNs can be used for many purposes, from illustrating a conceptual understanding of a system to calculating joint probabilities to make predictions, draw inference, and explore decision options (Nyberg, Marcot, and Sulyma, 2006). The arrows between the nodes represent causal dependencies based on understanding of process, statistical, or other types of association (Pollino, White, and Hart, 2007). BNs were included in the study for their ability to represent the strength of the causal relationship between variables, as a comparison with casual map methodology, particularly to compare the time required for development and the expected utility for management purposes.

State Transition

State transition (ST) models are diagrams that represent observed or theoretical states. Arrows represent the observed or theoretical transactions between these states (Jackson, Bartolome, and Allen-Diaz, 2002). ST models are used to conceptualize complex behavior of dynamic systems. They have the capacity and flexibility to accommodate various types of knowledge and information (Westoby, Walker, and Noy-Meir, 1989). The primary components of ST models are states, transitions, and thresholds (Stringham, Krueger, and Shaver, 2003) that are determined by the resilience of a system and its response to primary processes. They are intended to function on the basis of managerial, rather than ecological criteria (Westoby, Walker, and Noy-Meir, 1989).

METHODS AND RESULTS

Basic components of the ecosystem types that occur across Victoria were identified in a workshop undertaken by the PV research branch. This work has been used as a basis for further investigations into grassland systems, including a review of the literature, an elicitation process with experts and other stakeholders, and ongoing involvement and consultation with PV research, conservation, and on-ground staff.

The first step in the modeling process involved the mapping of a (conceptual) causal map for grasslands. This was carried out using CmapTools, which captured causal information and represented it in a Concept Map. The focus was to produce a model that was structured to represent, as clearly and concisely as possible, the relationships between threats and the values and processes that PV is aiming to protect.

The next step in the process involved a formal parameterization of the Bayesian network model, where the relationships between threats, values, and processes were informed by different types of data (i.e., quantitative and qualitative data, anecdotal evidence, expert opinion, and the output of other modeling processes). The linkages and interactions between values, threats, and processes were described numerically to indicate their strength. ST models were used to explore the different possible management interventions and their likely outcomes. The results from this part of the study are not presented here, except to illustrate the comparative strengths and weaknesses in each method.

Grassland Causal Map

An extensive literature review was conducted for Victorian grasslands, and a causal map was produced, shown in Figure 8.1. The boxes with the solid outline in Figure 8.1 represent the factors and processes that threaten

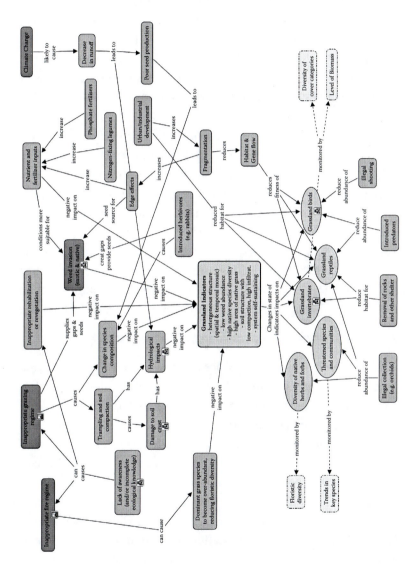

FIGURE 8.1

Causal map for *Themeda*-dominated grasslands.

grasslands, and impact on the indicators of grassland state that are outlined in the large central box, "Grassland Indicators," which in turn affect the things that we value about these grassland systems (represented by ovals). These values include threatened species and communities, and native plant, invertebrate, reptile, and bird species. Grassland values were sourced from Parks Victoria staff, the literature, land managers, and grassland experts. The boxes with the dashed outline represent what could potentially be measured in order to monitor the effectiveness of management strategies that aim to protect these values.

The key underlying threats to grassland persistence are represented by darker grey nodes. These include: inappropriate fire regime, inappropriate grazing regime, weed invasion, and climate change. The lighter grey nodes are used to describe the processes through which the key threats act to influence the state of grassland systems. For example, an inappropriate grazing regime will cause soil compaction, which damages the soil crust and impacts on hydrology by reducing infiltration (Bowker et al., 2006). Grazing also may change the species composition of the grassland as some species are more palatable than others, and species vary in their tolerance to repeated defoliation. Cultivation of introduced nitrogen-fixing species and the use of phosphate fertilizer have conferred a competitive advantage to weed species over many of the indigenous grassland plants. A change to the presettlement fire regime has had an impact on grasslands as well, which require periodic burning to reduce biomass and create intertussock gaps for indigenous plant and animal species.

The resources associated with a number of the nodes in Figure 8.1 indicate where extra information has been provided (e.g., ST models, subnetworks, photos, maps). Further details were provided for three of the key threats. The weed node has a Cmap attached to it, which describes in detail the factors that must be considered when planning weed management activities, and the likely outcomes from management actions. The fire and grazing nodes each have associated with them an ST model, which describes the potential states that a grassland (or section of grassland) may be in, and the potential management interventions that can be used to cause a transition between one state and another. Figure 8.2 presents the ST model for the management of fire in a *Themeda*-dominated grassland; the boxes represent the different states, the ovals the possible management actions, and the diamonds the moderating effect of the season of the burn.

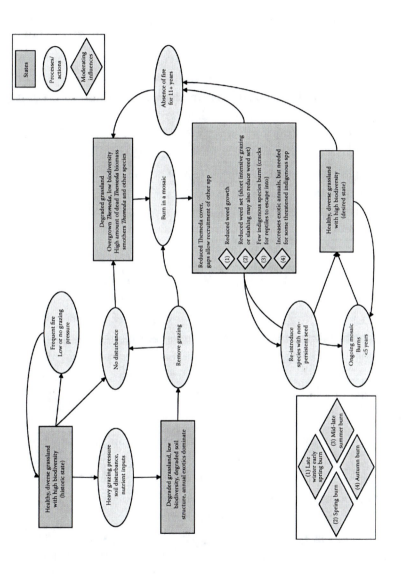

FIGURE 8.2

A state transition model for different fire regimes in a *Themeda*-dominated grasslands. This model outlines, in general terms, the different states of a *Themeda*-dominated grassland, and the likely consequences of various management actions related to the fire regime.

The states in the model are a theorized presettlement historical state, a degraded state that has resulted from heavy grazing, soil disturbance, and nutrient inputs (low floral biodiversity, degraded soil structure, and dominated by weed species); a degraded state that has resulted from a lack of disturbance (high *Themeda* biomass, low floral biodiversity); a state that has been burnt (but differs in its features depending on the season of the burn); and a healthy grassland that has resulted from regular burning and the reintroduction of species that have disappeared due to nonpersistent seed bank (the "desired" state). The healthy state requires periodic burning (interfire period less than five years) or it will revert to a degraded state.

The extra resources discussed above provide additional detail that cannot be included in the main model. Certain nodes are also annotated, and thus can display details of key references when the cursor is placed over the node (when viewed in CmapTools). These features enable the model to be used as a repository of information that is very easily accessed.

Values and Indicators

For ecological models to be useful in decision support, they must provide a link between management actions and ecosystem response. In addition, the decision support tool will be more effective if the ecosystem response is represented by an attribute that stakeholders care about (Reckhow, 1999; Borsuk, 2004). To do this, values and indicators that can be used to gauge the state of these values must be made explicit. Attributes used to gauge the condition of grasslands have been included in the Concept Map depicted in Figure 8.1, and include:

- Heterogeneous structure (spatial and temporal mosaic), which provides the niches for a diversity of flora and fauna species at a variety of scales (Eddy, 2002; Lunt et al., 2007).
- A low proportion of weed species, the corollary of which is that there is a high proportion of native plant species.
- Soil stability, which is essential to resist erosion; good soil structure is also important for infiltration of water, and the provision of habitat (McIntyre and Tongway, 2005; Pellant, Shaver, and Pyke, 2005).
- A self-sustaining ecosystem has natural cycles and ecosystem services intact (e.g., nutrient cycling, hydrology, seed supplies).

EVALUATION OF THE CASUAL MAP MODELING METHOD

The Concept Maps were found to be useful for communication and in stimulating discussion in the multiple rounds of feedback undertaken as a part of model development. Grassland management experts from Parks Victoria regional offices were consulted (in interviews), as were research and conservation staff in the city office (in a workshop and several meetings). There was broad consensus regarding the overall structure of the model and the representation of causal relationships. Differences arose around which of the many potential threats and management interventions should be included. In each case, an agreement was reached and the model component or relationship modified to reflect the consensus opinion. Priority values were also clarified, and several individuals argued successfully for the inclusion of additional values.

An important part of the feedback program was to get a sense of whether specific threats, processes, management actions, and values could be applied to grasslands across the state, and where it was likely that there would be differences. It was agreed that not all of the components depicted in the main Concept Map (Figure 8.1) would be important in all of the regions and parks where grasslands occur. It is expected that, in practice, managers would review the casual map and modify it for the conditions specific to their park. In this regard, the causal map could serve as an accessible knowledge repository and a medium for communication (Mingers and Rosenhead, 2004), as well as a checklist for the threats, processes, and management actions that should be considered and how these relate to the identified values. The Concept Maps also included recent grassland research, which has the potential to be incorporated in the management of these systems (e.g., novel approaches to manage specific threats in grasslands, such as the soil nutrient imbalance).

Strengths

The ability to represent complex ecological systems and the option to link to submodels (which contain extra detail) were perceived as useful features of this method. Links in causal maps indicate causation. As most people are able to express their understanding of a system in this manner, this method was accessible to those without formal training in modeling.

It was identified in the introduction to this chapter that an ideal modeling approach would be one that (1) effectively captures ecological interactions, (2) is simple enough for operational use, (3) communicates causal understanding effectively to managers and stakeholders, and (4) is not prohibitively expensive in the time and resources required for model construction. The Concept Maps developed here using CmapTools were able to achieve these aims. They were effective in capturing the important ecological interactions that occur in Victorian grasslands, using cause–effect relationships, which are straightforward and generally easy to understand. The main model (Figure 8.1) includes enough information to be considered as a stand-alone tool, though further detail is accessible (as resources attached to specific components within the main model). The Concept Maps also were able to be developed relatively quickly in comparison with the development of the BN for Victorian grasslands.

The BN model developed required considerably more resources when compared to the Concept Maps, and because of this it was decided by PV managers that these models would not be pursued as part of the current conceptual model program. However, in the future they may be considered for complex management problems, where their ability to make inferences (particularly with different combinations of management actions) and represent uncertainty would be advantageous.

The use of these models as a repository of knowledge and understanding of the ecosystem was considered to be of great value, especially in having all of the relevant facts and information in the same place. They were considered to be particularly useful for capturing the species, community, and ecological knowledge of individuals, that may have been built up over several decades, but which may not be captured by any other recording system. They would also be useful in communicating with external stakeholders, and for knowledge transfer when training new staff (reducing the impact of staff turnover).

Weaknesses

Causal maps were thought to not be well suited to inference. The net influence of multiple causal pathways is typically indeterminate. Causal maps cannot easily model uncertainty (all variables in the Concept Map presented here have the same level of certainty) and the representation of the decision variables is static (Huff, 1990; Laukkanen, 1996). Identifying the level of uncertainty can be very important in making inferences because observations of variables may be uncertain, information may be incomplete, or the variables involved may be vague.

The difficulty in representing threshold effects in Concept Maps was considered a drawback, though it was decided that these effects could be incorporated in the more detailed ST models in the model hierarchy.

CONCLUSIONS

Ecological interactions are complex and conservation management problems are typically ill-defined and poorly structured. The complexity of natural systems does not lend itself to structuring and formulation by elaborate quantitative models, or simple intuitive problem solving. Rather, making sense of these situations necessitates considering, and often times negotiating, alternative models of the ill-structured situation. Graphical capture of individual and collective narratives of cause and effect assists problem formulation by facilitating the sharing of alternative perspectives and working toward a collective perspective (Massey and Wallace, 1996).

Conceptual models are able to formally represent a summary of expert understanding about ecosystems, and can be used to identify and prioritize specific information needs associated with ecosystem management. In this way, conceptual models form a foundation for an integrated and holistic approach to management and research. The management of natural values in Victoria's parks would benefit from a comprehensive causal model for each ecosystem type, which would include all threats, values, important processes, and potential measurable components for monitoring purposes.

It was emphasized that the hypotheses, assertions, literature, and observations that justify the structure of each model could be fully documented by the use of Concept Maps, allowing model structures to be interrogated and to evolve. This was considered particularly important in the context of the adaptive management program (a structured, iterative process that employs the use of "management experiments" with the aim to improve decision making and reduce uncertainty over time via monitoring) pursued by PV (e.g., Robley and Wright, 2003).

REFERENCES

Axelrod, R. 1976. *Structure of decision: The cognitive maps of political elites*. Princeton, NJ: Princeton University Press.

Borsuk, M. E. 2004. Predictive assessment of fish health and fish kills in the Neuse River estuary using elicited expert judgment. *Human and Ecological Risk Assessment* 10, 415–434.

Bowker, M. A., J. Belnap, D. W. Davidson, and Goldstein, H. 2006. Correlates of biological soil crust abundance across a continuum of spatial scales: Support for a hierarchical conceptual model. *Journal of Applied Ecology* 43, 152–163.

Cain, J. 2001. *Planning improvements in natural resources management: Guidelines for using Bayesian networks to support the planning and management of development programmes in the water sector and beyond*. Oxon, U.K.: Centre for Ecology & Hydrology.

de Bruin, W. B., U. Guvenc, and B. Fischoff, et al. 2009. Communicating about xenotransplantation: Models and scenarios. *Risk Analysis* 29, 1105–1115.

Dorrough, J., A. Yen, and V. Turner, et al. 2004. Livestock grazing management and biodiversity conservation in Australian temperate grassy landscapes. *Australian Journal of Agricultural Research* 55, 279–295.

Eddy, D. 2002. *Managing native grassland: A guide to management for conservation, production and landscape protection*. Sydney: WWF Australia.

Holling, C. S. and C. R. Allen. 2002. Adaptive inference for distinguishing credible from incredible patterns in nature. *Ecosystems* 5, 319–328.

Huff, A. S. 1990. *Mapping strategic thought*. New York: John Wiley & Sons.

IHMC. 2008. Cmaptools 4.16. Pensacola, FL: Institute for Human and Machine Cognition: http://cmap.ihmc.us/conceptmap.html.

Jackson, R. D., J. W. Bartolome, and B. Allen-Diaz. 2002. State and transition models: Response to an ESA symposium. *Bulletin of the Ecological Society of America* 83, 194–196.

Klein, G., B. Moon, and R. R. Hoffman. 2006. Making sense of sensemaking 2: A macrocognitive model. *IEEE Intelligent Systems* 21, 88–92.

Laukkanen, M. 1996. Comparative cause mapping of organisational cognition. In *Cognition within and between organizations*, eds. J. R. Meindl, C. Stubbart, and J. F. Porac. Beverley Hills, CA: Sage.

Levins, R. 1966. The strategy of model building in population biology. *American Scientist* 54, 421–431.

Lunt, I. D., D. J. Eldridge, and J. W. Morgan, et al. 2007. A framework to predict the effects of livestock grazing and grazing exclusion on conservation values in natural ecosystems in Australia. *Australian Journal of Botany* 55, 401–415.

Mack, R. N. and J. N. Thompson. 1982. Evolution in steppe with few large, hooved mammals. *American Naturalist* 119: 757–773.

Massey, A. P. and W. A. Wallace. 1996. Understanding and facilitating group problem structuring and formulation: Mental representations, interaction, and representation aids. *Decision Support Systems* 17, 253–274.

McIntyre, S. and D. Tongway. 2005. Grassland structure in native pastures: Links to soil surface condition. *Ecological Management and Restoration* 6, 43–50.

McNay, R. S., B. G. Marcot, and V. Brumovsky et al. 2006. A Bayesian approach to evaluating habitat for woodland caribou in north-central British Columbia. *Canadian Journal of Forestry Research* 36, 3117–3133.

Mingers, J. and J. Rosenhead. 2004. Problem structuring methods in action. *European Journal of Operational Research* 152, 530–554.

Morgan, J. W. and I. D. Lunt. 1999. Effects of time-since-fire on the tussock dynamics of a dominant grass (*Themeda triandra*) in a temperate Australian grassland. *Biological Conservation* 88, 379–386.

Nadkarni, S. and P. P. Shenoy. 2001. A Bayesian network approach to making inferences in causal maps. *European Journal of Operational Research* 128, 479–498.

Neuhauser, C. 2001. Mathematical challenges in spatial ecology. *Notices of the AMS* 48, 1304–1314.

Norsys. 2005. Netica, www.norsys.com.

Nyberg, J. B., B. G. Marcot, and R. Sulyma. 2006. Using Bayesian belief networks in adaptive management. *Canadian Journal of Forest Research* 36, 3101–3116.

Pellant, M., P. L. Shaver, and D. A. Pyke, et al.. 2005. Interpreting indicators of rangeland health, Version 4. Technical Reference 1734-6. Denver, CO: U.S. Department of the Interior, Bureau of Land Management, National Science and Technology Center.

Pollino, C. A., A. K. White, and B. T. Hart. 2007. Examination of conflicts and improved strategies for the management of an endangered Eucalypt species using Bayesian networks. *Ecological Modelling* 201, 37–59.

Prober, S. M. and K. R. Thiele. 2005. Restoring Australia's temperate grasslands and grassy woodlands: Integrating function and diversity. *Ecological Management and Restoration* 6, 16–27.

Reckhow, K. H. 1999. Water quality prediction and probability network models. *Canadian Journal of Fisheries and Aquatic Science* 56, 1150–1158.

Robley, A. and J. Wright. 2002–2003. Adaptive Experimental Management of Foxes. Annual Report for Year 2, July 2002–June 2003. Parks Victoria Technical Series No. 2. Parks Victoria, Melbourne.

Stringham, T. K., W. C. Krueger, and P. L. Shaver. 2003. State and transition modeling: An ecological process approach. *Journal of Range Management* 56, 106–113.

Westoby, M., B. Walker, and I. Noy-Meir. 1989. Opportunistic management for rangelands not at equilibrium. *Journal of Range Management* 42, 266–274.

Walters, C. J. and C. S. Holling. 1990. Large-scale management experiments and learning by doing. *Ecology* 71, 2060–2068.

9

Influencing the Business Model and Innovations of a Research Organization through Concept Mapping

Robert R. Hoffman, Jan Maarten Schraagen,
Josine van de Ven, and Brian M. Moon

CONTENTS

INTRODUCTION

In this chapter, we describe several projects conducted at a Dutch research organization in which Concept Mapping influenced the organization's business model and its innovations. One project supported a collaborative activity in which a group of researchers and research program managers sought to define the business model of their unit within a large, national, applied-science organization. While two of us (Hoffman and Moon) had conducted a great many projects in which Concept Mapping had been used to facilitate the elicitation and representation of expert domain knowledge, the project we report in this chapter was a first for us, in that it was an attempt to use Concept Mapping to describe a business model. While the other two authors (Schraagen and Van de Ven) had extensive experience in business unit planning, the business model project we report in this chapter was a first for us in applying Concept Mapping. Since the execution of this project, the research organization has adopted Concept Mapping for use in its own research programs.

ABOUT TNO

TNO is the Netherlands Organization for Applied Scientific Research (Nederlandse Organisatie voor Toegepast Natuurwetenschappelijk Onderzoek). It was founded by an act of the Dutch parliament in 1932 and has as its core mission, the strengthening of the innovative power of government and industry. TNO conducts research for government organizations and for private sector companies, and also has close ties to universities through its 30 Knowledge Centers. It has significant international collaborations, especially in defense, security, aerospace, and the maritime industry. At the time of the project we describe in this chapter, the TNO was organized by these five core areas:

1. Quality of Life: To safeguard and improve health and well-being.
2. Defense, Security, and Safety: To ensure public safety and enhance the armed forces.
3. Science and Industry: To ensure that The Netherlands is economically competitive.
4. Built Environment and Geosciences: To develop ways of optimizing the use of space and natural resources.
5. Information and Communication Technology: To create innovative technology and applications in information management.

Through these core areas, TNO seeks to apply science to emerging needs of society and issues that are important from a policy perspective. As one can readily understand, given that The Netherlands is essentially a low-elevation river delta, there is a significant emphasis at TNO on research related to the theme of "living with water," which integrates many projects, such as wetlands information management and the science of climate change. Examples of other specific topic areas include: the optimum use of space in this small and densely populated country, issues of employment and participation by an aging population, innovation in construction and conservation of the natural environment, and efficient use of resources.

Each of the core areas has its own facilities for a number of business units. The Defense, Security, and Safety core area has five business units:

1. Observation Systems (e.g., electro-optics)
2. Information and Operations (command and control, policy studies)
3. Protection and Munitions (e.g., survivability, power technology)
4. Biological and Chemical Protection (e.g., threat detection, therapy)
5. Human Factors, which was the sponsor for the project we describe in this chapter

The Human Factors business unit is concerned with the work of professionals who operate on a 24/7 basis (i.e., military, emergency response, etc.). The unit has a number of state-of-the art laboratories, including some of the world's most advanced simulators. Its staff complement includes about 50 senior researchers, 100 researchers (including many graduate students), as well as administrative personnel. The scientific staff includes psychologists, engineers, physicists, and medical doctors. The majority of staff members are PhD-level and five also hold professorships.

The Human Factors business unit consists of four departments:

1. The Human in Command Department conducts research on decision making, teamwork, and cultural awareness.
2. The Human Interfaces Department conducts research on perception and interface design.
3. The Human Performance Department conducts research on traffic safety, workplace ergonomics, and sports performance.
4. The Training and Instruction Department conducts research on learning technology, team training, and learning simulations.

THE TNO STRATEGIC EVALUATION PROCESS

The TNO strategic plan, based upon agreements with the Dutch government and the TNO business partners, involves replanning every four years during which one of the business units undergoes a periodic "technology position audit" (TPA). The personnel of a business unit review their progress since the previous evaluation, taking into consideration significant changes in context and emerging policy-related issues (e.g., changes in funding mechanisms and priorities). Each department within the business unit reevaluates its capabilities and competencies, and the unit as a whole reevaluates its ambitions and goals. Next, a report of the self-evaluation is submitted to an audit committee consisting of national and international experts. That committee assesses the business unit in terms of its technology position, market attractiveness, technology maturity, and societal impact. Finally, the committee provides its recommendations to the TNO leadership.

As the time for the 2009 TPA approached, an opportunity arose for conducting a process of knowledge elicitation to support the preparation of the self-evaluation report. On a previous visit to TNO Human Factors by Hoffman, Concept Mapping had been described and its applications illustrated. That demonstration had suggested to TNO that Concept Mapping might help personnel express their goals and ambitions, and capture their business strategy for the upcoming TPA.

Thus, the TNO Concept Mapping activity was designed with two main purposes:

1. To create Concept Maps to support TNO Human Factors in its strategy development process and in its preparation for the TPA.
2. To train the TNO human factors scientists in Concept Mapping, which they might apply in various areas of TNO research. Furthermore, they might provide knowledge elicitation services both within the larger TNO organization.

Activity and Method

Four Concept Mapping sessions were held (October 28, 29 and December 17–19, 2008). One Concept Mapping expert served as the facilitator and another as the recorder. Descriptions of the process appear in Crandall, Klein, and Hoffman (2006) and IHMC (2009).

Knowledge elicitation (KE) sessions are usually devoted to interviewing the domain practitioners. Concept Mapping as one of the main KE methods is typically described in a session held prior to the actual knowledge elicitation. In the TNO sessions, however, it was necessary to spend some time in the sessions explaining the CmapTools and their applications. Part of the second session was devoted to demonstrating the process to the leadership of TNO. These distinct portions of the TNO activity, a segue from the knowledge elicitation itself, are taken into account in our evaluation of the process and the results.

First Session

Participants were seven senior researchers representing the four departments within the Human Factors business unit. In addition, the manager researcher of the business unit served as a key contributor to the KE session.

The Concept Maps focused on the following questions concerning the Human Factors business unit:

- What is a description of the unit?
- What is a description of the unit's facilities?
- What are its goals, ambitions, strategies, and SWOT (strengths, weaknesses, opportunities, threats)?
- What is the unit's action plan?

The Concept Mapping also focused on specific questions for each of the four departments:

- What is a description of the department?
- What are the department's goals, ambitions, SWOT, and actions?

Figure 9.1 and Figure 9.2 present Session 1 Concept Maps, showing their initial state of development and focus questions. Figure 9.1 illustrates the use of the "parking lot."

It was determined early in the process that there might be a use for *templates*. The first of these emerged in discussions while working on the

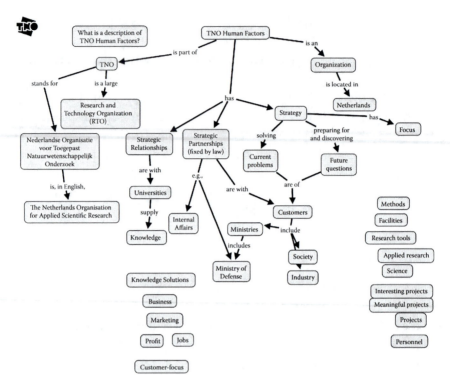

FIGURE 9.1

A Session 1 Concept Map about the TNO Human Factors business unit.

Concept Map shown in Figure 9.2. These are Concept Map structures that can be reused. One template was created for describing departments (topics, methods, facilities, etc.) and the other template pertained to goals, ambitions, strategies, and SWOT. It also became clear early on that most of the Concept Maps would benefit by using "nested nodes," which is a way of embedding a small Concept Map inside a node of a larger Concept Map. Figure 9.3 is also a Session 1 Concept Map, also partly completed, which illustrates the template for SWOT.

Total time spent in Concept Mapping was 450 min. The Concept Maps included a total of 420 concepts formed into 440 propositions. Thus, the yield was 440/450 = 0.98 propositions per task minute. Previous studies comparing Concept Mapping to other methods of KE (e.g., protocol analysis, interview methods, etc.) demonstrate that Concept Mapping is an efficient method for eliciting domain knowledge (Crandall, Klein, and Hoffman, 2006; Hoffman et al., 2002). The benchmark for effectiveness is

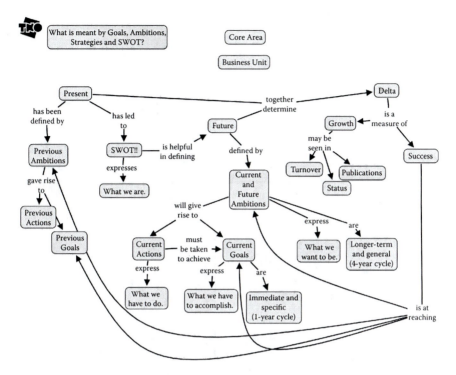

FIGURE 9.2
A Session 1 Concept Map about goals, ambitions, strategies, and SWOT.

2.0 informative propositions per task minute, which Concept Mapping can achieve. By contrast, the method of protocol analysis has been determined to yield less than 0.5 propositions per task minute. Part of the efficiency advantage for Concept Mapping is that the result from the KE session *is* the representation. In protocol analysis, and most other cognitive task analysis (CTA) methods, the statements generated in the CTA method must be transcribed and coded in terms of content or functional categories, which is very time-consuming. Sometimes in KE sessions, a high verbal expert can express knowledge and reasoning at a rate greater than that at which the Concept Mapper can effectively record all the concepts and relations. It can be more efficient, by orders of magnitude, to conduct more Concept Mapping sessions than to attempt to transcribe and code an audiotape (Hoffman et al., 2000; 2006).

Some of the time in Session 1 had been devoted to pointing out the capabilities of the CmapTools (e.g., discussing the uses of nested nodes), explaining the process of hyperlinking Concept Maps and resources, and

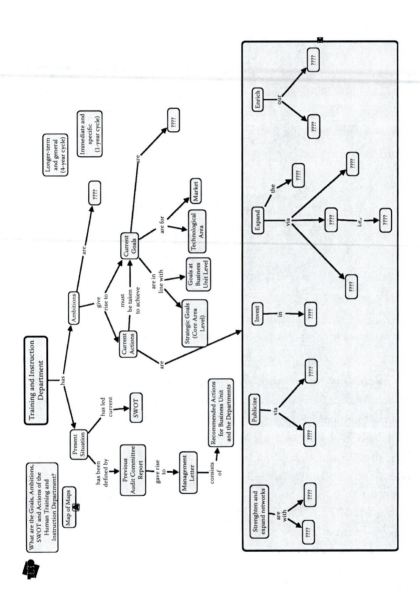

FIGURE 9.3

A Session 1 Concept Map illustrating the emergence of one of the template notions.

explaining the strategies used by the facilitator and the Concept Mapper to manage the KE sessions. Ordinarily, these activities are conducted in a workshop-like context held prior to the KE sessions themselves. With this in mind, a yield of 0.98 is considered to be a good yield.

This determination should be taken in light of the fact that it was not the purpose of this activity to result in a complete set of refined Concept Maps. In fact, the intent was to leave the work unfinished so that TNO personnel might gain experience and practice at the process. Thus, some of the Concept Maps had potential propositions (i.e., unlinked concept nodes), and these did not enter into the efficiency calculation.

Second Session

The second session was devoted to a review and refinement of the Concept Maps that had been created in the first session. Concept Maps that would "stitch together" the other Concept Maps were created (e.g., a Concept Map about how the departments are integrated). Attention also was paid to acquiring and integrating resources, specifically draft text to be included in the TPA document.

As the Concept Maps were reviewed, some "polishing" was conducted, i.e., adjustment of the Concept Map morphology and wordsmithing of the propositions in the Concept Maps. Figure 9.4 is one of the polished Concept Maps, describing the Human in Command Department.

Figure 9.5 illustrates a polished SWOT Concept Map, utilizing the template shown in Figure 9.3.

Third Session

This session was a demonstration of Concept Mapping in a brainstorming mode, with six directors and managers of the TNO organization. The rationale for the activity was that the Concept Map KE procedure might be used throughout the organization; that the other business units and their departments might forge Concept Maps to begin creating an organizational knowledge base for use in strategic planning.

The demonstration included a very brief presentation about Concept Maps, and then approximately 90 minutes in which the participants were guided in making Concept Maps about TNO strategy. The participants engaged in discussion of such concepts as "strategy," "adaptation," and "societal impact,"

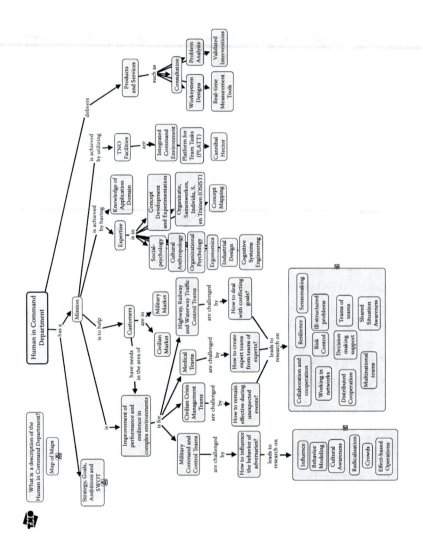

FIGURE 9.4

Concept Map describing the Human in Command Department.

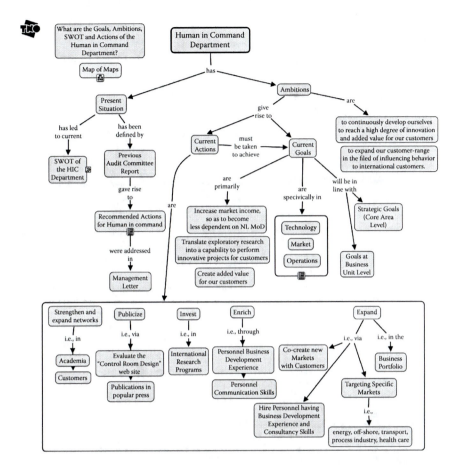

FIGURE 9.5
Concept Map describing a department's SWOT.

and "short-term market potential." The discussion was vigorous and suggested that the participants might benefit from further group sessions in which their key ideas, issues, and plans might be more clearly specified using Concept Mapping. Indicators of a need for improved shared understanding of a business model included disagreements about what is important as well as subtle differences in the interpretations of key concepts.

Fourth Session

The fourth session involved seven researchers representing two of the Human Factors Departments. Activity included refinement of the Sessions

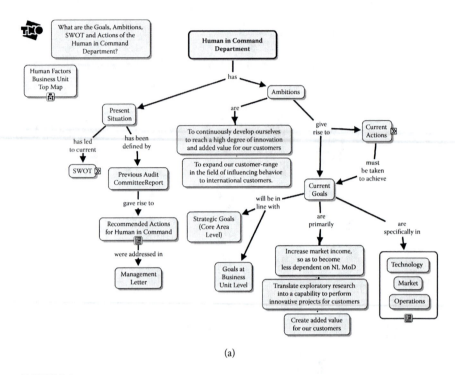

(a)

FIGURE 9.6a

Final Concept Map on strategies, goals, ambitions, and SWOT for the Human in Command Department.

1 and 2 Concept Maps. In some cases, it was decided that the templates that had been created in Sessions 1 and 2 could be simplified and that nested nodes could be used. Figure 9.6 illustrates the final Concept Map on strategies, goals, ambitions, and SWOT for the Human in Command Department. The left panel (Figure 9.6a) is the Concept Map and the right panel (Figure 9.6b) shows how the SWOT material that had previously been a template was revealed within a nested node.

The final session also involved hyperlinking additional resources (e.g., photographs of TNO facilities, additional text pieces). During the process of hyperlinking the Concept Maps together, the participants came to understand that material for all of the TNO core areas, all the departments within core areas, and all the business units within departments would need to be integrated. The TNO Concept Map business model would eventually organize Concept Maps about all the departments and not just the Human in Command Department within the Human Factors business unit. In this reorganization and integration of the Concept Maps, some of

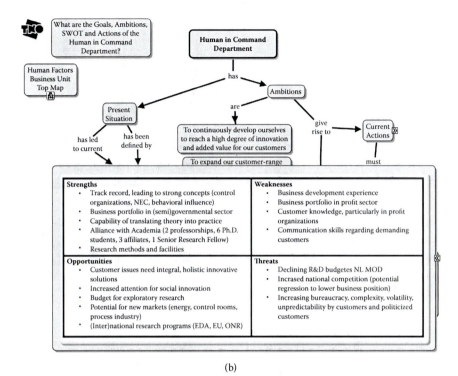

(b)

FIGURE 9.6b (continued).

the hyperlinking that had been done in Sessions 1 and 2 was undone, and new "maps of maps" (organizing Concept Maps, such as in Figure 9.7) were created and hyperlinked. It was determined that creating this new organizing structure would make it easier, in the ensuing months, to integrate additional Concept Maps. Figure 9.7 presents the highest-level Concept Map, the one that would integrate the Concept Maps for all of the TNO core areas. Figure 9.8 presents a Concept Map at the next level down in the model's organization, the Concept Map that organizes material about all of the business units within the Defense, Security, and Safety core area.

In addition, Concept Maps were created that described the four departments within the Human Factors business unit. Figure 9.9 is such a Concept Map, for the Human Performance Department. Additional Concept Maps described the business unit's customers and facilities.

Finally, a "presentation map" was created. This Concept Map would serve as the viewer's portal into the full set of Concept Maps. This is shown in Figure 9.10.

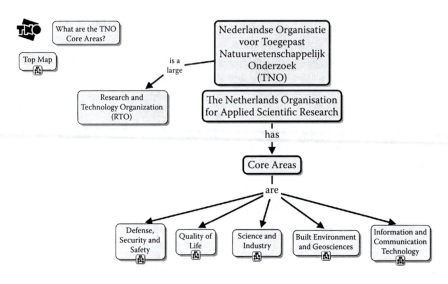

FIGURE 9.7
The highest level Concept Map for integrating across all of the TNO core areas.

At the end of Session 4, the TNO Concept Map business model consisted of 19 Concept Maps containing 522 concepts (not including template placeholders and Maps of Maps), whereas, at the end of the first session there had been 12 Concept Maps containing 420 concepts (not including template place-holders and maps of maps). Many of the new Concept Maps were maps of maps or were placeholders, to be refined subsequently by TNO personnel. Because Session 4 did not involve distinct KE activity, data from the fourth session were not used in an evaluation of yield.

Findings and Consequences

The Concept Mappers spent approximately 700 minutes at the activity of refining Concept Maps (including hyperlinking, resourcing, and refinement of Concept Map wording and morphology). The effort calculation would therefore be 700/19 = 37 minutes per Concept Map. This cannot be unequivocally interpreted because it represents the culmination from waves of refinement in which some changes were made and then, subsequently, undone. Considerable effort was taken in the change from the organization scheme created in Session 1 (which was intended primarily to organize material about the Human in Command Department), to the scheme created in Session 4, which would better enable subsequent integration of

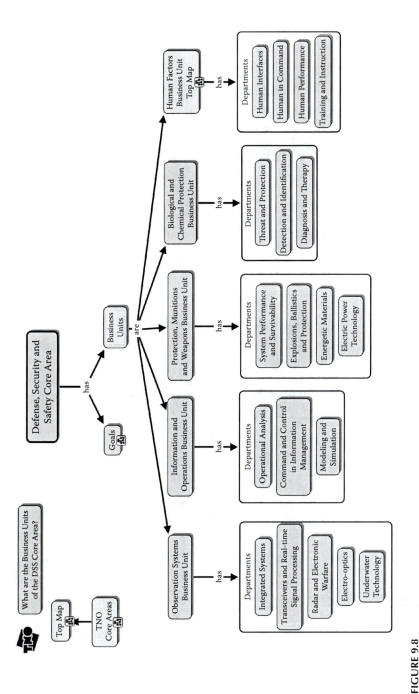

FIGURE 9.8

The Concept Map for integrating across all of the business units within the Defense, Security, and Safety core area.

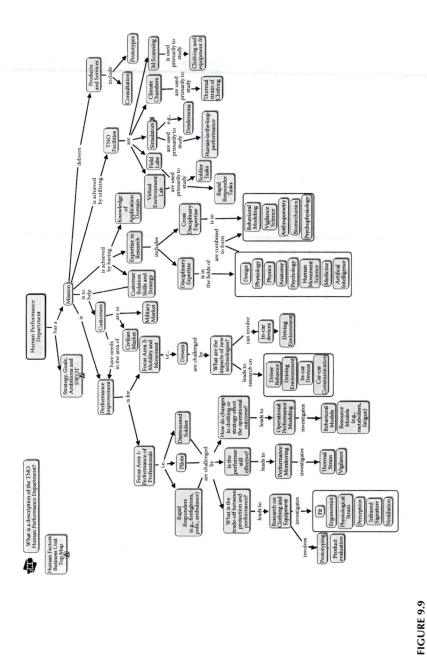

FIGURE 9.9

Final Concept Map describing the Human Performance Department.

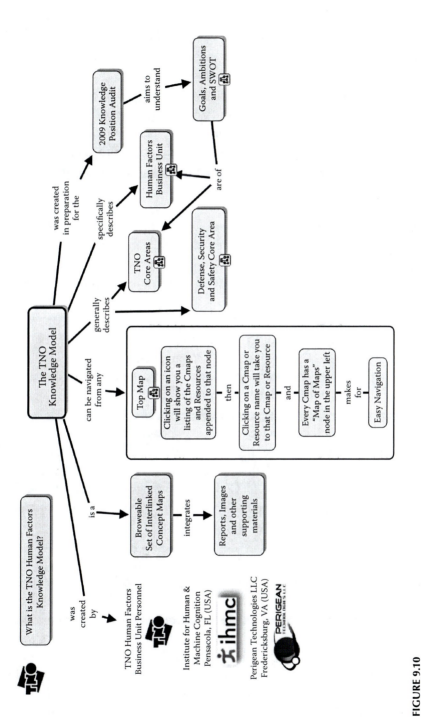

FIGURE 9.10

The "presentation Concept Map" that would be a viewer's portal into the TNO Concept Map business model.

Concept Maps about other departments and business units. Nevertheless, the Session 4 effort result underscores the previous experience: The refinement, integration and resourcing of Concept Map knowledge models can be a nontrivial exercise (Coffey and Hoffman, 2003).

None of the business model Concept Maps was used as a figure in the final department TPA report. The standard format, content, and associated page limitations on the TPA reports prevented it. However, in the view of TNO, the Concept Mapping process was more important than the product because, at the point in time of the KE sessions, the Human Factors business unit was still very early in the review process. Developing the Concept Maps helped to order their thoughts. In the judgment of TNO, the business model Concept Maps proved useful in the preparation for the TPA in a number of ways. First, the process pointed, early in Session 1, to a need for departments, units, and core areas to develop a shared understanding of a business model. There were disagreements about what was important, subtle differences in the interpretations of key concepts, and even disagreement about what the key concepts are. For instance, one key question was: "What is the difference between a goal and an ambition?" As it happened, the TNO policy and guidance material about the TPA process had not defined these key concepts. Thus, the Concept Mapping effort contributed significantly to the broader TNO leadership and management process.

Second, the process forced the different departments to be explicit about their ambitions—or we might say scaffolded them in a process in which they could effectively define their ambitions, including their action plans and their product portfolio. Concept Mapping is often not easy, and is certainly a skill (cf., Chapter 2). Propositional thinking does not come easily or immediately to everyone. It can be said that Concept Mapping forces one to achieve crystal clarity about what one means. Any concepts that are important yet have been left undefined make themselves apparent. In general, the TNO Concept Mapping process revealed knowledge that had been tacit.

Third, initial differences among the departments could be harmonized by using a common framework provided by the Concept Maps. This was useful in expressing a common picture of the departments.

Fourth, the departments obtained common ground by creating and refining technology roadmaps that used a common format. In preparation for the TPA, the Concept Mapping process brought all of the departments together and, for the first time, allowed them to exchange their business models and achieve a common purpose.

An interesting and striking emergent was the lack of shared understanding of the meanings of such basic business terms as "goal" and "ambition." Considerable time was spent Concept Mapping these notions, and this resulted in a useful understanding, in light of the purposes and goals of the TPA. Within TNO, it was proposed that Concept Maps about these review concepts would be found useful and valuable to other business units and to the participants in the TPA process.

The use of Concept Maps to represent the business model of an organization is an application that has claimed success in the past (cf., Chapter 1). The Concept Maps that were made in the activity reported here were suggestive of how this sort of application can be conducted for business processes and modeling. The TNO Concept Map templates might be useful to other human factors organizations, and other kinds of businesses and organizations, for business strategy modeling, for achieving shared understanding of core concepts, and for sharing of knowledge across units within an organization.

SUBSEQUENT APPLICATIONS

Since the completion of this project, Concept Mapping has been utilized in other TNO research. One of the projects had the goal of developing a new training concept—a "serious game"—for a target audience consisting of mayors of municipalities who had to work as a team during periods of emergency management. It was suggested within TNO that the researchers begin by using Concept Mapping to learn about the target audience. Three experts (one from TNO, two from outside TNO) from different professions used Concept Mapping to scaffold their discussions. They very soon came to the conclusion that they were using different labels for what might be the same problems. This reminded one of us (Van de Ven) of the discussion of the TNO business models about clarifying departmental goals and ambition.

Eventually, the group came to agreement on what were the most problematic key issues involving the information needs of a team of mayors, and the most likely origins of these key issues. This process proved to be very useful. The researchers were able to identify key questions that required answers before training design could commence. Eventually, the team prototyped a simple paper-and-pencil game that is very well liked by those who have played it. It will be converted into a digital game.

The goal of another TNO project was to generate the information requirements of the crew of a fire truck, in particular, the information the crew needs to know while en route to and at the scene of the fire. The researchers had only a few opportunities to interview firefighters. They could not afford to draft a list from a first interview and then get back to the firefighters to iteratively refine the list. The researchers, therefore, began by creating their own Concept Map using the official guidebooks for firefighters in The Netherlands.

Information about the incident and current situation is first the responsibility of the dispatch center and the team officer (of the truck) while en route. When on the scene, dynamic incident information is a responsibility of the team officer. Incident information includes, for example, the number of people involved, the hazardous material possible at the site, and whether there are any eyewitnesses. When more trucks are involved, as well as other services (e.g., police), the firefighting team officer needs dynamic incident information. There are two possible roles that will provide him with this information: a higher-ranking officer at the site or the dispatch center.

Only after this initial drafting of Concept Maps did the researchers interview a group of fire fighters, showing them the Concept Maps, and using those to facilitate a process of identifying gaps. Concept Maps of these basic information requirements were developed in anticipation of the interviews. After viewing these maps, the firefighters complemented the researchers on the completeness of coverage of the Concept Maps, and were able to provide additional and extremely useful information. They expressed some additional information that was not in the official guidebooks, but that they had learned during the years they served in the fire brigade. For example, when the fire is in a factory, there usually is a contact person pointed out for the fire brigade. The firefighting teams need to know the contact person and have that person available as soon as possible. This is usually the person who can provide the "the latest news," e.g., on new construction work, materials, people on the site, etc.

The Concept Mapping and Concept Map-based interviewing identified additional categories of information about site and location that firefighters need to know, but that typically are not readily available, e.g., the latest restructuring of a building, or the amount of hazardous material on the premises. For instance, the actual level of hazardous material in the air is measured by a process that takes several minutes and is usually not measured in the immediate vicinity of the firemen. The researchers generated a long list of information requirements and, because the requirements were linked to the firefighting processes, the Concept Maps show who needs the information, when, and why. One such example is shown in Dutch in Figure 9.11.

The focus on the information that was extremely important but not readily available presented an opportunity to develop new technologies or work methods to improve firefighting capacity and success. The Concept Maps continued to be a source of reference, not only by the TNO project team, but also by instructors of firefighters because the Concept Maps explain information needs and explain the place of the needs within the firefighting process.

We suspect that the positive results from Concept Mapping at TNO will continue to take hold, as the demonstrated benefits become more well-known and more researchers find that Concept Maps can be fruitfully deployed for a wide variety of applications.

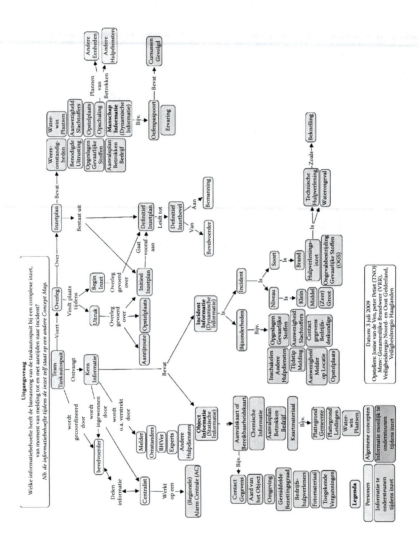

FIGURE 9.11
Dutch firefighting.

REFERENCES

Coffey, J. W. and R. R. Hoffman. 2003. Knowledge modeling for the preservation of institutional memory. *Journal of Knowledge Management* 7, 38–52.

Crandall, B., G. Klein, and R. R. Hoffman. 2006. *Working minds: A practitioner's guide to cognitive task analysis.* Cambridge, MA: MIT Press.

IHMC (Institute for Human and Machine Cognition). 2009. Protocols for cognitive task analysis: http://ihmc.us:16080/research/projects/CTAProtocols/.

Hoffman, R. R., J. W. Coffey, M. J. Carnot, and J. D. Novak. 2002. An empirical comparison of methods for eliciting and modeling expert knowledge. In *Proceedings of the 46th Meeting of the Human Factors and Ergonomics Society* (pp. 482–486). Santa Monica, CA: Human Factors and Ergonomics Society.

Hoffman, R. R., J. W. Coffey, K. M. Ford, and J. D. Novak. 2006. A method for eliciting, preserving, and sharing the knowledge of forecasters. *Weather and Forecasting* 21, 416–428.

Novak, J. D. 2010. *Learning, creating, and using knowledge: Concept maps as facilitative tools in schools and corporations.* New York: Routledge.

10

Concept Mapping Ecosystem Goods and Services

Susan H. Yee, John E. Rogers, Jim Harvey,
William Fisher, Marc Russell, and Patricia Bradley

CONTENTS

INTRODUCTION

Humanity's well-being is inextricably linked to the health of the Earth's ecosystems. Humans interact with the ecosystem in two ways: (1) they benefit from affordances ecosystems provide and (2) they create pressures on the ecosystem (Hassan, Scholes, and Ash, 2005). Ecosystems provide numerous benefits to humans, widely termed in environmental science as "ecosystem services," which include provisioning of food, fuel, and fresh water; regulation of climate and flooding; and cultural value through recreational opportunities. However, ecosystems can be stressed because they are rarely considered to an appropriate degree by individuals, businesses, or regulatory agencies while making economic and social decisions. As a consequence, many of the world's ecosystems are in decline, and the continuing supply of ecosystem services, falsely perceived as "free and limitless," is in jeopardy (Hassan, Scholes, and Ash, 2005). Many believe current declines are reversible, and sustainable use of the Earth's ecosystems is achievable. However, successful conservation may require that ecosystem services be more broadly considered in socio-economic decisions (Costanza, D'Arge, and de Grout, 1997; Boyd and Banzhaf, 2007).

The Ecosystem Services Research Program (ESRP) was established within the U.S. Environmental Protection Agency's (EPA) Office of Research and Development to provide information and methods needed by decision makers to assess and routinely consider ecosystem services in decision processes. The National Academy of Sciences underscored this concept in a 1997 report:

> Human society is dependent on the "goods and services" provided by ecosystems, including clean air, clean water, productive soils, and generation of food and fiber. A growing recognition of this dependence alters the way we conceptualize environmental problems. Reducing the harmful environmental impact of human activities on ecosystems, which in turn, provides humans with essential goods and services, is of direct benefit to society (NAS, 1997 p. 39–40).

Researchers, decision makers, and citizens pose questions such as: "What are the values of recreation and fisheries for a given acreage of wetland?" or "What are the human health benefits for maintaining urban and natural forests in terms of lower health costs or increased life expectancy?" It is this centrality to the human landscape that allows ecosystem services information to be so powerful and relevant in decision support, and why it is vitally important that tool development reflects the knowledge, concerns, and needs of local decision makers and stakeholders.

To achieve these goals, the ESRP has conducted research projects for several places, including Tampa Bay, Florida, and for several ecosystem types, including coral reefs. In this chapter, we describe how Concept Mapping has been used as a tool in the scientific research process toward development of decision support tools, such that decision makers can better understand the potential consequences of their decisions on the environment. We illustrate how Concept Mapping has contributed to prioritizing and organizing early research efforts for two ESRP projects, and provided the foundation for future research.

CONCEPT MAPPING AS AN ENVIRONMENTAL RESEARCH TOOL

Incorporating ecosystem services into the decision process requires a systems approach that conceptually links alternative human uses and decisions to changes in ecosystem condition, function, and the provision of ecosystem services. Ecosystems are complex, and environmental problems are rarely confined to a single resource. As with other complex systems, it is extremely difficult to anticipate the effects of alternative decisions on ecosystems or the value of ecosystem services. The problem is further compounded by the fact that standard environmental protection strategies are typically short-term and narrowly focused (Curran, 2009). Scientific research, business decisions, and management efforts are often limited by a particular expertise, economic concern, or level of authority. In many cases, the tools or information needed to consider the full value of ecosystems under alternative decision scenarios are not available.

Concept Mapping provides a tool for capturing, visualizing, and sharing the connections among human decisions, the pressures they create on the environment, and the value of ecosystem services. Concept Maps ("Cmaps") are an effective tool for representing relationships between ideas and synthesizing large amounts of information. In scientific research, Concept Mapping is a useful tool for visualizing a shared understanding of knowledge, communicating complex ideas, and detailing a single topic within the context of a larger system (Heemskerk, Wilson, and Pavao-Zuckerman, 2003). For example, Concept Mapping can be used to conceptualize consequences of alternative decisions on the provision of ecosystem services by linking anthropogenic and environmental stressors to ecosystem condition. The development of useful Cmaps for sustainability science requires judicious use of scientific, social, and economic information, and balancing knowledge of relationships with perceived importance.

The development of Concept Maps was central to the two ESRP research projects described in this chapter: a place-based study of Tampa Bay and an ecosystem study of coral reefs. The Tampa Bay Project illustrates how Concept Mapping can be used to quantify the knowledge and concerns of local experts and stakeholders for the purpose of prioritizing research plans. The Coral Reef Project illustrates how Concept Mapping can be used as an organizing framework for linking social and economic factors to their impacts on ecosystems.

CONCEPT MAPPING LEVELS OF KNOWLEDGE AND IMPORTANCE IN TAMPA BAY

The Tampa Bay Ecosystem Services Demonstration Project was a pilot study in ESRP designed to ultimately incorporate the value of ecosystem services into dynamic computational modeling tools that could be used by local governments, from the city to county level, in sustainable planning for future growth and development.

Tampa Bay is Florida's largest open-water estuary and is in a region that is undergoing substantial population and development pressures. The population of the Tampa Bay area is expected to increase 19 percent over current levels by 2015 and double by 2050 (Zwick and Carr, 2006). Current projections indicate that by 2040 urban development in central Florida, including Tampa Bay, will experience a dramatic loss of agricultural and native Florida lands. Virtually all of the natural systems and wildlife corridors in this region will be fragmented, if not replaced, by urban development. Alternative future scenarios are possible under smart growth, which preserves the availability of natural systems. However, if current trends continue, maintaining the water quality gains of recent decades and the ecosystem services derived from cleaner water will require more effort every year to compensate for increased pollution and pressures associated with population growth. By understanding the impacts and unintended consequences of uncontrolled growth and development, regional and local managers may try to constrain future growth so that ecosystem services are considered in the preservation and enhancement of human well-being throughout the watershed.

Dynamic computational models can be used to predict the probable impacts of change, such as population growth or climate change, on ecosystem services and human well-being in the future (Boumans and Costanza, 2007). The models are typically developed by first conceptually identifying relationships among key variables, and then relating changes in one variable to another with mathematical functions. For example, microbial activities contribute to reducing nitrogen-based pollutants in the water, and can be described by general mathematical formulations derived from laboratory conditions. However, microbial activity varies across the landscape, depending on levels of nutrient loading, soil type, or water level, in ways that require modifications to more general equations. Local stakeholder knowledge can identify location specific data and information about such processes, leading to more precise estimates of how rates may change depending on environmental and anthropogenic variables, and contributing to less uncertainty in model predictions. The most useful dynamic models to researchers and decision makers will be those soundly based on general scientific knowledge to clarify universal relationships among processes, but that incorporate local stakeholder knowledge (e.g., Gaddis, Vladich, and Voinov, 2007).

The first step in the ESRP Tampa Bay Project was to assess past and current research efforts, and identify key data sets and existing stressor response models that could be incorporated into a common dynamic modeling framework. Initial efforts involved a meeting in which the ESRP Tampa Bay team identified key ecosystem services for the Tampa Bay area and stressors that could possibly impact the delivery of those services. The six EPA scientists in this initial effort had expertise in biogeochemistry, landscape ecology, fishery science, wetland ecology, population modeling, atmospheric science, ecological economics, sea grass ecology, sustainability science, and climate change. A multidisciplinary approach was needed because of the size and complexity of the Tampa Bay watershed and the myriad interactions of stressors, ecosystem functions (physical and biological processes), and ecosystem types that are formative to ecosystem services. Due to variety and complexity of ecosystem types within the Tampa watershed, separate lists and corresponding Concept Maps were generated for each of five ecosystem types: wetlands, urban, open water, agriculture, and forests.

Concept Mapping was used to visualize the initial lists of stressors and ecosystem services, as in Table 10.1, and the perceived importance of relationships among stressors, ecological processes, and the ultimate delivery of services. The ESRP Tampa Bay team created five Concept Maps, one for each ecosystem type. In this chapter, we present only the open water Cmaps to illustrate the approach. Cmaps were created over the course of several group meetings using CmapTools software, projected on a large overhead screen to facilitate visualization of the links between stressors and services. With the help of a facilitator, this approach allowed all participants in the meeting to see real-time adjustments in the Cmaps as

TABLE 10.1

Key Stressors, Functions, and Ecosystem Services Used in Developing the Tampa Bay Project Open Water Cmap

Stressors	Functions Physical Processes	Biological Processes	Ecosystem Services
Temperature Change	Freshwater Inflow	SAV/Wetland Structure	Water Supply
Nutrient Loading	Ground Water Recharge	Decomposition	Flood Attenuation
Contaminants (Hg)	Salt Water Intrusion	Bioaccumulation	Water Quality
Sea Level Change	Salinity Change	Net Primary Productivity	Recreation
Precipitation Change	Depth	Secondary Productivity	Habitat and Biodiversity
Climate Change (CO_2)	Light Attenuation		Carbon Sequestration
Human Usage	Contaminants		Food and Fiber
	Evaporation		Storm Surge Protection
	Water contaminants		

they were being discussed, eliminating the need to take extensive notes or recreate Cmaps after the meeting.

The initial open water Cmap, shown in Figure 10.1, was constructed from the keyword list in Table 10.1 by placing stressors on the left side and ecosystem services on the right. Biological and physical processes were placed in the middle. In this way, a stress could be linked to a process or processes that could lead to change in a service. Connections were established by considering which stressors would impact a physical or biological process, and how these impacts would translate to a specific ecosystem service. A change in a stressor will ultimately result in a change in the level of a service. The complexity of the Cmap relates to the inherent complexity of the topic as well as the inclusion of all potential paths from a stressor through the affected processes to each of the potentially affected ecosystem services.

Though not shown, the Tampa Bay Concept Maps initially followed the logic of traditional Concept Mapping, with linking phrases between concepts to form propositions (Novak, 1998). The concepts in Figure 10.1 are implied to be linked by phrases such as: "could cause a change in." For example, a temperature change could cause a change in the level of net primary productivity (NPP), which could cause a change in carbon sequestration and storage.

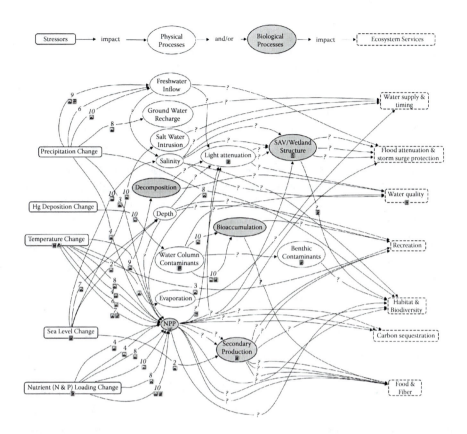

FIGURE 10.1

The initial Tampa Bay Project Cmap for an open water system. Lines with arrows indicate the direction of the interaction. The numerical values represent the relative weight of a given interaction with respect to all interactions. Question marks indicate that a relative weight could not be estimated from what was known. Icons represent either a list of relevant manuscripts or a graphical representation of the interaction. Acronyms and abbreviations: nitrogen (N), phosphorous (P), mercury (Hg), net primary productivity (NPP), submerged aquatic vegetation (SAV).

However, because a primary goal of the ESRP Tampa Bay team was to use Cmaps to assess research needs, linking words were replaced with numerical values in our Cmaps to quantify levels of knowledge and uncertainty.

After becoming familiar with the existing body of research, the ESRP Tampa Bay Project used the Cmaps to identify knowledge gaps where targeted research efforts could provide information for development of dynamic models and also to identify linkages where sufficient information was available for the development of dynamic models. By accessing the team's collective knowledge and conducting an initial literature review, a level of confidence in the supporting science was estimated for each of the individual connections. Confidence levels are indicated by the numerical values attached to connecting arrows in Figure 10.1 (10 = high confidence, 1 = little if any confidence, and ? = unknown). High confidence indicates that proposed relationships are backed by multiple independent research studies and are widely accepted among scientists. The Tampa Bay Region has been a focal point for ecological research over the past 30 years by local, state, federal, and academic researchers. Connecting arrows were annotated in CmapTools to attach literature citations and graphs illustrating the nature of each stressor response relationship, indicated by the picture or note icons in Figure 10.1. However, little was known about how stressors and processes contribute to provisioning of ecosystem services, as indicated by the numerous "?" on the right side of the figure.

To ensure that the ESRP Tampa Bay Project's efforts reflected the needs and concerns of local decision makers and stakeholders, the team's initial Cmap was presented and revised during a large workshop that included the internal EPA team, non-EPA partners, and members of the Tampa Bay core steering committee headed by the Tampa Bay Regional Planning Council and the Tampa Bay Estuary Program. This group was asked to examine the initial Cmap in Figure 10.1, generated by the ESRP Tampa Bay team, and propose changes in concepts or links based on their expertise and knowledge of the Tampa Bay watershed and research conducted there in the past. Changes were incorporated into the initial Cmap during workshop discussions, with participants viewing a large screen projection of the Cmap as a meeting facilitator edited maps using the CmapTools. The initial open water Cmap shown in Figure 10.1 evolved into the group consensus Cmap shown in Figure 10.2 through workshop discussions and compromise. Workshop participants were instrumental in tying temperature, precipitation, and sea level changes to increasing atmospheric CO_2 related to climate change, and members of the Tampa Bay core steering committee inserted human usage as a key stressor. Participants also added "sense of place," an eighth service. Participants removed much of the initial redundancy, modified confidence levels in a few cases, and provided confidence levels for all of the linkages that had been marked as unknown.

At the close of the workshop, participants were asked to review the Cmap over the following two weeks and to prepare a summary of the workshop. Summaries included their identification of the top three most important

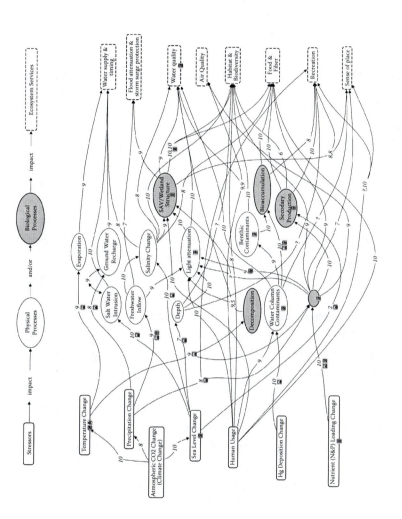

FIGURE 10.2

The consensus open water Cmap for the Tampa Bay Project that was generated during workshop discussions. (See Figure 10.1 caption for explanation of symbols and acronyms.)

ecosystem services for Tampa Bay, the most important stressors that would impact these ecosystem services, and any available information (supporting literature and data sources) on important linkages connecting stressors and ecosystem services. Through this process, water quality, food and fiber, and habitat and biodiversity were identified as the ecosystem services having greatest importance in the Tampa Bay watershed. Human usage and nutrient (nitrogen and phosphorous) loading change were identified as key stressors.

Key pathways were illustrated through use of heavy dark lines in the Cmap shown in Figure 10.3.

This final open water Cmap generated with the help of our six local experts, provided the framework for focusing the ESRP Tampa Bay Project research effort. In addition to mapping the current state of scientific knowledge, Concept Mapping also identified research gaps and linkages where adequate scientific support was available for dynamic modeling. Research gaps were prioritized as those with a low confidence rank, but considered by experts to be highly important. For example, the impact of human usage on SAV/wetland structure was not well known and would need further research. However, sufficient research was deemed available to support dynamic modeling of the link between SAV/wetland structure and habitat and biodiversity. Accuracy and reliability in predictive model development is directly linked to the level of certainty in data incorporated into model development. Therefore, field research in the ESRP Tampa Bay Project is being directed toward these identified research areas, with the goal, for example, of improving our knowledge base for the human usage: SAV/wetland structure linkage to reduce uncertainty in the pathway from human usage to Habitat & Biodiversity. (This is the circled concept in Figure 10.3.)

Continuing work in the next step of the ESRP Tampa Bay Project will develop a modular dynamic model for the Tampa Bay watershed based on the relationships, rate functions, and parameters identified through Concept Mapping. Computational models will be calibrated with data from the Tampa Bay watershed toward development of decision support tools where decision makers and scientists can assess the effects of alternative decisions on the provision of ecosystem services. Key to development of such models will be understanding the links between proposed policy or management approaches, the stresses human actions cause on ecological and physical processes, the impact the altered processes have on relevant and valued human well-being endpoints, and back full circle to proposed policy and management decisions. One approach to describing such links

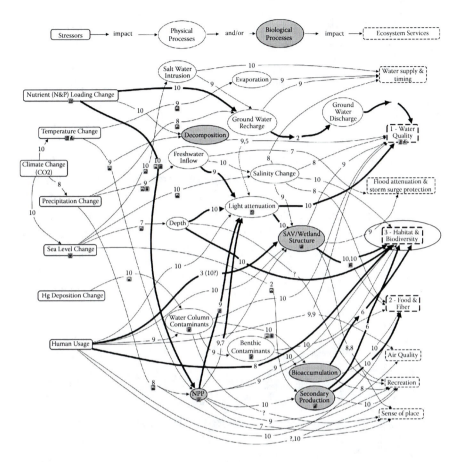

FIGURE 10.3
The final open water Cmap for the Tampa Bay Project, with dark lines indicating the primary concerns of local experts and stakeholders. (See Figure 10.1 caption for explanation of symbols and acronyms.)

between social, economic, and environmental concerns is through the use of Concept Mapping, and was illustrated in the next ESRP project.

CONCEPT MAPPING EFFECTS OF SOCIO-ECONOMIC DECISIONS ON CORAL REEFS

The ESRP Coral Reefs Project was a parallel project whose early efforts toward integrating ecosystem services into the decision process included elucidating the linkages between decisions, human activities, and the sustainability of coral reef ecosystem services. Sustainable use of environmental resources requires consideration of the environment with fulfillment of social and economic needs, and few programs exist that integrate all three (Curran, 2009).

Coral reef ecosystems provide the ecological foundation for productive and highly diverse fish and invertebrate communities that support multibillion-dollar reef fishing and tourism industries vital to regional economies (Burke and Maidens, 2004). However, reef ecosystem goods and services are threatened by a rapidly growing regional human population, climate change, and over-exploitation. Figure 10.4 illustrates how urbanization, fishing, and tourism contribute to loss of the reef. Efforts by numerous federal, state, academic, and nongovernmental organizations have generated a wealth of knowledge on coral reef ecology, yet reef ecosystems continue to decline (Wilkinson, 2008).

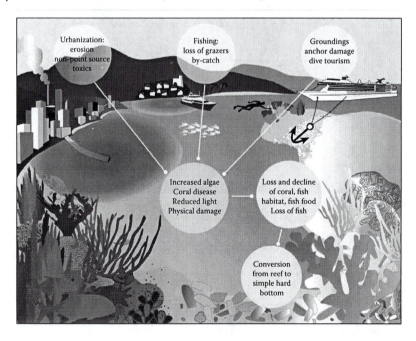

FIGURE 10.4

Illustration of how stressors can impact the coral reef ecosystem and the availability of natural benefits. (From P. Bradley, L. Fore, and W. Fisher. 2007. Coral reef monitoring needs assessment workshop in the U.S. Virgin Islands, hosted by USVI Department of Planning and Natural Resources (DPNR), Christiansted, St. Croix, USVI, September 11-13. Draft Summary Report (U.S. Environmental Protection Agency, 2007).

A key issue is that scientific and management efforts are often narrowly defined to a particular expertise or authority with little collaboration in monitoring, data assimilation, and modeling. For example, management efforts have been largely focused on activities that directly use the reef, such as fishing, yet many major stressors are derived from land-based activities and decisions. Consequently, information, such as monitoring data, watershed models, or land-use maps, has not been effectively integrated to identify gaps and prioritize research, nor have they been easily synthesized into concepts and tools for conservation that resonate with stakeholders and influence management. This leads to difficulty in accurately predicting benefits and consequences of management and regulatory decisions. Development of a comprehensive conceptual framework that considers the system as a whole will aid in better understanding of the impacts of human activities on reef ecosystem services.

The first step of the ESRP Coral Reefs Project involved developing a comprehensive conceptual framework using Concept Mapping to define relevant socio-economic and ecological factors, and to delineate potential cause and effect relationships among them. Reef Concept Maps were used to identify and organize areas of research, to catalog information and data, and to communicate connections between human activities and delivery of ecosystem services.

To develop Cmaps linking ecological and socio-economic factors, the ESRP Coral Reefs Project found it useful to employ an overarching framework to ensure that critical concepts were not overlooked. The Driver-Pressure-State-Impact-Response (DPSIR) scheme is a flexible framework that defines broad categories for concepts and characterizes the links between them. The DPSIR categories are defined in Table 10.2, and the links between them are illustrated on the left side of Figure 10.5. Within DPSIR, Drivers (D) are social and economic forces that lead to human activities, which create Pressure (P) on the State (S) of the environment, and Impact (I) the availability and value of ecosystem services. Decision makers may enact a Response (R) to reduce the impacts on environmental resources through regulations, policies, and other decisions, which may alter Drivers (D) or Pressures (P), or directly affect the State (S) of the ecosystem. DPSIR has been used to relate anthropogenic stresses to the state of the environment for management of water resources (Mysiak, Guipponi, and Rosato, 2005), biodiversity (Maxim, Spangenberg, and O'Connor, 2009), Marine Protected Areas (Ojeda-Martinez et al., 2009),

TABLE 10.2

Glossary of DPSIR Framework Used to Generate the Coral Reef Project Cmap

Term	Definition
Drivers	Social and economic forces, or more specifically socio-economic sectors that fulfill basic human needs for food, water, shelter, health, and culture, and motivate human activities
Pressures	Human activities that induce changes in the environment and are typically seen as negative or unwanted
State	The condition of the physical, chemical, and biological components of the ecosystem
Impact	Changes in the functioning of the ecosystem, namely ecosystem services, which benefit and impact the well-being of humans and the functioning of many socio-economic sectors
Response	Actions by groups or individuals in society to prevent, ameliorate, or adapt to changes in the perceived value of ecosystem services, by controlling changes in drivers or pressures, or restoring and maintaining the ecosystem state

and fisheries (Mangi, Roberts, and Rodwell, 2007). By placing concepts into five categories, the DPSIR framework visually and conceptually simplifies the complex connections between humans and the environment, allowing Concept Maps to be more readily understandable when soliciting expert knowledge, evaluating stakeholder concerns, or communicating with the public.

The ESRP Coral Reefs Project used the DPSIR framework to develop Cmaps linking socio-economic drivers to the provision of coral reef ecosystem services. Figure 10.5 shows the Coral Reef Cmap generated by listing and linking concepts among each of the five D-P-S-I-R categories. The ESRP Coral team used personal knowledge and literature searches to generate initial Cmaps, which were greatly improved with the help of focus groups of experts, representing federal, state, academic, and nongovernmental organizations. Each of five focus groups was tasked with listing key concepts within each of the five DPSIR categories (Drivers, Pressures, State, Impact, Response), as well as the uphill and downhill linkages showing the contributors and consequences related to a particular concept. Focus groups also reviewed initial Cmaps for missing concepts and accuracy of links, and suggested high priority research areas. For the Cmap presented in Figure 10.5, we grouped similar concepts to simplify links and included only major concepts. However, more complex Cmaps also were created by expanding concepts within and among groups.

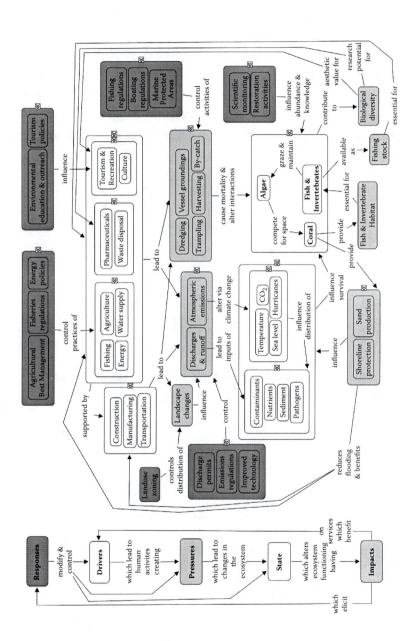

FIGURE 10.5

The Coral Reef Project Cmap that was generated within the DPSIR framework.

In the Coral Reef Project Cmap, seen in Figure 10.5, Drivers (D) were considered to be socio-economic sectors fulfilling basic human needs for food, water, and other raw materials, health, and culture. Socio-economic sectors function through human activities, including changes in land use, discharges, and direct contact use that create Pressures, shown in Figure 10.5, on the physical, chemical, and biological State of the reef ecosystem. For example, stony or reef-building corals (*Scleractinia*) are vulnerable to increasing seawater temperatures, land-based pollution, and over-exploitation through over-fishing and physical damage (Hughes et al., 2003). When reef-building corals die, they are often overgrown and replaced by algae, with subsequent loss of complex reef architecture (Alvarez-Filip et al., 2009), causing Impacts, shown in Figure 10.5, to humans through the loss of ecosystem services. The calcareous skeletons of stony corals form the foundation for reef structure, protecting the shoreline from storm surges, contributing to sand production for recreational beaches and the aquarium trade, and providing complex habitat for a diverse assemblage of fish and invertebrates, essential resources for fisheries, pharmaceutical development, and tourism. Table 10.3 gives examples of reef ecosystem services, and the attributes and processes of the coral reef ecosystem that provide them.

Economic sectors benefitting from reefs are often responsible for many activities that are causing their decline, including over-fishing and physical damage from boats or divers. This creates a cycle, which was represented

TABLE 10.3

Examples of Reef Ecosystem Services and the Attributes and Processes of the Coral Reef Ecosystem That Provide Them

Ecosystem Services	Attributes	Biophysical Processes
Fisheries	Large, abundant fish and invertebrates	Habitat provided by corals, sea grasses, and mangroves
Tourism and recreation	Rare and colorful fish and invertebrates; abundant sea urchins and parrotfish	Biodiversity, habitat, herbivory (algal cropping)
Shoreline protection	Large, abundant scleractinian (stony) corals and crustose coralline algae to bind them	Calcification and skeletal growth, photosynthesis, water clarity
Pharmaceuticals	High diversity, density, and trophic complexity	Biodiversity; competition, and predation

as a cyclic Concept Map representing dynamic changes or feedbacks within a system (Safayeni, Derbentseva, Cañas, 2005), illustrated by the upward arrows from Impact to Drivers in Figure 10.5. Availability of reef services may be sustainable if management strategies are vigorously implemented to prevent further loss of coral cover and maintain grazing fish that prevent algal overgrowth. Responses, illustrated in Figure 10.5, to reduce loss of ecosystem services may include water management, such as marine protected areas or mooring buoys that reduce damage from boat traffic and prevent overfishing, as well as land management, such as agricultural and construction practices designed to reduce sediment runoff into coastal areas. By linking Responses directly to changes in Drivers or Pressures in Cmaps, one can conceptualize the potential consequences of different decisions, balancing the costs to socio-economic sectors versus the benefits in provision of ecosystem services.

OTHER APPLICATIONS

The ESRP Coral Reefs Project has also used Concept Mapping for several other purposes. Concept Mapping in early research planning aided in summarizing and assessing the current state of knowledge and determining research needs. Keywords derived from Concept Maps were used to conduct scientific literature searches for a coarse assessment of numbers of research articles associated with different topics. In general, research related to decision science (D, R) or evaluation of ecosystem services (I) were generally lacking compared to research relating stressors (P) to the ecosystem (S). In writing our Coral ESRP Research Plan, we extended our traditional ecological research to include development of methods to evaluate ecosystem services, and evaluations of key socio-economic drivers in target jurisdictions and potential policy or regulatory options. As such, Cmaps were used as an organizing framework for integrating aspects of sociology, economics, and decision making into coral reef research. CmapTools is being used to accumulate information through annotations of concept nodes, allowing a visual organization of information, including available data, scientific literature, legislation, and possible management actions.

The Coral Reef Concept Map served as the conceptual foundation for ongoing research toward developing predictive mathematical models that are used to evaluate outcomes under alternative decision scenarios. The Coral Reef Cmaps, including the simplified Cmap in Figure 10.5, highlight key concepts and relationships that were included in model development. Literature searches were conducted to determine mathematical equations for linking changes in one concept to changes in another. These have been supplemented with lab and field research to determine dose–response curves relating levels of stressors to growth, survival, and diversity of reef organisms.

Finally, Cmaps have been useful for communicating with other scientists and decision makers. In particular, CmapTools has been used by ESRP in a decision-making workshop to generate Cmaps in real time with interactive participant feedback. The EPA workshop was hosted by the Florida Keys National Marine Sanctuary and included representatives from government, academia, and local stakeholders. In a workshop session, the DPSIR framework was used to encourage participants to consider uphill and downhill processes related to their local concerns, regardless of which single concept (e.g., a single driver, pressure, ecosystem service, or response) was used to initiate mapping. In other outreach efforts, the ESRP Coral team demonstrated Concept Mapping within the DPSIR framework to encourage scientists and decision makers to move beyond a single research area, economic concern, or management topic, and to think about their key issues within the context of a suite of complex interactions. Colleagues responded favorably to the DPSIR Concept Mapping approach, and have considered applying similar approaches for their own systems.

CONCLUSIONS AND MOVING FORWARD

For the ESRP Tampa Bay and Coral Reefs Projects, Concept Mapping has been valuable for learning, research planning, communication, organization of information, and for forming conceptual models to support the process of creating computational models. Concept Mapping was used to guide early research planning through a comprehensive and objective assessment of the current state of knowledge, with the help of literature searches and expert opinion. In ongoing outreach efforts, Cmaps provide a visual communication tool for soliciting expert opinion and communicating research plans to other scientists, stakeholders, and decision makers. Concept Mapping provided an efficient and interactive environment for brainstorming in large groups, and maps were developed within groups in real time, either to integrate multiple expert opinions or as a learning tool to demonstrate the benefits of Concept Mapping.

A primary goal of the ESRP is the development of dynamic computational models that predict the probable impacts of change, such as population growth or climate change, on ecosystem services and human well-being in the future (e.g., see Boumans and Costanza, 2007). The Concept Maps presented in this chapter lay the conceptual foundation for development of computational models in ongoing research that will evaluate the consequences of alternative decisions on the provision of ecosystem services. Computational models are inherently more complicated than the Concept Maps shown here, with complex interactions and feedbacks. However, the Cmaps do serve to highlight key concepts and relationships to include in model development, and provide an easy transition to object-oriented modeling languages.

The key to sustainable use of ecosystems is the integration of environmental, economic, and societal needs (Curran, 2009). Concept Mapping is ideal for synthesizing and visualizing large amounts of complex information. Through the simple idea that concepts are linked to other concepts, single topics are necessarily mapped within a complex web of concepts. Therefore, mapping encourages scientists and decision makers to move beyond their specialization and think about the "big picture." The power of ecosystems services is that they provide a direct link between anthropogenic stressors, ecological and physical processes, and human well-being. Business decisions and environmental protection strategies function within complex systems, and Concept Mapping is one tool for providing the shift from short-term narrowly focused strategies to long-term comprehensive strategies that is needed.

ACKNOWLEDGMENTS

The Tampa Bay Project is grateful to discussion and insights from workshop participants, including members of the Tampa Bay core steering committee headed by the Tampa Bay Regional Planning Council and the Tampa Bay Estuary Program. The Coral Reefs Project Cmaps were greatly improved through discussions with expert focus groups including participants from the National Oceanographic and Atmospheric Administration, U.S. Department of Agriculture, U.S. Fish and Wildlife, U.S. Geological Survey, Florida Department of Environmental Protection, Florida Fish and Wildlife Research Institute, Nature Conservancy, World Resources Institute, Coastal Ocean Values Center, Commonwealth of the Northern Mariana Islands, Atlantic and Gulf Rapid Reef Assessment Program, and academia.

REFERENCES

Alvarez-Filip, L., N. K. Dulvy, and J. A. Gill, et al. 2009. Flattening of Caribbean coral reefs: Region-wide declines in architectural complexity. *Proceedings of the Royal Society, B* 276: 3019–3025.

Boumans, R. and R. Costanza. 2007. The multiscale integrated Earth systems model (MIMES): The dynamics, modeling and valuation of ecosystem services. In *Global assessments: Bridging scales and linking to policy.* Report on the joint TIAS-GWSP workshop held at the University of Maryland University College, Adelphi, May 10–11. 2007. GWSP Issues in *Global water system research,* no. 2, ed. C. Van Bers, D. Petry, and C. Pahl-Wostl, (p. 104–107). Bonn, Germany: GWSP IPO.

Boyd, J. and S. Banzhaf. 2007. What are ecosystem services? *Ecological Economics* 63: 616–626.

Burke, L. and J. Maidens 2004. *Reefs at risk in the Caribbean.* Washington D.C.: World Resources Institute.

Costanza, R., R. D'Arge, and R. de Groot, et al. 1997. The value of the world's ecosystem services and natural capital. *Nature* 387: 253–260.

Curran, M. A. 2009. Wrapping our brains around sustainability. *Sustainability* 1: 5–13.

Gaddis, E. J. B., H. Vladich, and A. Voinov. 2007. Participatory modeling and the dilemma of diffuse nitrogen management in a residential watershed. *Environmental Modelling and Software* 22: 619–629.

Hassan, R., R. Scholes, and N. Ash. 2005. *Ecosystems and human well-being: Current state and trends,* Vol. 1. Washington, D.C.: Island Press.

Heemskerk, M., K. Wilson, and M. Pavao-Zuckerman. 2003. Conceptual models as tools for communication across disciplines. *Conservation Ecology* 7: 8.

Hughes, T. P., A. H. Baird, D. R. Bellwood, et al. 2003. Climate change, human impacts, and the resilience of coral reefs. *Science* 301: 929–933.

Mangi, S. C., C. M. Roberts, and L. D. Rodwell. 2007. Reef fisheries management in Kenya: Preliminary approach using the driver-pressure-state-impacts-response (DPSIR) scheme of indicators. *Ocean & Coastal Management* 50: 463–80.

Maxim, L., J. H. Spangenberg, and M. O'Connor. 2009. An analysis of risks for biodiversity under the DPSIR framework. *Ecological Economics* 69: 12–23.

Mysiak J., C. Giupponi, and P. Rosato. 2005. Towards the development of a decision support system for water resource management. *Environmental Modelling and Software* 20: 203–14.

National Academy of Sciences (NAS). 1997. *Building a foundation for sound environmental decisions.* Washington, D.C.: National Academy Press.

Novak, J. D. 1998. *Learning, creating, and using knowledge: Concept maps as facilitative tools in schools and corporations.* Mahwah, NJ: Lawrence Erlbaum Associates.

Ojeda-Martinez, C., F. G. Casalduero, J. T. Bayle-Sempere, et al. 2009. A conceptual framework for the integral management of marine protected areas. *Ocean and Coastal Management* 52: 89–101.

Safayeni, F., N. Derbentseva, and A. J. Canas. 2005. A theoretical note on concepts and the need for cyclic concept maps. *Journal of Research in Science Teaching* 42: 741–766.

Wilkinson, C. 2008. *Status of the coral reefs of the world: 2008.* Townsville, Australia: Global Coral Reef Monitoring Network and Reef and Rainforest Research Centre.

Zwick, P. D. and M. H. Carr. 2006. Florida 2060, A population distribution scenario for the state of Florida: Report to 1000 Friends of Florida. Gainesville: University of Florida.

11

Concept Mapping in Corporate Education: Experiences at Petrobrás University

Acacia Z. Kuenzer, Wilson L. Lanzarini, and Eleonora B. Taveira

CONTENTS

INTRODUCTION

In order to lead in a competitive and dynamic market, a company has to be prepared to face the challenges of the globalized world. It must combine the production of innovating strategies, such as intensive investment in science and technology, while counting on the learning capacity of its workforce. These new demands, in their turn, imply the development of new forms of education for the workforce. Instead of rigid professionals who are just competent at their jobs, flexible professionals must be able to succeed in the face of technological changes arising from the dynamics of contemporary scientific–technological production. Perhaps the most important of these is the changing axis in the relationship between work and education.

215

According to Zarifian (2001), the evidence of this change in the axis can be seen through the change in the nature of work, which no longer means "tasks" or "intervention." No longer can the worker only be thought of as a resource for use when equipment or systems malfunction and require qualified actions. It is no longer sufficient to only have practical knowledge. On the contrary, workers are increasingly required to learn to work intellectually, developing complex cognitive competences that overlap systematized knowledge. Work now means dealing with events and adapting to changing circumstances.

This growing complexity requires the development of cognitive competencies that are complex, to include analyzing and synthesizing, establishing relations, innovating solutions, working with priorities, dealing with differences and clear and precise communications (Kuenzer, 2002). In the education of this new workforce, the axis has changed from memorizing repetitive procedures to a new form of competence, which requires creativity, communications capacity, and ongoing learning. To these new educational requirements, for companies operating in the petroleum, gas, and energy sector, can be added the capacity to act with social and environmental liability (Petrobrás, 2008).

This chapter reports on the use of Concept Mapping by professionals from the corporate university (Petrobrás University) of an international-sized company in the energy generation sector, Petrobrás. The company has enjoyed over 50 years of corporate success, owing to the development of human resources (Caldas, 2005; Petrobrás, 2009a), research and development, and its high operational efficiency. Petrobrás recognizes that the complex cognitive competencies are fundamentally important, not only to remain competitive, but also to preserve the environment, people, and the company itself. To achieve this throughout the workforce, Petrobrás University has embarked on the adoption of the Meaningful Learning (Ausubel, 1964; Novak, 2010) as a pedagogic paradigm, which has included the use and evaluation of Concept Mapping.

The chapter begins with a review of the Petrobrás University and the challenges it seeks to address. It continues with a review of the epistemological bases for adopting Meaningful Learning to address these challenges. Next, we review the guided implementation of Concept Mapping. We conclude by assessing the value of Concept Mapping in corporate education.

PETROBRÁS UNIVERSITY

The use of teaching frameworks and activities at Petrobrás is considered a major supporting pillar of the company's development. Every year, Petrobrás University develops teaching programs (graduate degrees and ongoing education) for thousands of professionals employed at Petrobrás, in partnership with the technological, operational, and management business areas. Its teaching area, restructured as a corporate university in early 2000, implemented an organizational framework in the form of technology and corporate management schools, with administrative and pedagogic support activities (Petrobrás, 2005).

In the development of its pedagogic activities, and awareness of the strategic role of organizational knowledge, Petrobrás faces a double challenge. It must innovate through intensive investment in science and technology by training professionals who are technologically and ethically prepared, while simultaneously preserving and disseminating the knowledge and culture that constitute its corporate identity.

In order to face this double challenge, Petrobrás focuses on the permanent learning capacity of the organization. Starting with the pedagogic project, Petrobrás is establishing a learning program capable of promoting the development of individual competencies that can support organizational competencies. Ultimately, these competencies will enable the company to generate better results concerning targets set by Petrobrás in its strategic plan (Petrobrás, 2008).

With these challenges and foci in mind, Petrobrás University sought a learning theory and strategies that enable the articulation of new scientific and technological knowledge, and the tacit knowledge of the most experienced members of the workforce, which stems from previous professional, educational, or life experiences. This stimulated the adoption of the concept of Meaningful Learning, as developed by Ausubel, with a humanist connotation provided by Novak (1981). Concept Mapping, because it enables the systematization of the subjective forms of apprehension, understanding, presentation, and negotiation of concepts regarding their relations, was considered the teaching and learning strategy for implementing Meaningful Learning.

EPISTEMOLOGICAL BASIS FOR ADOPTING MEANINGFUL LEARNING

The Petrobrás University formalized its epistemological point of view in its pedagogic proposal (Petrobras, 2009b). The assumption that served as the basis for adopting Meaningful Learning (ML) is that the incorporation of new knowledge results from the attribution of a meaning. Meaning is directly dependent on previous experiences and knowledge that are to be found in the cognitive framework of each student, and includes heavily subjective content. In ML there is a substantive, nonarbitrary, and nonliteral incorporation of the new knowledge into the cognitive framework. This incorporation implies a deliberate effort to articulate new and old knowledge, capturing relationships between concepts and also finding new relations, so that the constituted meanings constitute superior qualitative synthesis. When incorporated into the cognitive framework, these connections allow permanent development in the building of knowledge and, thereby, enable creativity. Another result of ML is the development of the capacity to transfer previous knowledge to new situations, connecting tacit knowledge to scientific knowledge and, thus, creating original solutions (Novak, 1981).

Although the construction of meanings is subjective, this process is not individual because it occurs in cultural historical contexts. ML, therefore, connects the individual and the collective, as it integrates man and society. In this perspective, it is a humanizing learning theory.

Based on this concept of knowledge, Petrobrás University understands competence as a result of articulation between theory and practice, i.e., as the capacity to act under foreseen and unforeseen situations, in a quick, responsible, and efficient manner, articulating tacit and scientific knowledge to life and labor experiences. It implies the capacity to mobilize knowledge, skills, and aptitudes to solve problems. In this context, learning will be meaningful when the superior synthesis between previous and new knowledge is translated into new thinking, feeling, and ways of doing.

With the goals and epistemological bases of Petrobras University's adoption of ML and Concept Mapping established, we next report on the guided implementation of Concept Maps and their practical application throughout a program for the qualification of junior geologists at Petrobras University (Lanzarini, 2010). Junior geologists are selected candidates who undergo approximately eight months of initial preparation at Petrobras University. Only after completing the course do they take up their positions at work.

GUIDED IMPLEMENTATION OF CONCEPT MAPPING

Concept Mapping was introduced at Petrobras through workshops and practical application throughout 2008 and 2009.

Workshops

The introduction of Concept Mapping into Petrobrás was through two workshops, hosted by professor Dr. Marco Antonio Moreira from the Instituto de Física da UFRGS, Brazil, under the guidance of Dr. Joseph Novak. Among the participants were geologists, systems analysis, professors, didactic coordinators, and librarians, many from the exploration and production (E&P) business area, and Petrobrás University Science and Technology School. The qualification of the professional geologists, and the development of personal and technological competencies in the field of petroleum geology, are aimed at supporting the operational activities of the company in operating E&P. The E&P management, including that of petroleum and natural gas reserves, is directly related to its financial performance, and is influenced by politics and market scenarios, or so-called "petroleum geopolitics." Thus, involvement from the E&P was deemed particularly important for evaluating the value of ML and Concept Mapping.

The workshops included the methodology underlying ML and Concept Mapping, and the instruction on the use of CmapTools. It was observed that the course participants showed high levels of motivation and perception of the potential practical application of Concept Maps in their work.

The participants were asked to prepare Concept Maps in their own fields. Several of the geologists elaborated a first Concept Map of petroleum geology, guided by Moreira and Novak. Initially drawn by hand, it included no linking phrases. Following some discussion with one of the participating professors, it was redrawn with CmapTools. Linking phrases

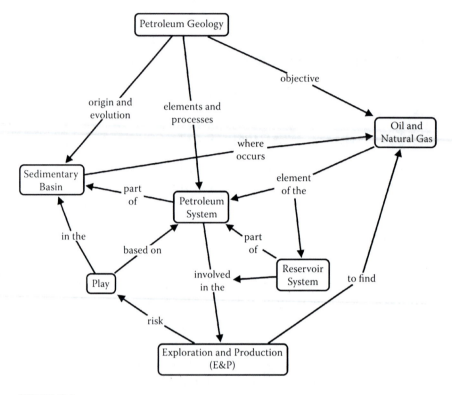

FIGURE 11.1
Concept Map of petroleum geology.

were added, and other improvements were considered. The final Concept Map is shown in Figure 11.1.

For the participating geologists, petroleum geology was understood as an application of geological knowledge in the oil and natural gas E&P. It studies the evolution of the sedimentary basins, with a view to the discovery and production of commercial reserves of petroleum and gas. It focuses on understanding the elements and processes of the petroleum and of reservoir systems that are involved in E&P. The technical corporate activities involved in these systems include financial risks, characterizing the "play." Reservoir geology constitutes a subarea of petroleum geology, focusing on the elements and processes of the reservoir subsystem.

Concept Maps also were drawn for the questions asked on geologist selection tests that candidates take prior to being hired by the company. These tests are conducted by geologists who have graduated from a number of geology courses at different universities located all over Brazil. The

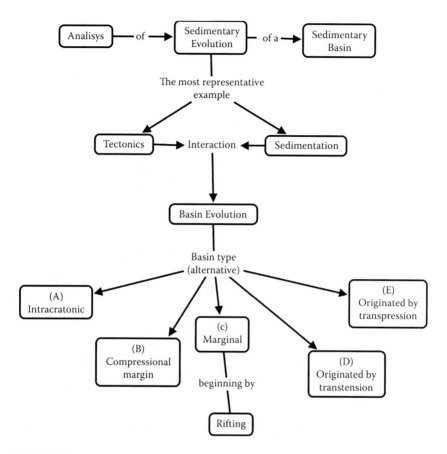

FIGURE 11.2

Concept Map of a question from the 2008 test for the candidates of the Petrobrás Junior Geologist Program.

reasoning underlying the drawing of these Concept Maps was to evaluate the range covered by the test and to map the presented and/or required knowledge. At first, a Concept Map was drawn for each of the test questions. An example is shown in Figure 11.2. In the upper part of this Concept Map are the concepts related to the question and at the bottom, the concepts related to the alternatives to the question. The correct alternative in Figure 11.2 is "C." When analyzing the concepts shown in this question, together with the concepts or Concept Maps of other questions related to the subject "sedimentary basin," it was possible to point out the elements (concepts, links, and connection words) that are presented or questioned and others that are not.

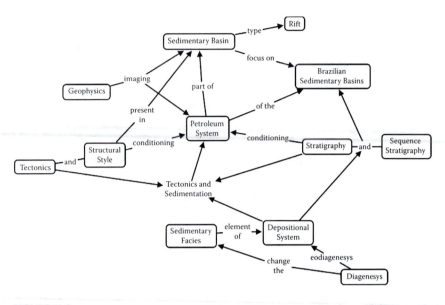

FIGURE 11.3

Concept Map of the main areas of Petroleum geology from the 2008 public test for the candidates of the Petrobrás Junior Geologist Program.

The questions and corresponding Concept Maps were assembled according to broad themes of petroleum geology and a Concept Map was collectively drawn encompassing these broad themes, as shown in Figure 11.3. As a result, comparing the two Concept Maps in Figure 11.1 and Figure 11.3, it was possible to determine that the test covered the main themes of petroleum geology.

Next, the participating geologists elaborated a broad Concept Map of petroleum geology, as shown in Figure 11.4, in which the petroleum geology concept was represented in a large and integrated form. Secondary Concept Maps of more specific or restricted concepts, e.g., petroleum system, reservoir system, sedimentary basin, exploration and production, etc., could also be constructed to the limits of knowledge concerning the subject. These main concepts are related to some themes mapped in the test, e.g., petroleum system, sedimentary basin (see Figure 11.3), and other themes also represent the secondary concepts of geological competence, e.g., tectonics, stratigraphy, sedimentary facies.

Subordinate Concept Maps were prepared as well for the purpose of providing examples of more specific Concept Mapping (Concept Map of

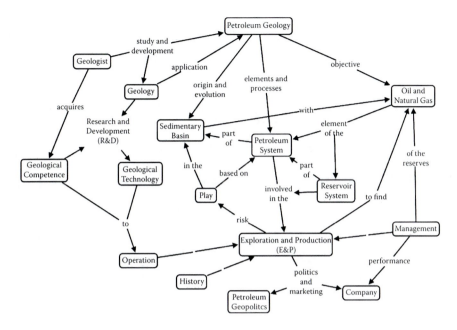

FIGURE 11.4
An enlarged Concept Map of petroleum geology.

the petroleum system, reservoir system, E&P, competence development, etc.) and the potential use of Concept Maps during the training programs for new geologists and in E&P.

Practical Application in a Learning Program

Springing from the workshops, the participants assimilated the principles of Meaningful Learning, and developed practical activities using Concept Maps.

Continuing into early 2009 and in the context of training geologists who had recently passed the test, the Concept Map of petroleum geology was used as teaching material in the first training program module, "Introduction to Petroleum Geology." As an exercise, some concepts and interrelations were removed from the original Concept Map (see Figure 11.4) and the students were challenged to complete the Concept Map (as shown in Figure 11.5).

Concept Maps of concepts subordinated to those presented and/or completed by the students were requested after some hours of class time

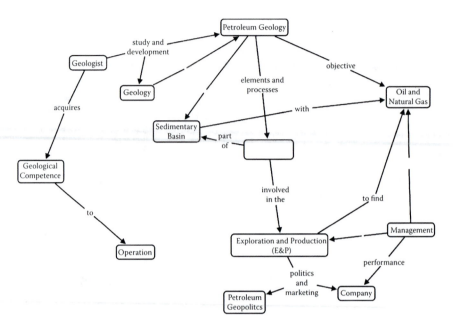

FIGURE 11.5
A reduced Concept Map of petroleum geology.

devoted to the theme, as a learning evaluation. As a result, it was noted that the Concept Maps completed and/or drawn by the students reflected considerable previous knowledge of the major themes of geological knowledge or affinity, and to a lesser degree, their recently acquired knowledge of the discipline.

After six months of training in the classroom, geology professionals were sent to onshore and offshore drilling rigs for training in mud logging and formation evaluation for a period of approximately two months, which was completed with the elaboration of a report on the work conducted and acquired learning. Upon returning from this activity, one of the geologists appointed to develop his professional career at Petrobrás University, was asked by one of the professors who had participated in the workshops to develop a Concept Map of the area and/or recently conducted activity. In the words of the geologist: "[Concept Mapping provides] a very efficient method to help you remember, visualize, and relate all that was seen and learned during the training in the activity."

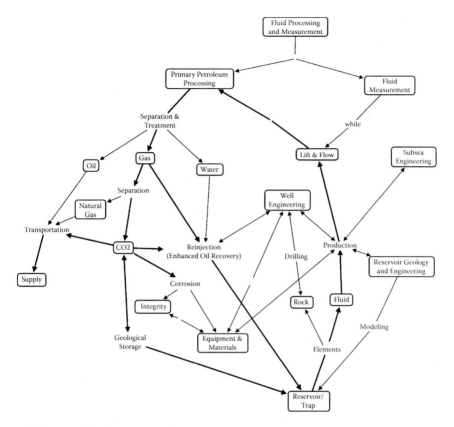

FIGURE 11.6
Concept Map of a technological problem "CO_2 Production Management."

Some other Concept Maps also were produced based on the present problems, both operational and technological, raised by company professionals. One was on the topic of how to visualize the CO_2 management question in the context of the petroleum and natural gas E&P process. This Concept Map is shown in Figure 11.6.

Another was on the topic of how to specify concepts in the field of maintenance and inspection engineering, with the aim of defining a taxonomy for the related practice community. A third was on the topic of how to relate the several alternative energy areas, research, teaching, and action of the company. These company problems are, in general, too complex and interdisciplinary to be described or presented only by means of tables and other conventional resources.

ASSESSING THE VALUE OF CONCEPT MAPPING

In 2009, Petrobrás initiated a review of the Corporate Pedagogy Project in order to adapt and define its pedagogic perspective and procedures, with the inclusion of Meaningful Learning and Concept Mapping as part of its methodological principles (Petrobrás, 2009b). The proposal for the inclusion of Meaningful Learning and the several experiences reported in the pedagogical plan of Petrobrás University for training, disclosure, and use of Concept Maps, allows us to reach some initial conclusions.

The first finding has to do with the potential for the use of Concept Maps to train teachers, program coordinators, and professionals connected with company knowledge, especially in connection with the concept of Meaningful Learning. During events conducted for this purpose, we noticed that these professionals were motivated to use the studied principles and techniques in their specialized field.

In relation to the use of Concept Maps in one of Petrobrás University's main training programs, we observed that this technique is an excellent way to represent the petroleum geology concept in a broad and integrated manner. Concept Mapping was also useful in evaluating the new geologist admission tests, measuring the initial knowledge level of recently hired professionals and their development during the first program discipline, and building the experiential knowledge further elaborated by one of the geologists who created the program.

The Concept Maps enabled the identification of prior knowledge, the representation of the cognitive structure of the student, and the creation of situations in which this knowledge may be articulated with the scientific knowledge to be transmitted. When dealing with experienced professionals in the process of continued education, Concept Maps demonstrated themselves as useful instruments for the elaboration of qualitatively superior synthesis obtained from the articulation between tacit and scientific knowledge. When dealing with professionals being hired by the company, they enabled the articulation of previous experiences and the corporate knowledge that has to be gained, thereby leading to meaningful learning.

Furthermore, the Concept Maps allow for cooperation between the students and their professors, meaning that they can work together on constructions that lead to collective learning. The Concept Maps also encouraged the establishment of partnerships that were projected beyond the time allotted to training for the exchange of knowledge among professionals in their work experiences.

Based on the experiences of the workshop and practical applications, Petrobrás University professionals in several knowledge management areas of the company continue to evaluate the knowledge modeling application. We will continue to evaluate the potential to support company processes, such as competence mapping, technological monitoring, knowledge evolution and training in specific areas or programs, and the establishment of practice communities.

REFERENCES

Ausubel, D. P. 1963. *The psychology of meaningful verbal learning.* New York: Grune and Stratton.

Caldas, J. N. 2005. *Uma História de Sucesso—50 anos de desenvolvimento de recursos humanos.* Rio de Janeiro: Peteróleo Brasileiro S/A—Petrobras, 111.

Kuenzer, A. Z. 2003. Competência como práxis: Os dilemas da relação entre teoria e prática na educação dos trabalhadores. *Boletim Técnico do SENAC, Rio de Janeiro,* 29 (1).

Lanzarini, W. L. 2010. *Aplicação de mapas conceituais no desenvolvimento do Programa de Formação Geólogo Júnior 2009.* Petrobras, Recursos Humanos, Universidade Petrobras, Relatório Interno, p. 20.

Novak, J. D. 1981. *Uma teoria de educação.* São Paulo: Pioneira. Tradução do original. (*A theory of education*).

Novak, J. D. 2010. *Learning, creating and using knowledge: Concept maps as facilitative tools in schools and corporations,* 2nd ed. New York: Routledge.

Petrobrás. 2005. *Projeto pedagógico empresarial. Recursos humanos/universidade Petrobras.* Rio de Janeiro: Petrobras, Publicação International, p. 45.

Petrobrás. 2008. *Dicionário de dompetências. Recursos humanos.* Rio de Janeiro: Petrobras, Publicação International, p. 32.

Petrobrás. 2009a. Relatório anual 2008. Petrobras, p. 128: <http://www.hotsitespetrobras.com.br/rao2008/i18n/pt/index.aspx>

Petrobrás. 2009b. *Plano educacional corporativo. Recursos humanos/Universidade Petrobras.* Rio de Janeiro: Petrobras. Versão preliminar. Documento interno., p. 61.

Zarifian, P. 2001. *Objetivo competência: For uma nova lógica.* São Paulo, Atlas.

12

Using Concept Maps within the Product Design Process in Engineering: A Case Study

Barbara J. Daley, Michael R. Lovell, Ronald A. Perez, and Nathaniel E. Stern

CONTENTS

INTRODUCTION

Engineering in the United States has changed dramatically over the past 20 years leading to significant challenges confronting both engineering education and the practice of engineering. For example, college graduation rates in the United States increased 26 percent from 1985 to 2004, while graduation rates for engineers decreased 23 percent during the same period. Additionally, during the economic declines of 2001–2003 and 2008–2009 the first job cuts made by many companies included engineering positions, most notably in the research and development departments (Douglas, Iversen, and Kalyandurg, 2004).

According to the National Science Board (NSB, 2007), engineering education faces three essential challenges: (1) being able to respond to the changing global context of engineering, (2) changing the perception of engineering to attract individuals from diverse backgrounds, and (3) retaining those students initially attracted to the field of engineering. Particularly important is the need to adapt to the changing global context. As the NSB states:

> … engineering thinking needs to be able to deal with complex interrelationships that include not only traditional engineering problems, but also encompass human and environmental factors as major components. In addition to analytical skills … companies want engineers with passion, some systems thinking, an ability to innovate, an ability to work in multicultural environments, an ability to understand the business context of engineering, interdisciplinary skills, communication skills, leadership skills, an ability to adapt to changing conditions, and an eagerness for lifelong learning (p. 2).

As a result, for the United States to remain competitive in the global marketplace, engineering education and practice must work together to foster the development of the next generation of engineers. This type of collaboration needs to focus on developing thinking skills in future engineers and using these thinking skills in creating new products through design innovation and process efficiency. As Florida and Kenny (1990) indicate, U.S. firms need to "actualize the important follow-through innovations in products and manufacturing processes that are needed to turn new technologies into a constant stream of commercial products" (p. 10).

Because of changes in the type of thinking needed by engineers and the need to remain competitive, many companies in the United States are now looking to universities to help drive the research and development of the next generation of products. At the University of Wisconsin–Milwaukee (UWM), a new type of partnership has been created between businesses and the university for this purpose. The focus of this partnership is to provide a mechanism for training students to be more innovative and entrepreneurial while simultaneously fostering the economic growth and development of partnering industries. The belief is that if students are given access to state-of-the-art product realization tools and actual day-to-day industrial problems, they can learn to be more innovative.

The goal of this chapter is to describe how Concept Maps (Cmaps) and, specifically, CmapTools are being used as state-of-the-art product realization tools. This case study demonstrates how Concept Maps are being used to foster meaningful learning, innovative thinking, design innovation, and process efficiency among engineering students, art students, and business partners.

CONCEPT MAPS AND ENGINEERING: WHAT DO WE KNOW?

Before discussing the use of Concept Maps in this case study, we review the many ways Concept Maps are being used in engineering and engineering education.

Concept Maps for Innovation

Engineers use Concept Maps to foster communication within teams, develop knowledge models and knowledge management systems, create visual designs, and promote innovation. For example, McCartor and Simpson (1999) demonstrated how Concept Maps were used at Boeing Corporation by the systems engineering group to develop and communicate a new vision for airplane level engineering. Additionally, they described how one team used Concept Mapping to develop preferred processes for an electrical/electron enterprise group. In these examples, they show that Concept Maps helped engineers communicate across disciplines; develop new detail and rigor in thinking about tasks and relationships; design a visual, compact, and nonlinear way to present complex concepts; discover missing concepts; illuminate faulty connections; foster in-depth discussions; and, during disagreements, focus on the task instead of individuals (McCartor and Simpson, 1999).

In a similar project, Salustri, Eng, and Weerasinghe (2008) indicate that the early stages of the engineering design process tend to be represented with text documents. Instead, they used Concept Maps to visualize information during these early stages, demonstrating that this can promote new ideas and lead to deeper insights. They state, "… as the team members grew more accustomed to the CmapTools software, the authors noticed that (a) convergence to a common understanding of the goals and structure of the project occurred very quickly, and (b) interactions between the team members increased in frequency" (p. 5).

Concept Maps also are being used in business and industry to create knowledge models. Ugwu, Anumba, and Thorpe (2004) describe the development of knowledge models for automated constructability assessment. They created Concept Maps to "identify the roles, level of task decompositions, and constructability assessment processes/issues from different disciplines and perspectives. The study shows that in addition to design review processes, other factors, such as procurement route selection and effective communication of design parameters between the stakeholders, are all essential to realize the goals and objectives of constructability in infrastructure engineering and project management" (p. 191).

Moon, Hoffman, and Ziebell (2009) also describe using Concept Maps and knowledge models to capture knowledge of experts and develop systems for structuring and representing this organizational knowledge.

> At NASA's Glenn Research Center, for example, concept mapping and knowledge elicitation sessions were conducted with a retiring senior engineer who specialized in the Delta rocket motor. The resulting knowledge model of 11 Cmaps and 140 other resources thoroughly expresses and organizes his deep knowledge (p. 25).

Moon et al. indicated that such knowledge models can be used as organizational resources to develop on-the-job training programs and memory aids.

Finally, Dubberly (2008) describes using Concept Maps as a way to develop an understanding and a visual model of innovation. Dubberly, quoting computer scientist Alan Kay, notes, "We do most of our thinking with models. They are 'boundary objects,' enabling discourse between communities of practice. This is what makes models so powerful" (p. 36).

Concept Maps for Instruction

Engineering education, according to Sheppard, Macatangay, and Colby (2009), "is holding on to an approach to problem solving and knowledge acquisition that is consistent with practice that the profession has left behind. There are, however, pockets of innovation" (p. xxi). Innovative practices in engineering education include using Concept Maps in a variety of ways, including as a teaching and learning method, as an assessment strategy, and as a part of the curriculum design process.

For example, Muryanto (2006) used Concept Maps as a teaching strategy in an upper-division chemical engineering laboratory to enhance student learning. In this project, students created both individual and group Concept Maps before, during, and after their lab practice sessions. Results indicate that student learning deepened, leading to a greater understanding of the concepts taught in the lab, and that students had increased confidence in their learning and understanding.

Similarly, Vega-Riveros, Marciales-Vivas and Martinez-Melo (1998) used Concept Maps in an undergraduate engineering course on neural networks. They indicated that one advantage of the maps is that they can be directly translated into a computer language to build a knowledge base. Ibrahim, Morsi, and Tuttle (2006) are developing wireless communication modules using Concept Maps as an active learning media.

Finally, Ryve (2004; 2006) has been using Concept Maps to facilitate engineering students' discussions of mathematical concepts. Ryve demonstrates that Concept Maps helped students communicate effectively and engage in mathematically productive discourse. Ryve (2004) indicates that the collaborative construction of the Concept Maps in linear algebra:

> ... gives many opportunities for the students to communicate and clarify their intended foci to themselves and each other. The encouragement to clarify their intended foci could be one reason why the discourses of these students show the characteristics of a mathematically productive discourse (p. 174).

Concept Maps for Assessment

Engineering educators are going beyond just using Concept Maps in teaching and learning; they are also using them to connect teaching and assessment strategies. For example, Van Zele, Lenaerts, and Wieme (2004) used Concept Maps to assess engineering students' understanding of atoms. Coller and Scott (2009) used Concept Maps to assess student learning following participation in a video game course designed to teach mechanical engineering and found that students in the game-based course had deeper learning than those in traditional courses.

McClellan et al. (2004) describe the use of Concept Maps in a signal processing course. The goal of this course was to acquaint students with course content by using Concept Maps the students developed to connect to an extensive repository that included demonstrations, tests, exercises, and homework problems. The Cmaps were then assessed in three ways. First, a simple visual evaluation was used to determine if the maps were good, average, or poor. Second, a subset of the maps was evaluated for the types of links that were created: good links, average links, or erroneous links. Finally, Cmaps were assessed on three parameters: correctness, size, and complexity. McClellan et al. indicate that students with better course grades created Cmaps that were larger, but not necessarily more correct or complex.

Turns, Atman, and Adams (2000) describe using Concept Maps in various engineering courses to support an array of assessment functions, including as a method to quickly gauge understanding, as a final exam, and as a tool to assess learning at the course level. At the program level, they describe using maps to characterize the level of statistics expertise of students in industrial engineering, to explore students' understanding of the conceptions of their discipline, and to explore students' conceptions of their profession. Turns et al. indicate, "Clearly Concept Maps are not a perfect assessment solution. They can require extensive time to interpret and can still remain ambiguous" (p. 172). Yet, they continue, "Concept Maps represent an innovative way to assess and gain insight into student learning about the relationships among concepts" (p. 172).

Sims-Knight et al. (2004) extended this work on using Concept Mapping as an assessment method in engineering. In their work, they assessed student-constructed Concept Maps in three senior engineering courses. The Cmaps focused on the design process and were created by students in software engineering, computer engineering, and electrical engineering. Sims-Knight et al. found that four basic patterns of maps were developed: branching, cat's cradle (or integrated), web, and linear. The Cmaps revealed the students' underlying understanding of design and also fit into the domain-specific expertise of the students. The electrical engineering students created more linear maps, while the computer and information science students created more integrated (or cat's cradle) maps. The authors indicate that this may reflect how the design process varies between engineering disciplines.

Finally, Borrego et al. (2009) used Concept Maps to assess interdisciplinary knowledge integration. Their year-long research study of a design course in green engineering assessed how students developed an interdisciplinary understanding of green engineering processes. Researchers compared student-generated Concept Maps constructed at the beginning of the year and the end of the year. Their findings indicate that Concept Maps are a viable approach to engineering knowledge assessment. Additionally, Borrego et al. (2009) highlight "important issues in faculty scoring of interdisciplinary Concept Maps that may not be present when maps are used in traditional single-discipline settings. The interdisciplinary setting revealed differences in: (1) evaluation criteria, (2) expertise, and (3) investment" (p. 1). They advocate careful selection and training for faculty using Concept Maps across disciplines.

Concept Maps for Curriculum Design

Engineering educators also have begun to use Concept Maps in the curriculum design process. Upadhyay et al. (2007) conducted a study to identify the parameters that influence the quality of an engineering education curriculum. Using a quality improvement process, they developed a Concept Map to depict both the hierarchical structure and the basic concepts necessary to develop engineering proficiency. The Cmaps they developed identified the major concepts and subconcepts needed for quality engineering education. They state:

> Such concept maps would help decision makers, planners, and administrators to understand the necessary linkages in the complex and co-evolving system of engineering education. This hybrid model also can be useful in presenting a knowledge scenario of any engineering education system for further analysis, evaluation, or projections. The overall pattern of concept maps can be used as a basis for continuous improvement and can provide pointers for organizational and performance assessment (p. 32).

It was the intention of these researchers to use the Concept Maps developed for further longitudinal curriculum development and assessment.

Based on the above studies, we believe that Concept Mapping could have a positive impact on both the education of engineers and the practice of engineering. Previous research indicates that Concept Maps have been successfully used within engineering to foster innovative thinking, student learning, and to assist in the product design process. We believe that Concept Maps can foster the integration of teaching, learning, and product development within the profession and, thus, we chose to integrate their use within the Industrial Product Innovation Center formed at UWM.

THE CASE

The Industrial Product Innovation Center was formed at UWM through the cooperation of business partners and the College of Engineering and Applied Sciences at the university. The business partners included: GE Health Care Systems, Briggs and Stratton, Badger Meter, Inc., Eaton Corporation, TAPCO–Traffic and Parking Control Company, Inc., The Great Lakes Water Institute, and ReGENco.

A major purpose of this center is to link business problems that need research and development with students and faculty in the College of Engineering and across the university. The center has fostered the development of research partnerships between businesses and the university as well as nurturing grant development and technology transfer programs. One of the most recent activities of the center was to foster the development of a capstone course in product realization. Seniors in electrical, mechanical, industrial, and computer engineering were invited to enroll in the course, as were art and graphic design students. The students formed eight teams, each of which included a variety of engineering students and an art or graphic design student.

Eight business groups, each with a unique product needing research and development, met with the student teams and explained the product needs and customer requirements. The student teams, with faculty and business advisors and a small budget, were then asked to create product design prototypes to solve the business problems presented. Most of the products to be developed were extremely specific, for example, a water valve that can be controlled remotely or a physical interface that lets customers know when their lawnmowers need more oil. Other products included an apparatus to test components in the next generation of computerized tomography (CT) scanners, a digital unit that can trip a relay after detecting a ground fault leak, a new solar-powered illuminated street sign, and a marine-rated servo robot.

The teams were taught how to develop Concept Maps and how to use CmapTools. Each team then worked through the product realization process for their specific business problem. They developed a project plan; specified the customer needs; established product requirements; generated multiple product concepts; selected concepts; designed, tested, and redesigned the product; developed production plans; and prepared to launch the product.

In this chapter, we focus on how two of these teams used Concept Maps in the design process. First, we present one of the team projects that did not result in a particularly high level of innovation. The first team used Concept Maps in a way that facilitated completing their project, but not in a way that created a highly innovative outcome. The second team used Concept Mapping in a manner that led to a greater innovative success. Although we cannot claim a statistical causal role in these outcomes, we can argue that the differences in the Concept Mapping by the two teams played some role, in that richer Concept Maps developed at the design conception stage were useful in guiding the refinement of design notions.

Development of a Mass Property Device

The objective of the first team was to build a device that more accurately measures the mass and center of gravity of components placed inside the newest generation of CT scanners. These new, higher-resolution CT scanners rotate at significantly greater angular velocities than the previous models (up to 8 g). At the higher rotational velocities, there is an increased requirement for the rotating mass of the combined scanner components to remain precisely balanced. For this reason, the project required the development of a method to more accurately determine the mass and center of gravity of the components within the scanners. The sponsor of the project specified that the device must be able to measure components with a mass between 2.5 kg and 250 kg and a volume between 0.001 m^3 and 0.192 m^3 and must be accurate within 0.1 kg for mass and 0.01 m^3 for volume. Using background information and requirements provided by the sponsor, the team developed a Gantt chart to formally plan the development of their project over the 14-week semester. Interviews to clarify the product

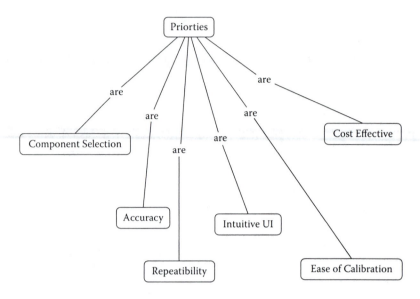

FIGURE 12.1
Priorities for developing mass property device.

requirements with potential users of the device led the team to identify additional criteria including that the device (1) be easy to operate, (2) be inexpensive to manufacture, (3) yield reliable results, (4) be easy to calibrate, and (5) use off-the-shelf components. These priorities were placed in the Concept Map-like diagram depicted in Figure 12.1.

The group then investigated technologies that could be used to measure center of gravity and mass. These technologies included electrical, hydraulic, pneumatic, and gravity techniques. After analyzing and discussing the project individually and as a team, searching online, and interviewing experts, the team broke the available technologies down further to include concepts such as digital force transducers, potentiometers, hydraulic load cells, air pressure gauges, and amoeba methods. These technologies were organized into a Concept Map-type diagram, presented in Figure 12.2.

As shown in Figure 12.3, the concepts the students identified for the mass property devised were then sketched. The sketch in Figure 12.3 represents the students' thinking on two different types of mass property devised that they could create.

Following the development of the sample sketches in Figure 12.3, the students performed calculations to determine their viability for meeting the device requirements.

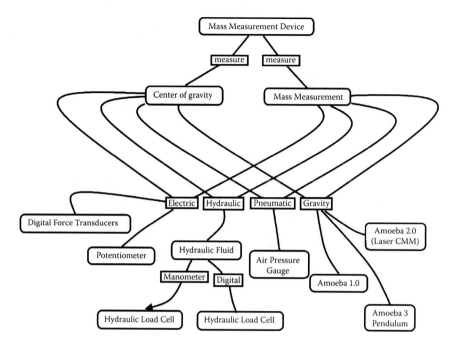

FIGURE 12.2
Technologies for mass property device.

Based on the sketches in Figure 12.3 and the calculations, the team reviewed the concept generation and feasibility of their design. Then the team used a concept screening and scoring technique developed specifically for this course. The concept screening and scoring technique were designed to assist the students in reviewing the concepts they generated and help them to determine which of these concepts would be used in further investigation or product development. This is a two-step process. In concept screening, the team narrows the number of concepts in the product design, and then scores the concepts to apply priorities to various attributes of the product so that a final selection can be made.

Based on this analysis, the team decided to move forward with both the load cell and pressure transducer design concepts. The load cell method would measure the support reaction forces and integrate data acquisition software and a computer to perform mass and center of gravity calculations. The load cell device design was tested to determine its accuracy.

The pressure gauge design is used with pneumatic cylinders to support and measure loads. This method did not have the errors associated with the load cells, but had lower resolution. The pressure gauge values had to

AMOEBA METHOD (ORIGINAL)   HYDRAULIC PLATE WITH ATTACHED CYLINDERS

PRESSURE GAUGE

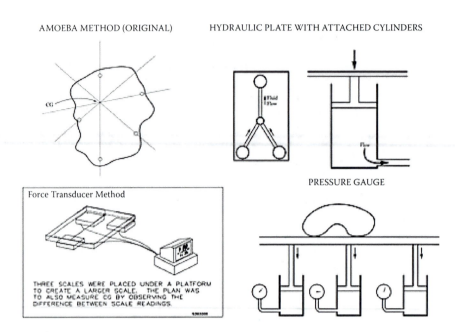

FIGURE 12.3
Sample sketches for mass property device.

be recorded manually and entered into a spreadsheet to calculate the mass and center of gravity values. As with the load cell method, the pressure gauge design was tested by placing known loads onto the system to determine the optimum components to be used in the final device design.

In this first example, the team developing the mass property device created two rather simplistic diagrams that contained some features of Concept Maps. The first diagram, depicted in Figure 12.1, was created in a linear fashion and did not show integration across components of the map or between the concepts. Additionally, in both the diagrams created by this team (Figure 12.1 and Figure 12.2), linking words between concepts were all but absent. Thus, the meaning to be represented in these diagrams was not readily apparent. We believe that this team struggled with conceptualizing their product in the form of a Concept Map and, therefore, the product outcome, though satisfactory, was not highly creative.

Development of a Remote Shut-Off Valve

The objective of the second team project within the capstone course in product realization was to develop a ¾-in. residential water shut-off valve that could be remotely opened, closed, or set in various positions. The team had to create a functional prototype that met all specifications as well as develop a control system, a schematic, and the required software protocol.

After interviewing the sponsor of the project, the team determined the valve should also:

1. Have no significant pressure loss when open
2. Be adjustable in 10 percent increments
3. Have an enclosure that provides protection from environmental damage and tampering
4. Be battery powered
5. Be able to operate at 150 psi and withstand burst pressure of 450 psi
6. Be made of low lead brass or stainless steel materials
7. Have a useful lifetime of 15 years

The team then developed a project plan and Gantt chart to make a prototype of the water shut-off valve. To further refine the product requirements and begin mapping their ideas, the team developed the Concept Map displayed in Figure 12.4.

The team used the Cmap to link high-level concepts and mechanisms to the requirements. They started with the potential applications and existing product lines of the sponsor, drilled down to the electrical and mechanical aspects of the product design, and finally related those to fulfilling the requirements. Through the development of the Concept Map, the team achieved an excellent understanding of the breadth and scope of the project at an early stage.

After mapping the requirements, the team set about developing Concept Maps for specific aspects of the product: the valve design, motor, control card, and power source. Figure 12.5 shows the Concept Map generated for the shut-off valve design.

As Figure 12.5 shows in the three major nodes (i.e., concepts) beneath the parent node, the group developed concepts in three areas related to the water valve: the valve design, the controller, and a possible solenoid design. Each of these areas was taken to several subsequent levels of detail, and crosslinks between areas were identified. This shut-off valve design Concept Map allowed the group to organize multiple concepts for each component of the product. These concepts supported the creation of detailed design drawings for several possible valve solutions, as illustrated in Figure 12.6.

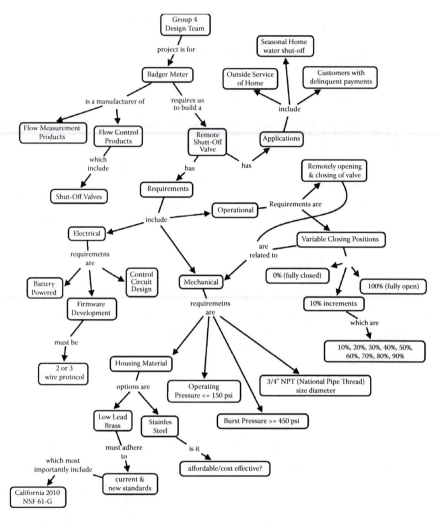

FIGURE 12.4
Initial Concept Map for developing remote shut-off valve.

Also illustrated are the detailed designs developed by using the Concept Maps to incorporate different valve component technologies, including ball (bottom left), globe (bottom middle), and screw (bottom right).

After creating the design for the different components of the product, this team, like the first, generated a concept-scoring matrix to help determine which of the concepts identified would be used in the final product. The scoring procedure assisted in evaluating the designs on a number of pertinent dimensions, such as torque and corrosion propensity. The

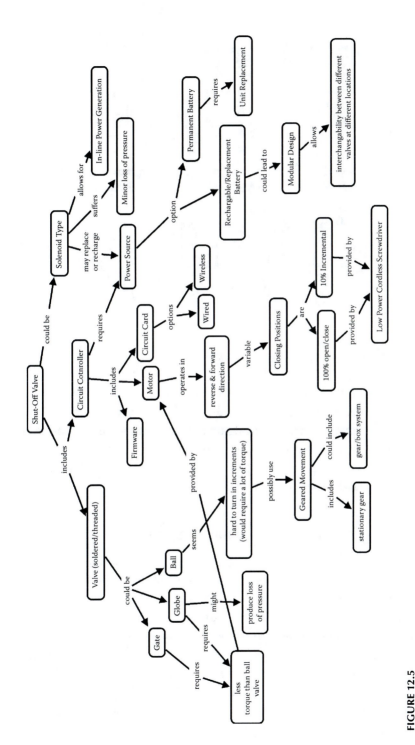

FIGURE 12.5

Final design Concept Map for remote shut-off valve.

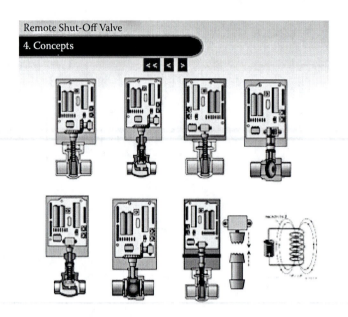

FIGURE 12.6
Remote shut-off valve design concepts

combination of the Concept Maps and the scoring matrix provided students with alternative ways to view the product they were creating and facilitated the team decision making on product design. The second team then constructed a prototype and developed a stringent test plan to meet the project requirements. This test plan established pass/fail criteria and included a listing of necessary modifications.

Comparison of Product Development Processes Used by Both Teams

Both the mass properties device and the remote water shut-off valve teams successfully developed working prototypes that met requirements of the project sponsors. However, there were differences in the level of creativity in each of the product designs.

The mass measurement team developed two working prototypes: one based on load cells and the other based on pressure gauges. Both the load cell and pressure gauge designs met the minimum requirements of the sponsors, but neither was viewed by the faculty as having a very high level of sophistication. Similarly, the Concept Maps developed by this team lacked the three essential mapping components identified by Novak and Gowin (1984): subsumption, progressive differentiation, and integrative reconciliation. In the subsumption process, lower order concepts are subsumed under higher order concepts. This subsumption process creates a hierarchy of knowledge structures. In the progressive differentiation process, concepts are broken down into finer and finer components. In this way, progressive differentiation is similar to an analysis process. Finally, integrative reconciliation is a process where the learner attempts to reconcile and link together concepts from the left side of the Cmap to those on the right side of the Cmap. This is similar to a synthesis process. As can be seen in Figure 12.1 and Figure 12.2, these three processes are missing. The Cmaps created by this team depict a rather linear thinking process as a central component of their product development work. Faculty teaching this course believed that the lack of specificity on the Concept Maps led to the development of products that were functional, but not necessarily innovative.

On the other hand, the remote shut-off valve (Figure 12.6) not only met all of the customer requirements, but also included several novel features. The control system for closing the valve in 10-degree increments was particularly complex and innovative; most likely the greatest accomplishment of the team. It can be hypothesized that this team's more complex Concept Mapping led to more complex product concepts, and, ultimately, a more innovative product. As can be seen in Figure 12.4 and Figure 12.5, this team did subsume lower order concepts under higher order concepts, progressively differentiated concepts into finer and finer components, and created crosslinks from one side of the Cmap to the other through a process of integrative reconciliation. Additionally, the propositional statements and the linking words students used in these Cmaps (Figure 12.4 and Figure 12.5) show a greater understanding, not only of the overall product, but of the component parts of the product as well.

Student Responses

Student responses to using Concept Maps in the product development process were solicited in the form of course evaluations from all eight teams. Overall, students from all the teams within the course indicated that the Cmaps helped them think in different ways. For example, one student indicated that part of what he learned over the course of the semester was just how linear his thinking had become. He stated that the Concept Maps forced him to think in a different way and to search out a variety of ways to create a product. Another student indicated that his team had tried to use the Cmaps not only to understand the products, but also to come up with creative ideas in their development.

Nonetheless, the thought processes needed for product design were still difficult for some students, as indicated by one team at the conclusion of their project:

> Over the course of the semester our team learned a great deal about the product development process. We learned about all the steps that make up the process as well as the tools needed to complete those steps or manage the process. The first critical lesson we learned was the importance of identifying and clarifying customer requirements. We found that digging deep into the requirements on the front end of the process would probably help to minimize the potential for scope creep in the project later. In our case, some scope creep occurred on the maximum g-force to be applied to the components. This required us to reevaluate our design selection and redesign the disk. We also learned about the C-Mapping tool (*sic*) to aid in outside-the-box thinking about potential solutions. We found this tool to be more challenging to apply than we had expected. Even with using this tool, we still had difficulty developing outside-the-box solutions to the problem. The scoring and selection tools were very useful in identifying which combination of concepts for the disk, shaft, and base would best meet the customer requirements.

In summary, comments from the students throughout the semester indicate that they found Concept Maps to be nontrivial to learn and to apply, and yet a very useful tool that helped them in many different ways, such as:

- Enhancing communication within the team, which was particularly beneficial since the team members were students from different disciplines.
- Promoting innovation and providing a visual road map to explore ideas and build a knowledge base.
- Visualizing relationships which sparked new ideas.
- Facilitating discussions by providing a detailed context of the tasks.
- Facilitating the integration of interdisciplinary knowledge.
- Understanding the breadth and scope of the project and the different tasks.

These comments were received both from teams who struggled to develop their products and teams who excelled at developing their products.

Business Responses

Following completion of the class and the product realization process, all business partners were surveyed for their input. The survey consisted of a 12-item questionnaire on which participants completed a Likert scale rating with 1 on the low end of the scale and 5 indicating exceptional. The items asked business partners to evaluate such things as the students' understanding of the project requirements, the team's ability to communicate, the effectiveness of course instructors, and interaction between students and sponsors. The overall means for each item on the survey ranged from 3.75 to 4.25, indicating a general level of satisfaction demonstrated by business partners. One part of the survey, in particular, asked the business partners to evaluate the effectiveness of the teams' creative solutions. This item was linked directly to the students' use of Concept Maps in the course, and the mean score on this item was 4. Finally, overall qualitative responses from the business partners indicated that the product realization process was a positive experience for them and the students.

IMPLICATIONS FOR USING CONCEPT MAPS IN PRODUCT DEVELOPMENT

Students, business partners, and engineering faculty involved in this case all indicated that Concept Maps have a potential role to play in new product development. In this case, as in the literature, the Cmaps were instrumental in a number of areas. First, the Cmaps seemed to help the teams communicate. Faculty and business partners observed that in the first half of the semester, the Cmaps facilitated discussion as the teams generated ideas, developed concepts, and selected concepts for their products.

Second, for all teams in this course, the Cmaps functioned as a visual representation of the product development process. The teams appreciated that the Cmaps were easily modified to reflect their changing ideas during the design process. Students commented that CmapTools was not only easy to learn, but easily modified as their ideas shifted.

Third, the teams seemed to find that the Cmaps helped them understand their thinking and learning processes. For example, one team discussed, with an instructor, how the Cmaps helped the engineering and the graphic arts students to understand how differently each of them analyzed ideas and created their own thought processes. In this team, the students were intrigued by comparisons of linear versus fully integrated Cmaps.

Additionally, the engineering literature suggests that the structure of a Concept Map, i.e., branching, cat's cradle (or integrated), web, or linear (Sims-Knight et al., 2004), may be indicative of the domain-specific expertise of the map creator. Studies indicate that meaningful diagrams of domain concepts can differentiate expert versus nonexpert knowledge and that Concept Mapping can support the formation of consensus among experts (Gordon, Schmierer, and Gill, 1993). Evidence from studies of experts versus novices indicates that expertise is usually associated not just with more detailed knowledge, but knowledge that is better organized than that of novices (Glaser, 1987).

Hays and Kinchin (2006), in the education literature, describe a similar typology of maps and indicate that as individuals develop Concept Maps they tend to use a linear (or chain) format, then a spoke format, or network format. However, Hays and Kinchin do not attribute these different structures to domain-specific knowledge or expertise per se; rather, they indicate that the type of map created reflects the type of thinking. Furthermore, different types of thinking serve different purposes, and being able to switch back and forth between types of thinking is an important skill. Hays and Kinchin posit that an individual's ability to switch between "chain" and "network" thinking may be a component of expertise. Hays and Kinchin (2006) go on to state, "Chain thinking has considerable utility in practical situations. Nevertheless, an ability to retain complex networks in an underlying structure while moving quickly to prescriptive chains is likely to be the hallmark of the successful manager and leader" (p. 140).

In the work of the two teams described in this chapter, it is unclear if the Concept Map structure created by each team is related to the type of product being developed, the expertise of the team, or the complexity of the design process. This is an area that needs further research and exploration. Do engineers in the product development and design process engage in switching between chain thinking and network thinking as described by Hays and Kinchin? Is switching thinking processes a hallmark of creativity and the development of domain-specific expertise? Further work in this area could assist in understanding the underlying dynamics in the product development and realization process.

Finally, as Novak and Cañas (2006) state:

> While at first glance concept maps may appear to be just another graphic representation of information, understanding the foundations for this tool and its proper use will lead the user to see that this is truly a profound and powerful tool. It may at first look like a simple arrangement of words into a hierarchy, but when care is used in organizing the concepts represented by the words, and the propositions or ideas are formed with well-chosen linking words, one begins to see that a good concept map is at once simple, but also elegantly complex with profound meanings (p. 31).

As demonstrated in this case study, Concept Maps can play a useful role in the process of product realization. Integrating Concept Maps within the product development process can help with group collaboration, achieving common ground and shared purpose, generating concepts, selecting concepts, and presenting complex ideas in a simplified format.

REFERENCES

Borrego, M., C. B. Newswander, and L. D. McNair, et al. 2009. Using concept maps to assess interdisciplinary integration of green engineering knowledge. *Advances in Engineering Education*, 1–26.

Coller, B. D. and M. J. Scott. 2009. Effectiveness of using a video game to teach a course in mechanical engineering. *Computers & Education* 53: 900–12.

Douglas, J., E. Iversen, and C. Kalyandurg. 2004. Engineering in the K-12 classroom: An analysis of current practices and guidelines for the future. Washington, D.C.: The American Society for Engineering Education. Retrieved from http://www.engineeringk12.org

Dubberly, H. 2008. Toward a model of innovation. *Interactions* (January–February), 28–36.

Florida, F. and M. Kenney. 1990. *The breakthrough illusion: Corporate America's failure to move from innovation to mass production*. New York: Basic Books, Inc.

Glaser, R. 1987. Thoughts on expertise. In *Cognitive functioning and social structure over the life course* (pp. 81–94), eds. C. Schooler and W. Schaie. Norwood, NJ: Ablex.

Gordon, S. E., K. A. Schmierer, and R. T. Gill. 1993. Conceptual graph analysis: Knowledge acquisition for instructional system design. *Human Factors* 35, 459–481.

Hays, D. B. and I. M. Kinchin. 2006. Using concept maps to reveal conceptual typologies. *Education & Training* 48 (2–3): 127–42.

Ibrahim, W., R. Morsi, and T. Tuttle. 2006. Concept maps: An active learning and assessment tool in electrical and computer engineering. Paper presented at the American Society for Engineering Education, Indiana University /Purdue University, Fort Wayne. http://ilin. asee.org/Conference2006program/Papers/Ibrahim-P66.pdf (accessed January 10, 2010).

McCartor, M. M. and J. J. Simpson. 1999. Concept mapping as a communications tool in systems engineering. Paper presented at the proceedings of the 9th Annual International Symposium of the International Council on Systems Engineering, Brighton, England.

McClellan, J. H., M. Borkar, and V. Rajbabu, et al. 2004. Concept maps for navigating signal processing education resources. Available online at http://users.ece.gatech. edu/~rajbabu/publications/CMAP_DSPWS2004.pdf

Moon, B., R. Hoffman, and D. Ziebell. 2009. How did they do that? *Electric Perspectives* 34: 20–29.

Muryanto, S. 2006. Concept mapping: An interesting and useful learning tool for chemical engineering laboratories. *International Journal of Engineering. Education* 22 (5): 979–85.

National Science Board. 2007. Moving forward to improve engineering education. NSB -07-122. Retrieved from http://www.nsf.gov/pubs/2007/nsb07122/index.jsp

Novak, J. D. and B. Gowin. 1984. *Learning how to learn.* Oxford, U.K.: Cambridge University Press.

Novak, J. D. and A. J. Cañas. 2006. The theory underlying concept maps and how to construct them. Technical Report IHMC CmapTools 2006-01, Florida Institute for Human and Machine Cognition. http://cmap.ihmc.us/Publications/ResearchPapers/ TheoryUnderlyingConceptMaps.pdf (accessed June 12, 2009).

Ryve, A. 2004. Can collaborative concept mapping create mathematically productive discourses? *Educational Studies in Mathematics* 26: 157–77.

Ryve, A. 2006. Making explicit the analysis of students' mathematical discourses—Revisiting a newly developed methodological framework. *Educational Studies in Mathematics* 62: 191–209.

Salustri, F. A., N. L. Eng, and J. S. Weerasinghe. 2008. Visualizing information in the early stages of engineering design. *Computer-Aided Design and Applications* 5: 1–18.

Schvaneveldt, R. W., F. T. Durso, and T. E. Goldsmith, et al. 1985. Measuring the structure of expertise. *International Journal of Man-Machine Studies* 23, 699–728.

Sheppard, S. D., K. Macatangay, and A. Colby. 2009. *Educating engineers: Designing for the future of the field.* San Francisco: Jossey-Bass, Inc.

Sims-Knight, J. E., R. L. Upchurch, and N. Pendergrass, et al. 2004. Using concept maps to assess design process knowledge. Paper presented at the 34th ASEE/IEE Frontiers in Education Conference, Savannah, GA. http://fie-conference.org/fie2004/papers/1167. pdf (accessed January 10, 2010).

Turns, J., C. J. Atman, and R. Adams. 2000. Concept maps for engineering education: A cognitively motivated tool supporting varied assessment functions. *IEEE Transactions on Education* 43: 164–73.

Ugwu, O. O., C. J. Anumba, and A. Thorpe. 2004. The development of cognitive models of constructability assessment in steel frame structures. *Advances in Engineering Software* 35: 191–203.

Upadhyay, R. K., S. K. Gaur, and V. P. Agrawal, et al. 2007. ISM-CMAP-Combine (ICMC) for hierarchical knowledge scenario in quality engineering education. *European Journal of Engineering Education* 32: 21–33.

Van Zele, E., J. Lenaerts, and W. Wieme. 2004. Improving the usefulness of concept maps as a research tool for science education. *International Journal of Science Education* 26 (9): 1043–1064.

Vega-Riveros, J. F., G. P. Marciales-Vivas, and M. Martinez-Melo. 1998. Concept maps in engineering education: A case study. *Global Journal of Engineering Education* 2 (1): 21–27.

13

Improving Organizational Learning with Concept Maps: A Business Case Study

David Barberá-Tomás, Mónica Elizabeth Edwards Schachter, and Ernesto de los Reyes-López

CONTENTS

INTRODUCTION

In the past decades knowledge has increasingly been considered as an organization's most important resource for achieving and maintaining a competitive advantage (Drucker, 1993; 1999; Leonard-Barton, 1995; Grant, 1996; Nonaka, Reinmoeller, and Senoo, 1998). A considerable number of studies have demonstrated that many of the world's most successful and innovative organizations are those that are best at managing their knowledge. Numerous theorists have contributed to the evolution of the knowledge management (KM) field with different perspectives. While several authors have stressed the growing importance of information and explicit knowledge as organizational resource (Drucker, 1993; Nonaka, 1994; Wilkens, Menzel, and Pawlowsky, 2004; Nonaka, Von Krogh, and Voelpel, 2006), others have focused on the cultural dimension and the "learning organization" concept (Slater and Narver, 1995; Argyris, 1982; Argyris and Schon, 1996). Other trends emphasize aspects of KM related to the organizational learning (OL) and the dynamic capabilities (Leonard-Barton, 1995; Teece, Pisano, and Shuen, 1997) and, more recently, the OL alignment with the business and innovation strategies (Johannessen, Olson, and Olaisen, 1999; Teece, 1986; 2000; Hung, Lien, and McLean, 2009).

KM includes a multidisciplined approach to achieving organizational objectives by making the best use of knowledge, focusing both on processes, such as acquiring, creating, and sharing knowledge, and the cultural and technical foundations that support them. Typically, focus is placed on organizational objectives, such as improved performance, competitive advantage, innovation, the sharing of lessons learned, integration, and continuous improvement of the organization, overlapping synergistically with organizational learning.

OL is a concept dating from the early 1960s and defined in a wide variety of ways by researchers (Argyris and Schon, 1978; 1996; Dierkes et al., 2001; Lähteenmäki, Toivonen, and Mattila, 2002). By the 1990s, OL had become increasingly debated by economists and organizational studies' practitioners and scholars. Although there is a widespread acceptance of the OL notion and its importance to strategic performance, no theory or model of OL is still widely accepted (Daft and Huber, 1987; Dodgson, 1993; Kim, 1993; Lähteenmäki, Toivonen, and Mattila, 2002; Templeton, Lewis, and Snyder, 2002). Questions about the interrelationships between individual learning and OL and how OL can contribute to improve knowledge management are still without a clear response (Argyris, 1992; Pawlowsky, 2001).

Kolb (1984, p. 38) states that learning "is the process whereby knowledge is created through the transformation of experience." Both parts of his definition are important: what people learn (*know-how*) and how they understand and apply that learning (*know-why*). Presumably, learning facilitates behavior change that leads to improved performance and the organizational learning (Fiol and Lyles, 1985; Lyles and Schwenk, 1992;

Senge, 1990). Accepting the idea that OL means the process of improving individual and group actions through better knowledge and understanding, we are facing the problem of explain how transference and "appropriability" of knowledge occur and the nurture of the links between individual learning with an organizational one. Knowledge transfer is the process through which one unit (e.g., group, department, or division) is affected by the experience of another, while appropriability represents the person and organization's ability to capture both explicit and tacit knowledge (Davenport and Prusak, 1998).

We agree with Argyris and Schön (1996) in that learning, to be considered organizational, must be incorporated by means of epistemological artifacts (maps, memoranda, and programs) that are found in the context of the organization. Collaborative environments and the application of social computing tools can be used for both creation and transfer of knowledge, contributing to organizational learning and knowledge management in alignment with business strategy (Lee, Courtney, and O'Keefe, 1992; Davenport and Prusak, 1998). Learners can function as designers using the technology as tools for analyzing the world, accessing information, interpreting and organizing their personal knowledge, and representing what they know to others (their "mental models").

At present, considerable diversity of methods and software tools is used with the purpose of enabling the transference knowledge and supporting KM, but most of these tools are being developed under a technological thrust. They are more concerned with new ways of storing and communicating information than with the actual ways in which people create, acquire, and use knowledge (i.e., how people learn in organizational environments and how organizational learning is improved).

Also OL is viewed as the process of acquisition or development of competences at different levels of aggregation (individuals, groups, networks) within the organization (i.e., an ability to apply new knowledge to enhance the performance of an existing activity or task or to adapt to new circumstances). Ahmed, Lim, and Loh (2002, p.16) wrote:

> … organizational learning, therefore, seeks to describe a process of increasing the overall performance of an organization by encouraging knowledge creation and use in each of its value chain functions, in order to render each a source of competitive advantage or core competence.

Concept Maps can be used to gather knowledge from both individuals and groups, facilitate knowledge creation process, act as a discussion and communication tool, and assist in the diffusion of knowledge and learning processes within an organization (Cañas et al., 2004). Nevertheless, utilization of Concept Maps and Concept Mapping tools is still very limited in the business environment when compared to educational settings. Additionally, relatively little research has been done on the contribution of Concept Maps to knowledge transference, organizational learning, and knowledge management (cf., Fourie, 2005; Henao-Cálad and Arango-Fonnegra, 2007).

In this chapter, we analyze some theoretical perspectives exploring the links between individual and organizational learning (Ausubel, Novak, and Hanesian, 1978; Kim, 1993; Pawlowsky, 2001). We also inquire into the potential of Concept Maps for supporting processes of organizational learning (OL) (de los Reyes López and Barberá, 2004; Sutherland and Katz, 2005). Finally, we present a case study applying Concept Maps (using CmapTools) to improve understanding of organizational learning and, in particular, the alignment of knowledge transfer with business strategy in a technological firm.

LEARNING TO LEARN IN ORGANIZATIONS: APPROACH TO AN ANALYTICAL FRAMEWORK

What's the meaning of the expression "learn to learn" in relation to organizational learning? Is it possible, for example, to achieve the integration between the Theory of Meaningful Learning (ML) and the theoretical frameworks of organizational learning?

Several authors disagree with the possibility of comparability between individual learning and organizational learning, but a considerable amount of literature considers that organizations can learn. The problem of the conceptualization of OL goes beyond the conception that organizations can learn despite the fact that they cannot read a book or attend a course, implying psychological and epistemological constraints (Cook and Brown, 1999; Lähteenmäki, Toivonen, and Mattila, 2002). G. P. Huber (cited by Argyris, 1992, p. 7) suggests that:

an organization has learned if any of its components have acquired information and have this information available for use, either by other components or by itself, on behalf of the organization.

Organizational learning must take into account the interplay between different levels of aggregation: actions and interactions of individuals and the actions and interactions of high-level entities, as departments, divisions, and networks within the organization. Kim (1993, p. 12) appoints that:

> although the meaning of the term *learning* remains essentially the same as in the individual case, the learning process is fundamentally different at the organizational level. A model of organizational learning has to resolve somehow the dilemma of imparting intelligence and learning capabilities to a nonhuman entity without anthropomorphizing it.

Meaningful learning (as contrasted with *rote* learning) is differentiated from other types of learning due to the following key characteristics:

- It is nonarbitrary and consists in a substantive incorporation of new knowledge into the learner's cognitive structure.
- It is necessary for development of conceptual understanding.
- Sometimes it is characterized as *deep* or *dynamic* learning (opposite to *surface* or *static* learning); suppose a deliberate effort to link new knowledge with the previous knowledge (prior learning) is related to experiences with objects and events, and the learner must be encouraged to learn meaningfully.

ML depends on the quality of the materials and knowledge resources, an appropriate didactic instruction, the learner motivation, and the learning environment (Novak, 1998). The theory of meaningful learning has been essentially applicable to individuals, but its ultimate constructivist interpretations and applications embrace the possible empowerment of each learner and the interrelationships between learners as members of teams and groups.

Ausubel's theory of learning (Ausubel, Novak, and Hanesian, 1978; Novak, 2010) claims that new concepts to be learned can be incorporated into more inclusive concepts or ideas in a hierarchical structure. Meaningful learning results when the learner chooses to relate new information to ideas the learner already knows, and the more inclusive

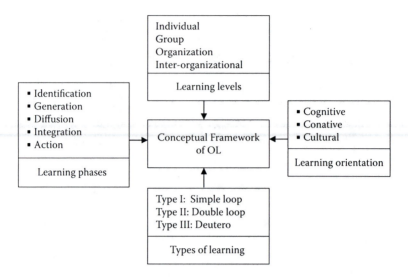

FIGURE 13.1

Conceptual framework of organizational learning. (Adapted from Pawlowsky, P. 2001. The treatment of organizational learning in management science. In *Handbook of Organizational Learning and Knowledge*, eds. M. Dierkes, A. Berthoin-Antal, J. Child, and I. Nonaka. New York: Oxford University Press.)

concepts or ideas can subsume or anchor new ideas. Advance organizers can be verbal phrases or a graphic and, in any case, the advance organizer is designed to provide what cognitive psychologists call the "mental scaffolding" to learn new information. As we can observe in Figure 13.1, cognitive learning may be representational (acquisition of concept names or labels), concept learning (acquisition of concept meanings), and propositional learning (acquisition of propositional meanings). All of these kinds of cognitive learning may be used or shown in a Concept Map (Novak, 1998, p. 41).

ML occurs at individual levels and also at organizational levels throughout the integration and through sharing of the *minds* (cognitive structures and mental models) of the organizational members (Wilkens, Menzel, and Pawlowsky, 2004). But the empirical evidence obtained by an ample research at individual level is still scarce in the *black box* of the organizations and their complex environments, where *learn to learn* seems be a more complex activity. In an organization, agents (learners) are members of an interacted system and the environment can best be characterized as *enacted*. Weick (1969) created the phrase "enacted environment," which means that "the human being creates the environment, to which the system then adapts. The human actor does not react to an environment, he enacts it" (Weick, 1969, p. 64). Subjective construction of meaning is developed on the basis of symbols and language and organizational reality is constructed by interaction of organizational members who develop a joint interpretation. Thus, the key element of knowledge is not the intellectual capacity but the capacity to interact and develop a common understanding and pattern of interpretation in turbulent fields.

Organizational knowledge results from former experiences in the enacted system and leads to organizational images, organizational theories-in-action (Argyris and Schön, 1978; Weick and Bougon, 1986), and organizational interpretation systems or shared mental models (Senge, 1990). From this constructivist perspective, organizational knowledge can be defined as a result of the subjective interpretation of its members and is not understood as an "objective" mental reflection of reality, but essentially as a co-existing and conflicting interpretation of reality that is based on the history of each participating member of a joint interaction system.

Pawlowsky (2001) has developed a conceptual framework for OL based on the common elements of the different approaches since it first appeared in the literature (Cyert and March, 1963). This model identifies the fundamental dimensions of the learning process, in order to analyze the specific actions undertaken and to understand better their origins, their development, and their effects, as shown in Figure 13.1.

The first of these dimensions is the level of the system at which the learning takes place (individual, group, organization, interorganizational). The second dimension is the orientation of the learning undertaken: cognitive, cultural, or conative (or learning through action), similar to the three orientations proposed by the Theory of Meaningful Learning (Ausubel, Novak, and Hanesian, 1978). The third dimension is the type of learning achieved by means of the tool used or the action taken. Because the concept of OL arose as an attempt to incorporate within a theory the efforts made by organizations to survive in increasingly competitive environments, the types of learning described in Pawlowsky's model have a strongly evolutionist character. Thus, the types described refer essentially to the degree of complexity and of self-awareness of the subject in his or her relationship to the environment and with him/her as a learner.

Type I (or "simple loop") learning is conceived as a correction of deviations in the behavior of the organization carried out through "normal" operations within the working of the organization. Type II (or "double loop") learning implies an adaptation to the environment and, therefore, an awareness (and perhaps a modification) of the models assumed by the organization in its relationship with it. Type III learning (or "deutero-learning") refers to a type of analysis in depth of the cognitive and behavioral structures of the organization.

Finally, Pawlowsky distinguishes between the various phases of the process of OL in order to be able to assign to each of these phases the resources and tools adequate for their objectives: identification, generation or creation, diffusion or dissemination, integration, and transformation.

The phase of *identification* consists of locating the information that may be relevant for the learning; the *generation* or *creation* phase refers to the creation of new knowledge; the third phase is the *diffusion* or *dissemination* of the knowledge through the different levels (individual, group, organization) that participate in the process; the fourth phase consists of the *integration* of the knowledge generated and disseminated into the cognitive structures, usually called the knowledge systems of the organization (Pawlowsky, 2001). The fifth and last phase is the *transformation* of the knowledge into action and its effect on the standard conduct of the organization and its enacted environment. In the Theory of Meaningful Learning, the three operational phases include the advance organizer, the presentation of learning task or material, and the phase of strengthening cognitive organization. In the cognitive structure of the learner, it produces a process of assimilation of knowledge (obliterative subsumption, progressive differentiation, integrative reconciliation, or superordinate learning). In sum, ML participates in OL processes, but is not equivalent to it. Its presence may or may not improve the OL, i.e., individuals and a group within the organization can learn significantly determined knowledge, but it does not mean that the organization is learning as well.

The role of socialization processes is very important for disseminating a meaningful organizational learning. Nonaka and Takeuchi (1995) have called externalization the process through which tacit knowledge of individuals within the organization can be made explicit or codified by the organization. In contrast, internalization is the reverse process, identifying how formal rules and procedures and process are captured by the employees. These researchers have chosen the term *socialization* to denote the sharing of tacit knowledge, and the term combination to represent the diffusion of codified knowledge. According to this model, knowledge creation and organizational learning take a path of socialization, externalization, combination, internalization, socialization, externalization, combination … etc., in an infinite spiral.

With these theoretical concerns in mind, we turn next to their practical application.

CONCEPT MAPS FOR KNOWLEDGE TRANSFERENCE

In this section, we outline our theoretical considerations for using Novakian Concept Mapping to advance the goals of OL.

Mapping Tacit Knowledge

From the perspective of knowledge management, Concept Mapping can be a useful tool for acquiring and representing tacit knowledge. Although the graphical display of tacit knowledge has been in use for centuries as a method of expressing individual thinking, Concept Maps (Cmaps) enable the user to share his or her knowledge, to collaborate with others, and to show the logical connection between concepts (Huff, 1990). Although there are other tools for elaborating ideas and cognitive maps, Cmaps enable describing objects and explaining events, formalizing and displaying tacit knowledge, as well as to transfer it with the help of pictures, movie clips, voice, text, structure, or other forms of description to explicit knowledge. Cmaps facilitate sense-making and meaningful learning on the part of individuals who make or use Concept Maps because they are constructed to reflect organization of the declarative memory system.

Knowledge Transfer

Knowledge transfer mechanisms between individuals and an organization are at the heart of organizational learning; they represent the process through which individual learning becomes embedded in an organizations memory and structure (Kim, 1993; Busch, Richards, and Dampney, 2001). Although technical expertise is of great importance in organizations that compete in technological and scientific contexts, knowledge about how to transfer and improve the appropriability of technological knowledge and expertise inside the organization is not widespread (Teece, 2000).

Moreover, the knowledge to be transferred in a firm is not only about technical specifications of a product, or not simply technological. Knowledge about competitors, customers, and suppliers is also part of the mix and is an important tacit dimension that is difficult to transfer without the transfer of individuals (Teece, 2000). In this sense, knowledge is often widely diffused in an organization. Some of it may lie in R&D laboratories, some on the factory floor, and some resides in the executive or manager's knowledge. Sometimes what is critical is the capacity to weave it all together, and, in many circumstances, organizations contract knowledge brokers and other specialists in technology transfer for translating knowledge within the firm.

A Concept Map can be seen as a tool for process of knowledge transfer, i.e., an instrument that allows one or more persons to collaborate synchronously or at different times in the process of representing explicitly their understanding of a domain of knowledge. Related to this process, Vygotsky (1978) stressed the importance of social exchange in learning, especially with learners who are at about the same zone of proximal development (ZPD); that is, learners who are at about the same level of cognitive development (same ZPD) on a given topic will enhance each other's learning if they engage in active exchange of ideas.

From the perspective of the knowledge transfer, we consider that it also occurs even in those cases of individuals with different ZPD or who have a gap in a determined knowledge area. For example, a Concept Map can be useful to explain the expert ideas on a specific topic or question to other persons who do not have this expert knowledge. According to Henao-Cálad and Arango-Fonnegra (2007, p. 44):

> ... if experts are involved, the concept maps can continue representing the problem as the profile of the problem becomes clearer. If the concept maps are stored, they constitute part of the collective history and they serve as a starting point for the methodological memory of the topic.

We agree with these authors considering that Cmaps constitute a strategic instrument for knowledge preservation and transfer and KM. However, the use of Cmaps is a necessary, but not sufficient, condition for the success of organizational learning. The existence of a proper environment and the individuals' motivation are key premises for the meaningful learning and organizational learning as well. Motivation is intrinsically related with the concept of the alignment between the staff and the business strategy (Teece, 2000). Also alignment implies that the firm must have the potential to learn, unlearn, or relearn based on its past behaviors. In this sense, the process of learning involves both individual and organizational levels at the creation and manipulation of this tension between constancy and change. Hedberg (1981, p. 6) states it this way:

> Although organizational learning occurs through individuals, it would be a mistake to conclude that organizational learning is nothing but the cumulative result of their members learning. Organizations do not have brains, but they have cognitive systems and memories. As individuals develop their personalities, personal habits, and beliefs over time, organizations develop world views and ideologies. Members come and go, and leadership changes, but organizations' memories preserve certain behaviours, mental maps, norms, and values over time.

The following section details an empirical case study involving the use of Cmaps with the aim of investigating the links between knowledge transfer and organizational learning in alignment with the business strategy in a technological firm.

COMPLEX KNOWLEDGE TRANSFER: A CASE STUDY

The Context

The case study presented here deals with a company specialized in design, development, production, marketing, and sales of implants and instruments for orthopedic and trauma surgery. This firm is a leader in the Spanish orthopedic industry and exports worldwide to more than 40 countries competing in all continents. Its products include implants made from advanced biomaterials with osteoinductive and resorbable properties like implants and gene-activated matrix, designed to support the regenerative activity of the stem cells.

Since the date of its establishment in 1993, this firm followed a precise innovation policy with the clear goal of introducing to the market its own innovating products in the traumatology and orthopedic surgery areas. Today it is a medium-size firm with 40 employees, totally consolidated in its sector with a diversity of products (surgery instruments, cervical and lumbar cages of porous material, prosthesis) and positioned in the highest part of a market dominated by multinational companies.

The Problem

In 1997, the firm was developing spinal column implants, which is the sector with highest growth potential in the market for surgical implants. These implants are considered to be high range because they are highly complex and destined for a type of surgery treating pathologies of the spinal column of recent application. To pursue this business opportunity, the firm increased the size of the R&D and the sales departments, hiring three new representatives for the Spanish market and maintaining the same resources for the international market (e.g., a sales manager with wide experience in the market for spinal implants). By mid-2000, the firm had a product ready for market—an implant considered to be the gold standard of spinal surgery and necessary for the future development of a line of products for this type of intervention.

Two and a half years later, the sales results of this product in Spain were well below expectations, whereas international sales were growing as planned. Multiple possible causes of this problem were analyzed, concluding that the main reason lay in the slowness of local sales staff in acquiring the necessary knowledge about the product to face the market. Complicating matters, three sales representatives were hired by other firms, and were replaced by new representatives with no experience in the sector.

An efficient appropriability of knowledge was extremely important in the commercialization process, so much so that it can be defined as one of a firm's principal strategic objectives. Any representative should be able to maintain a dialog with the surgeon in scientific terms, at least with regard to the matters surrounding the application of the implant. In this sense, a large part of the marketing of the sector was dedicated to providing the manufacturer with a certain scientific legitimacy, which must be confirmed by the firm representative to the customer.

The firm was faced with the problem of providing fast training with a complex knowledge package to the sales representatives. New staff had to quickly learn how to deal with information, especially information acquired by staff in the course of their previous years of experience in the organization. The key to the challenge lay in how to transfer this expertise to novice employees (Heijst, Spek, and Kruizinga, 1997).

Methodology and Problem Resolution

The firm decided to join an organizational learning project with the support of a knowledge institute researcher who has experience in using technological tools for KM, particularly in the elaboration and use of Concept Maps. The project objectives were:

- Problem identification and search of possible resolution, i.e., to identify the knowledge gap that caused the problem and locate the specific knowledge capable of plugging this gap.
- Knowledge generation, through elaborating Concept Maps, which corresponded with conceptualization, included research, clarification, and modeling of existent knowledge.
- Knowledge diffusion at the intraorganizational level (i.e., knowledge transference of Concept Maps and their elicited contents).
- Integration of this new knowledge content into the knowledge systems of the organization.
- Transforming the transferred knowledge into organizational conduct, in alignment with the business strategy of the firm.

In this project, Cmaps were used in three of the five phases of the Pawlowsky theoretical framework: generation, diffusion, and transformation. The use of this technique also can be described in terms of the other dimensions in the analytical framework (Pawlowsky, 2001). Related to the learning levels, Cmaps were applied to individuals and groups, since they express the propositional hierarchies realized by the members of an R&D department. The learning was Type II or double loop, because it involved adaptation of the organization to the specific characteristics of the spinal implants sector, which is more complex than the other sectors of the

TABLE 13.1

Methodology and Process of Application of Cmaps

Tool	Level of Learning	Type of Learning	Orientation of Learning	Phase of Learning
Concept Maps	Individual/ group	Type II or double loop	Cognitive/cultural	Generation/diffusion/ transformation

market for implants for orthopedic surgery and traumatology. The organization also had to commit itself to modifying its usual way of operating in order to undertake this adaptation. Finally, the orientation of the learning was predominantly cognitive, but the cultural learning involved in the use of a tool, such as Cmaps, was taken into account. Table 13.1 summarizes this description of the Concept Maps within the theoretical framework of organizational learning.

Throughout the exposition of the results of the first two phases of the project (identification and generation of knowledge), we used concepts taken directly from the Theory of Meaningful Learning. In the phase of identification, several important obstacles were identified: the decontextualization of the learning with respect to the salespersons ZPD (Vygostky, 1978), the lack in the previous knowledge and expertise level of the learners (with a very heterogeneous background), and limitations of materials and training. Normally, the training of sales staff was limited, on the one hand, to the reading of a series of basic medical manuals orientated to doctors or nurses and, on the other, of a biomechanical description of the product provided by the R&D department. Salespersons were overwhelmed by concepts of pathological anatomy or biomechanics, and it was difficult to provide them with a clear knowledge related to the product they must sell. However, available schemes were elaborated by the R&D department employees and while they considered them clear and appropriate, they were not understood by salespersons. One specific error in the schemes was a lack in the concepts identification of the product and a deficient conceptual propositional hierarchy.

These conditions did not favor a meaningful learning and hindered the construction of new meanings. The errors arose from the so-called limited or inappropriate propositional hierarchies (LIPHS); as the meaning of every concept is constructed by means of the series of propositions in which it is immersed. A learning based on LIPHS will lead to the erroneous incorporation of new meanings or will paralyze their effective incorporation (Gonzalez, Morón, and Novak, 2001). In addition to the technological support of knowledge management, employees received training with regard to the exchange of knowledge, especially for the diffusion of best practices. The company concentrated very much on product training and best practice seminars to facilitate knowledge creation and its distribution.

The first step was to identify the experts whose knowledge could solve the detected gaps. The experts were identified by qualitative methods, given the small size of the firm. The method of nomination was used, based on the existence and acceptance of a qualified opinion. In this case, the technical director, who was responsible to the general management of the R&D and manufacturing departments, was chosen as the possessor of a qualified opinion, because he had held this post since the foundation of the firm and had been in charge of the R&D department of another multinational firm in the same sector for four years. Another expert chosen was the R&D engineer in charge of the development of products for the spinal column. This expert operated under several disciplines, but all of them were product-oriented because his work is the development of the product.

We conjectured that the propositional hierarchy that could be provided by the representation of the expert's knowledge was the resource that would make clear the deficiency detected in the sales department, if the knowledge generation phase could be carried out correctly. Concept Mapping formed the basis for generation.

The first Cmap made was for cervical plates. In this map, it was decided to start from a concept that would include a range of implants because the firm intended to launch at least two products of different characteristics within this range. The Cmap, shown in Figure 13.2, explains the general attributes of cervical plates related to those of the most usual types of this range of implants. The Cmap was elaborated considering a set of focal questions to delimit the problem:

What is cervical plate?
What is cervical plate for?
In which context is cervical plate used?

What are the principal technical characteristics of a cervical plate?
How does a cervical plate function?

The next Cmap was that of the tic-tac lumbar plate. This product was the most innovative, being based on a new surgical approach to a set of pathologies. We labeled the conceptual peak Tic-Tac Plate Project instead of the specific product, in order to develop in greater depth links between surgery and biomechanical aspects whose innovation would be fundamental in achieving the initial acceptance of the product by the market. Figure 13.3 presents this Concept Map.

Finally, we created the Cmap of the POROBloc intersomatic boxes, a specific product, whose distinguishing characteristic is the use of a new material. The Cmap in Figure 13.4 illustrates the general characteristics of the product, those of the new material, and the functional advantages of this new material over those normally used.

The remaining phases of the project were the elaboration and diffusion of an instruction package for the commercial department of the three products, followed by the integration within the sales department's usual training procedure before the launch of a new product. Last was the transformation of the knowledge into action, which can be evaluated and measured by reviewing the Cmaps in the light of the learner's commercial experience with the new product, adding new concepts or modifying the existing hierarchies. Once the use of Concept Maps had been incorporated into the normal working of the organization, consideration could be given to making new Cmaps, more focused on marketing strategies, to support the transformation of knowledge into action.

When the salespersons were asked to evaluate their experience with regard to Concept Maps, they stated that Concept Maps were an excellent tool for eliciting a clear representation of knowledge. Also, both salespersons and R&D employees value positively the self-explanatory structure of the Cmaps. They also considered that the mapping process provided them the opportunity to be conscious of their latent ideas and discover hidden relationships about their expertise, fostering the staff's effectiveness. Deepening understanding and possibilities to develop new products or to plan new research were indicated as other important benefits of Cmaps by the R&D department employees.

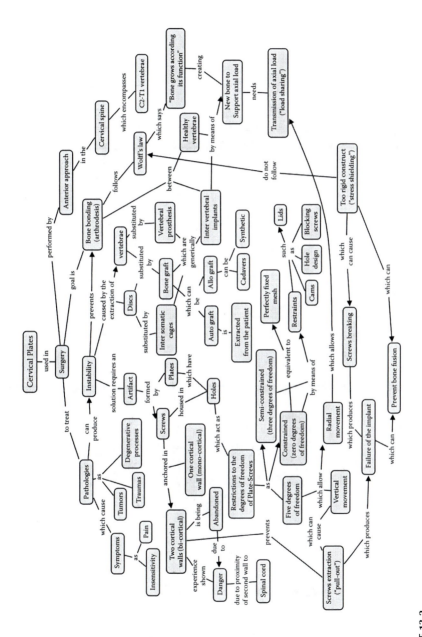

FIGURE 13.2
Concept Map of cervical plates.

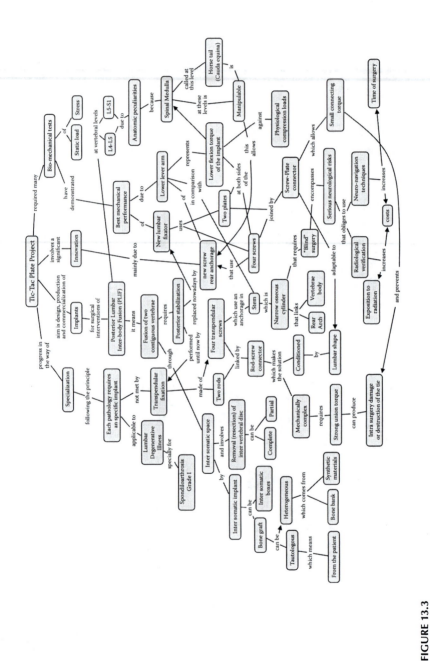

FIGURE 13.3

Concept Map for the development of a Tic-Tac Plate Project.

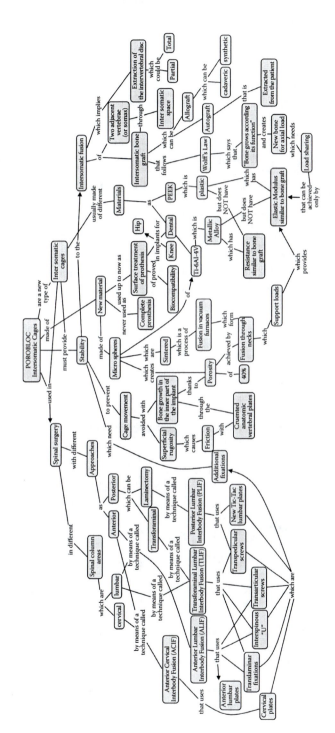

FIGURE 13.4

Concept Map for the development of POROBloc intersomatic cages.

CONCLUSION

We believe that Cmaps are potent and low cost tools for improving the transference of knowledge process and the organizational learning integrating both content and context learning aspects. CmapTools software provide excellent facilities for knowledge sharing and acquiring processes in a complex technological environment. Experts can make their knowledge available to other employees, reinforcing the commitment in alignment with the business strategies of the firm. In this case study, it was observed that both salespersons and R&D experts acquired new knowledge meaningfully. For this reason, we consider that the Theory of Meaningful Learning and the use of tools, such Concept Maps, can make important contributions to investigate and to improve the organizational learning and the knowledge management in business organizations.

REFERENCES

Argyris, C. 1982. *Reasoning, learning, and action: Individual and organizational.* San Francisco: Jossey-Bass.

Argyris, C. 1992. *On organizational learning.* Boston: Blackwell Publishing.

Argyris, C. and D. A. Schon. 1978. *Organizational learning: A theory of action perspective.* Reading, MA: Addison-Wesley.

Argyris, C. and D. A. Schon. 1996. *Organizational learning: Vol. 2. Theory, method, and practice.* Reading, MA: Addison-Wesley.

Ausubel, D. P., J. D. Novak, and H. Hanesian. 1978. *Educational psychology: A cognitive view.* New York: Rinehart and Winston.

Busch, P., D. Richards, and C. Dampney. 2001. Visual mapping of articulable tacit knowledge. Proceedings of the 2001 Asia-Pacific Symposium on Information Visualization, Vol. 9, Sydney, Australia, 37–47 .

Cañas, A. J., G. Hill, and R. Carff, et al. 2004. CmapTools: A knowledge modeling and sharing environment. In *Concept maps: Theory, methodology, technology, Proceedings of the First International Conference on Concept Mapping,* eds. A. Cañas,, J. Novak, and F. González. Pamplona, Spain.

Cyert, R. M. and J. G. March. 1963. *A behavioral theory of the firm.* Englewood Cliffs, NJ: Prentice-Hall.

Cook, S. D. N. and J. S. Brown. 1999. Bridging epistemologies: The generative dance between organizational knowledge and organizational knowing. *Organization Science* 10 (4): 381–400.

Daft, R. L. and G. P. Huber. 1987. How organizations learn: A communication framework. *Research in the Sociology of Organizations* 5: 1–36.

Davenport, T. H. and L. Prusak. 1998. *Working knowledge*. Cambridge, MA: Harvard Business School Press.

Dierkes, M., A. B. Antal, J. Child, and I. Nonaka. 2001. *Handbook of organizational learning and knowledge*. Oxford, U.K.: Oxford University Press.

Dodgson, M. 1993. Organizational learning: A review of some literatures. *Organization Studies* 14 (3): 375–394.

Drucker, P. F. 1993. *Post-capitalist society*. London: Butterworth Heinemann.

Drucker, P.F. 1999. *Management challenges for the 21st century*. New York: Harper Business.

Fiol, C. M. and M. A. Lyles. 1985. Organizational learning. *Academy of Management Review* 10 (4): 803–813.

Fourie, L. C. H. 2005. *Computer-based concept mapping tools in business*. Proceedings of San Diego International Systems Conference, San Diego, State University, California, July 8–10.

González, F. M., C. Morón, and J. D. Novak. 2001. *Errores conceptuales. Diagnosis, tratamiento y reflexiones*. Pamplona, Spain: Eunate.

Grant, R. M. 1996. Prospering in dynamically competitive environments: Organizational capability as knowledge integration. *Organizational Science* 7 (4): 375–387.

Heijst, G., R. Spek, and E. Kruizinga. 1997. Corporate memories as a tool for knowledge management. *Expert Systems with Applications* 13: 41–54.

Henao-Cálad, M. and M. P. Arango-Fonnegra. 2007. Concept maps as a strategy to convert knowledge in knowledge management. VINE: *The Journal of Information and Knowledge Management Systems*. 37 (1): 41–48.

Herdberg, B. 1981. *How organizations learn and unlearn: Handbook of organizational design*. Oxford, U.K.: Oxford University Press

Huff, A. S. 1990. *Mapping strategic thought*. New York: John Wiley & Sons.

Hung, R. Y., B. Y. Lien, and G. N. McLean. 2009. Knowledge management initiatives, organizational process alignment, social capital, and dynamic capabilities. *Advances in Developing Human Resources* 11 (3): 320–333.

Johannessen, J., A. B. Olson, and J. Olaisen. 1999. Aspects of innovation theory based on knowledge-management. *International Journal of Information Management* 19 (2): 121–139.

Kim, D. H. 1993. The link between individual and organizational learning. *Sloan Management Review* Fall, 37–50.

Kolb, D. A. 1984. *Experiential learning: Experience as the source of learning and development*. Englewood Cliffs, NJ: Prentice-Hall.

Lähteenmäki, S., J. Toivonen, and M. Mattila. 2002. Critical aspects of organizational learning research and proposals for its measurement. *British Journal of Management Volume* 12 (2): 113–129.

Lee, S., J. F. Courtney, and R. M. O'Keefe. 1992. A system for organizational learning using cognitive maps. *OMEGA International Journal of Management Science* 20 (1): 23–36.

Leonard-Barton, D. 1995. *Wellsprings of knowledge—Building and sustaining sources of innovation*. Cambridge, MA: Harvard Business School Press.

Lyles, M.A. and C. R. Schwenk. 1992. Top management, strategy and organizational knowledge structures. *Journal of Management Studies* 29 (2): 155–174.

Nonaka, I. 1991. The knowledge creating company. *Harvard Business Review* 69 (6 Nov-Dec): 96–104.

Nonaka, I. 1994. A dynamic theory of organizational knowledge creation. *Organization Science* 5 (1) :14–37.

Nonaka, I., H. Takeuchi, and K. Umemoto. 1996. A theory of organizational knowledge creation. *International Journal of Technology Management* 11 (7/8): 833–845.

Nonaka, I., P. Reinmoeller, and D. Senoo. 1998. The art of knowledge systems to capitalize on market knowledge. *European Management Journal* 16 (6): 673–684.

Nonaka, I., G. Von Krogh, and S. Voelpel. 2006. Organizational knowledge creation theory: Evolutionary paths and future advances. *Organization Studies* 27 (8): 1179–1208.

Novak, J. D. 2010. *Learning, creating, and using knowledge: Concept maps as facilitative tools in schools and corporations.* Mahwah, NJ: Lawrence Erlbaum Associates.

Pawlowsky, P. 2001. The treatment of organizational learning in management science. In *Handbook of Organizational Learning and Knowledge*, eds. M. Dierkes, A. Berthoin-Antal, J. Child, and I. Nonaka. New York: Oxford University Press.

de los Reyes, E. and D. Barberá. 2004. Los mapas conceptuales como herramienta de aprendizaje organizacional: Aproximación a un Marco Teórico y presentación de Resultados Parciales de un Proyecto. In *Concept maps: Theory, methodology, technology, Proceedings of the First International Conference on Concept Mapping*, eds. A. Cañas, J. Novak, and F. González. Pamplona, Spain.

Senge, P. M. 1990. *The fifth discipline.* New York: Doubleday.

Slater, S. F. and J. C. Narver. 1995. Market orientation and the learning organization. *Journal of Marketing* 59 (3): 63–74.

Sutherland, S. and S. Katz. 2005. Concept mapping methodology: A catalyst for organizational learning. *Evaluation and Program Planning* 28 (3): 257–269.

Teece, D. 1986. Profiting from technological innovation. Organizational arrangements for regimes of rapid technological progress. *Research Policy* 15 (6): 285–305.

Teece, D. 2000. Strategies for managing knowledge assets: The role of firm structure and industrial context. *Long Range Planning* 33: 35–54.

Teece, D. J., G. Pisano, and A. Shuen. 1997. Dynamic capabilities and strategic management. *Strategic Management Journal* 18: 509–533.

Templeton, G. F., B. R. Lewis, and C. A. Snyder. 2002. Development of a measure for the organizational learning construct. *Journal of Management Information Systems* 19 (2): 175–218.

Vygotsky, L. 1978. *Mind in society: The development of higher psychological processes.* Cambridge, MA: Harvard University Press.

Weick, K. E. 1969. *The social psychology of organizing.* Reading, MA: Addison-Wesley.

Weick, K. E. and M. G. Bougon. 1986. Organizations as cognitive maps: Charting ways to success and failure. In *The thinking organization: Dynamics of organizational cognition*, eds. H. Sims and D. Gioia. San Francisco: Jossey-Bass, pp. 103–135.

Wilkens, U., D. Menzel, and P. Pawlowsky. 2004. Inside the black-box: Analysing the generation of core competencies and dynamic capabilities by exploring collective minds. An organisational learning perspective. *Management Revue* 15 (1): 8–26.

Section III

Pushing the Boundaries

14

Conceptual Mapping as a First Step in Data Modeling

Hector Gómez-Gauchía and Ron McFadyen

CONTENTS

INTRODUCTION

Almost all database teaching approaches are based on the assumption that students or designers have a clear idea of the domain, its concepts, and the needed functionality. In our experience, we discovered this is a huge assumption that fails frequently. In professional database development database design is performed using artifacts produced from requirements analysis, but it is very common to find out that specifications are not clear and, sometimes, just do not exist at all. Domain experts may be very vague when they describe the domain and do not use the proper terms of database modeling, like *entities* or *attributes*. In these situations, we found it very useful to use a tool that helps the conceptualization process. This is the process of describing explicitly those elements that are part of the domain, such as concepts and the relationships that exist amongst them.

After teaching database design courses for several years, we found a similar problem. It is difficult for students to understand the conceptualization process that is needed to obtain a correct and complete data model of the database, such as an Extended Entity/Relationship (EER) model, object model, or a Unified Modeling Language (UML) diagram. We summarize the problem from two perspectives. First, it is a complex task for a domain expert to explain the details of a domain to the database designer. Second, it is a complex task, too, for database designers to understand an unknown domain. The students, as designers, see the domain as a fuzzy cloud of ideas. They are confused about many topics, including:

- What constitutes a concept and what is a relationship among concepts.
- Understanding the semantics of relationships among concepts.
- Distinguishing concepts, attributes, and values.
- How to map domain terms into the EER diagram elements (entities, relationships, keys, cardinality, and participation).
- Finding which relationships are needed for specific domain functionality.
- How to navigate through the concepts and relationships of the domain.

As a result, the EER diagrams they produce are often ambiguous, incomplete, or just incorrect. They do not reflect the domain and the functionality needed by the user.

This situation arises for two specific reasons. First, natural language is ambiguous, and there is a tendency to use generic verbs and terms when the domain is not well understood. A direct consequence is that it is very difficult to be precise with these generic and abstract concepts and verbs. Second, students generate incorrect data models because they forget the purpose of the database, due to overwhelming domain details, i.e., students cannot "see the forest for the trees."

The proposed solution is to modify the database design process to include new phases with a tool that helps to reason about the domain. We call this the concept formation process or conceptualization.

In the next section, we review several theories that may serve for purpose. We chose Concept Maps as the more adequate tool because they address both of the reasons underlying confusion. In Concept Mapping, there are no restrictions on semantics. Concepts and linking phrases can state anything, and their abstraction and precision is imposed by their creator. Concept Maps give a big picture of the whole domain. This is highly important in database development because the data model is very different depending on the purpose, i.e., functionality affects the data structure and content we need in our project. In the section following, we explain our proposed Concept Map-building process that leads to the creation of an EER model. In the final section, we describe a case study, the teaching strategy applied to it, the evaluation, and the results.

THEORIES TO IMPROVE CONCEPT FORMATION: BRIEF SURVEY

In looking to overcome the challenges for database design, our goal was to find a theory that facilitates conceptualization. This relates to talking, thinking, and reasoning with the domain elements, and includes representing the elements explicitly. We studied theories that could fit our conceptualization process.

First, we looked at affinity diagrams. The affinity diagram, also known as the "KJ method" (Ohiwa, 2003), was developed to help discover meaningful groups of ideas within a raw list of brainstormed ideas. When creating an affinity diagram, it is important to let the groupings emerge naturally into affinity sets. The original KJ method, heavily used in Japan, uses separate cards with one idea each to be grouped by hand. Commercial software is available that implements this method. The goal of this theory was not appropriate for our purpose because its goal is to find new ideas, and our goal is to clarify domain concepts and relationships that we already have.

Next, we explored cognitive maps, which represent the mental process that acquires, codes, stores, recalls, and decodes information. These can show the shape of a system and its dynamic evolution over time. The technique was founded on the personal construct theory introduced by George Kelly (1955) and fuzzy cognitive maps (Kosko, 1986). Cognitive maps use diagrams with loops to represent the topics that influence the domain over time. This technique could have fit our goal, but it is complex to learn, has many features that we do not need, such as domain evolution over time (whereas a database design is more like a snapshot in time of the domain), and would have added an additional load to our students.

Next, we considered mind maps (Buzan and Buzan, 2000). In some respects, mind maps are related to Concept Maps, but their goal and their graphical structure are different. Mind maps are graphical representations of knowledge that often take on a star shape with branches and subbranches to indicate relationships between concepts. They describe a general view of a topic and its related ideas, e.g., the main ideas of a talk are shown as lines radiating from the middle of the graph, and from each main idea more lines radiate outward for its component ideas. Mind maps can express ideas broader than individual concepts, working at a high level of abstraction. Mind maps do not use labels to connect concepts. Rather, a line that represents an idea connects to another line (i.e., idea) without a description of the relationship between those two ideas. Mind maps may include a lot of icons to help to clarify the topic and to provoke visual emphasis, but the exclusion of linking phrases rendered mind maps inappropriate for our goals.

Next, we looked at Vee diagrams (Gowin, 1987). Vee diagrams are used as a problem-solving tool. They involve two aspects represented in the shape of the letter V. On the left side of the Vee is the conceptual description and on the right side the methodological steps for solving the problem. Vee diagrams do not have any specific representation of the conceptualization itself. We could not use Vee diagrams for our purpose because they are precisely oriented to solve problems using activities, and we needed a static view to relate concepts, i.e., to create a map of a domain.

Finally, we examined Concept Maps (Novak and Gowin, 1984). We determined that Concept Maps were appropriate for our goal. Concept Maps are very flexible and have few constraints. They allow conceptualization at different levels of abstraction, including a low level of basic elements, such as a simple concept, and a very high level, such as a complex concept described by a phrase. Concept Maps may be built incrementally, similarly to the database design. Concept Maps are simple to learn and use, and new, research-based refinements to the basic guidelines for developing Concept Maps have been recommended (cf., Åhlberg, 2004). Most importantly,

Concept Maps have been shown to be appropriate for knowledge conceptualization in an ontology environment (Gómez-Gauchía, Díaz-Agudo, and González-Calero, 2004). This use was closest to our goals.

We describe in the next section how Concept Maps help to deal with the problems of database design mentioned in the first section, i.e., the ambiguity of natural language and the overwhelming amount of detail.

EXTENDING THE DATABASE DESIGN PROCESS

When specifications for a database are not clear or just do not exist at all, we have found Concept Maps very useful for supporting the design process. The Concept Map is created through interactions with domain experts, and is a visual representation that makes explicit the concepts and their relationships.

Based on our experience with students, we have defined four phases in the database design process. We do not describe the last phase in this chapter because we follow the standard procedure that can be found in any database book (cf., Elmasri and Navathe, 2007). We describe the phases and the obtained products:

> Phase 1: Concept Map building process for conceptualization of database design
> Phase 2: Constraining the Concept Map toward the EER diagram
> Phase 3: Creating the EER diagram
> Phase 4: Transformation of the EER diagram into the relational model.

Figure 14.1 shows these phases in order.

Phase 1: Concept Map Building Process for Conceptualization of Database Design

We have adapted the guidelines of building Concept Maps to database design. To illustrate the guidelines, we use an example domain about clients having investments, clients buying products and services, and clients having job positions. The building process is a refinement cycle with five steps. In step 1, we

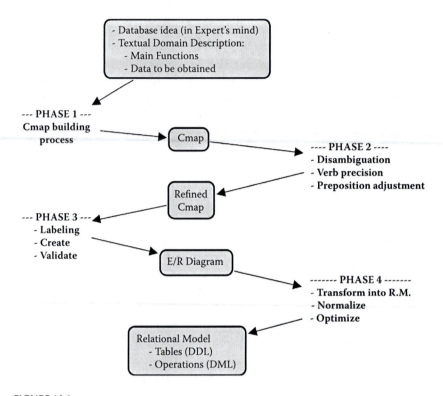

FIGURE 14.1
Extended database design process.

build a list of concepts that are known in the domain we are modeling. A concept refers to anything that is nameable. No relationships are accounted for in this step. The domain is seen only from the point of view of our database purpose. For step 2, we select the most general concepts from the list as starting points to build the Concept Map. These concepts are added to the Concept Map and then crossed off the list. We have in our example *client* and *investments*.

In step 3, we group (using the rest of the concept list) those concepts that are related by some meaningful criteria and create (if necessary) a more abstract concept that describes these criteria. We also add these concepts to the Concept Map and cross them off the list, and continue to connect the more abstract concept to the others in a hierarchical manner with directed lines with a label (linking phrase). In this way we create relationships. For example, the expert talks about the treatment of *address* and *phone.* We may decide to group these two concepts using the "has" label, as properties of a more abstract concept named *client.*

In step 4, we create relationships connecting the rest of the chosen concepts with directed lines and labels. Performing this step, we try to answer the question: "What relates the concepts of the previous steps?" The linking phrase written on the directed line. In our example, this is demonstrated in *"client has investments."*

In step 5, we finish the process by applying step 4 to the remaining concepts in the list, one by one. If there is a concept left without any relationship to the others, it will be treated in step 6. It may be deleted or connected to its missing linking phrase.

Finally, in step 6, we verify and validate the Concept Map with domain experts or documents. It may be necessary to modify some of the Concept Map parts already built and go back to previous steps.

Normally, in this phase, the obtained Concept Map, shown in Figure 14.2, has several drawbacks, which are treated in the next phase.

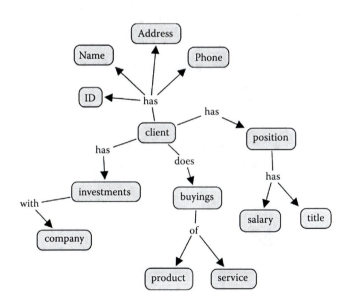

FIGURE 14.2
Cmap example.

Phase 2: Refining the Concept Map toward the EER Diagram

The goal of this phase is to refine the linking phrases in the Concept Map to facilitate a transformation to an EER diagram. The Concept Map is an expression in the natural language of the system designers and domain experts. Two Concept Maps for the same problem, but expressed in different languages, may be quite different. For example, in Spanish, the subject of a phrase is not mandatory, in English it is. Due to this difference, in Spanish, there is an ambiguity that, combined with the use of generic verbs, makes it difficult to model a phrase. To avoid such ambiguities, we define guidelines for our transformation process. When we worked with students in English and Spanish, we analyzed the kind of language they used and defined appropriate transformations, which we applied to the Concept Map of Figure 14.2 to obtain the Concept Map of Figure 14.3. This five-step process is described next.

Step 1 is "disambiguation." If the same term appears more than once in the Concept Map, it must be used with the same meaning. As a corollary, different terms must have different meanings. In step 2, term precision, we expel all generic verbs, such as "to have," "to be," "to do," and "to get." Better Concept Maps are produced when linking phrases are more accurate (Kharatmal and Nagarjuna, 2006). If we cannot expel all of them, we apply the next guideline.

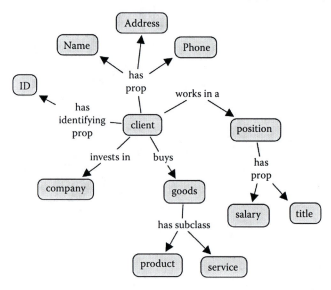

FIGURE 14.3
Refined Concept Map example.

TABLE 14.1

Linking Phrases and Their Meanings

Linking Phrase	Means a Concept That:
has-part	is a physical component (aggregation)
has-subclass	is a subtype (specialization)
has-value	acts as a possible value, a concept that expresses an example (example)
has-property	is a characteristic or descriptive property of another concept (attribute)
has-identifying-property	serves to uniquely identify instances of another concept (key attribute)
has-derived-property	can be derived from other characteristics (derived attribute)
has-composite-property	is a composition of other property characteristics (composite attribute)
has-values-in	represents the set of valid values for a property characteristic (domain)
has-category-superclass	represents a subset of other supertypes (category)

We transform generic verbs into precise action verbs, or transform them, if possible, into linking phrases that map to elements of the EER model. These are shown in Table 14.1. The proper choice of linking phrases makes the Concept Map more precise and facilitates the transformation to a data model (McFadyen, 2008; Sien and Carrington, 2007; Xiao, 2007).

Step 4 is "transform prepositions." Prepositions that appear alone as linking phrases are transformed into phrasal verbs. In step 5, "transform two relationships into one," we look for any prepositions that appear alone as a linking phrase. Where the preposition may be part of the previous linking phrase, we revise it accordingly. For step 5, "validate the refined map," the Concept Map is validated with the aid of domain experts.

Figure 14.3 shows these guidelines applied to the Concept Map of Figure 14.2. It is a simple example due to space constraints, but several relevant transformations are present. In Figure 14.2, the generic verb "has" refers to several different actions: *has-property* in "client has name," *has-identifying-property* in "client has id," *invests* in "client has investments," and *works-in-a* in "client has position." The preposition *of* appearing in "buyings of product" is more precisely stated as "goods has-subclass product." The preposition appearing alone in the linking phrase "client has investments *with* company" refers to the previous linking phrase. It collapsed into *invests-in* following the last guideline.

Phase 3: Creating the EER Diagram from the Refined Concept Map

In this phase, knowledge sources are the refined Concept Map and specifications of the textual domain descriptions, if they exist. Table 14.2 shows tasks (1, 2, and 3) in this phase and knowledge involved in the tasks.

The tasks are as follows. First, element classification determines the mapping between the Concept Map and the EER diagram. A summary of mappings is given in Table 14.2. When doing this, we label the elements of the Concept Map with names of the EER elements, including relationship cardinality and participation or existence. We obtain a labeled Concept Map. Next, we build the preliminary EER diagram following the meanings of the labels of the labeled Concept Map. Finally, we verify the EER diagram with the textual domain descriptions and the experts. We check to determine if something is missing, incorrect, or useless. In

TABLE 14.2

Creating the EER Diagram: Tasks and Knowledge

Task 1. Classify Elements: Put These EER Labels to Refined Cmap Elements	Using These Elements of Refined Cmap
Entity, attribute, value .... (depending on linking phrases)	Concepts
Relationships	Linking phrase Special verbs:
Attribute.. and an entity for the part (if it has another parts)	*...has-part*
Is-a relationship	*...has-subclass*
Category relationship	*...has-category-superclass*
Value (no mapping in EER)	*...has-value*
Attribute or entity..	*...has-property*
Task 2. Build Preliminary EER Diagram	**Using Labeled Cmap**
Task 3. Verify the EER Elements and Add These Specific EER Elements	**Using Documents and Experts to Verify These Aspects**
Add Constraints:	Domain
Entity:	Purpose:
• Primary keys	• General Functions
• Weak or Strong	• Queries
Relationship:	• Semantic Assertions
• Participation	
• Cardinality	

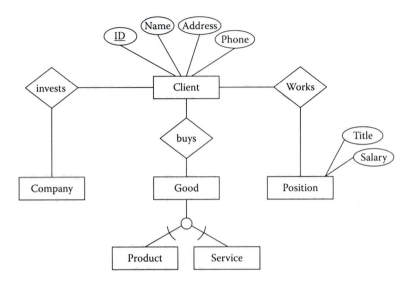

FIGURE 14.4
EER derived from the refined Concept Map.

this step, we add missing elements that are EER specific, such as weak entities and identifying relationships. This is done applying entity/relationship theory.

We can see in Figure 14.4 the EER diagram derived from the refined Concept Map of Figure 14.3 after performing the tasks of the current phase. Some transformations are affected by the surroundings of a concept, which makes the design decisions difficult.

The solution then is to modify the design according to pure database design theory. Figure 14.5 presents an example of this situation; there are

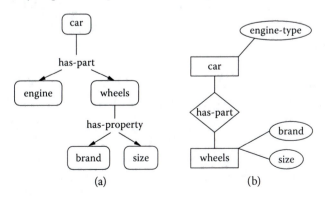

FIGURE 14.5
An example of Concept Map transformation with *has-part*.

two concepts pointed to by a *has-part* linking phrase and another two concepts pointed to by a *has-property* linking phrase. They are transformed in two different ways based on Table 14.2 directions. Because we do not know any more data or attributes for *engine*, we create an attribute *engine-type*. However, we do need an entity *wheels* to accommodate attributes *brand* and *size*. We need the *has-part* relationship to connect *wheels* and *car*.

CASE STUDY: STUDENTS USING THE DATABASE DESIGN PROCESS

For evaluation purposes, we incorporated the design process into a third-year database design course of the computer science degree. There were two classrooms of 80 students each where the students were organized into groups of two.

Teaching Strategy

We designed a strategy to measure the improvements of the students related to those problems described in the introduction section. The teaching strategy for the course is based on the learning by doing paradigm that is guided by exercises with three hours of lectures per week. We spent six hours teaching the basics of Concept Maps. Students worked on small Concept Maps, assisted by the professor. To teach the database design process, three hours were allocated for each phase; students applied the phases to their small Concept Maps. Subsequently, students were asked to follow the design process with a domain of medium size, including the implementation of the model. An additional 18 hours was required to teach the standard theory of the EER model, the Relational Model, the transformation process, and SQL (structured query language).

To induce some introspection, the students were asked to create a *student problem list* to record difficulties they encountered after each of the database design phases. This encouraged students to learn through their problems, instead of forgetting them when engaged in a pure trial and error strategy. The lists were reviewed by the professor to solve the more relevant issues.

Evaluation and Results

To evaluate the impact of our methodology, we compared the students' work with a control group of students from the previous year who did not use Concept Maps. We established an evaluation process centered on four ad hoc techniques to measure our main goals. First, we sought to measure the overall comprehension of the new design process. We compared the problems described in the student problem lists. The new lists had fewer problems overall, and they were less related to conceptualization.

Second, we sought to measure the comprehension of the database domain concepts and needs. We compared the database domain questions asked by the students of the professors during the design process. In general, comparing the current students to the students of the previous year, there were fewer questions overall and the questions were more elaborate, indicating a deeper comprehension of the domain.

Third, we sought to measure the final deviation on the data model. We compared the importance of the changes required to the final relational model implemented. These changes were noted when the experts evaluated the students' models. In this part, the improvement was clear. The models had few errors and none were critical.

Finally, we sought to measure the customer appreciation of the process. We compared student surveys regarding their satisfaction with the process. We considered three aspects: easiness to understand, to follow, and to debug the process. Although several answers were positive, the survey was not conclusive. We suggest the reason for this is because many students are not conscious of their subtle improvements and doubts.

Although it is a subjective evaluation, we summarize the overall improvement of the learning process as positive. The ability of our students to effectively design a database can be measured by considering the problems they encountered and by the correctness of their final product (the database). When we compared the current students to the control group, we observed a reduction in the size and in the nature of the student problem lists and domain questions, and we have seen that fewer and less significant adjustments were required to their final product. Our analysis of student work suggests to us that the worst students showed the greatest improvement in the ability to design databases. Average students showed the next highest level of improvement, and the best of our students also showed some improvements.

The main effects we observed in the learning process were as follows. Students needed only a short period of time to learn the Concept Map tool. Students encountered fewer difficulties related to conceptualization, for reasons mentioned in the introduction. The methodology helps to resolve language ambiguity and gives an incremental structure to the overwhelming amount of domain details. Students discovered their mistakes in earlier stages of the process instead of at the final stages, when they had already implemented the database. This is a very important advantage.

Students also spent less time learning database theory, and it was easier for them to put into practice. As a consequence, students were more motivated to learn. Most importantly, the student designs and implemented databases were more accurate, i.e., closer to the needs originally described.

CONCLUSIONS

After teaching database design for several years, we recognized an important problem. Students are not able to understand easily the conceptualization process needed to obtain a database design, such as an EER diagram. It was a problem that students encountered prior to where the current design process starts.

Our proposed solution is to modify the database design process to include new phases with a tool that assists the concept formation process, i.e., the conceptualization. We defined a specific Concept Map-building process to be used as a previous step to create the EER diagram. We defined a teaching strategy to teach this new database design process, based on the "learning by doing" paradigm. We developed some ad hoc techniques for evaluation purposes.

We presented a case study applied to our students. We described the evaluation techniques and showed objective and subjective results that suggest the new design process is more appropriate for students.

Our proposed database design process formalizes an approach followed by many data analysts. They begin by jotting down in an informal way various ideas and concepts, and connecting them with links and relationships. Initially the analyst is not concerned with distinctions between entity types, attributes, domains, etc. He/she is capturing information that will evolve to attributes, entity types, etc., according to the linking phrases used.

Concept Maps only involve two constructs (concept and linking phrase) and so they are easy to use, and represent a good tool for a novice data modeler. Advanced modeling concepts can be introduced to the student as refinements that help to make his or her thinking more accurate and consistent.

ACKNOWLEDGMENTS

Supported by the Spanish Committee of Education (TIN2009-13692-C03-03), by D.G.U.I. de la Conserjería Educación de Comunidad Madrid, and by Universidad Complutense (research group 910494).

REFERENCES

Åhlberg, M. 2004. Varieties of concept mapping. In *Concept maps: Theory, methodology, technology, Proceedings of the First International Conference on Concept Mapping*, eds. A. Cañas, J. Novak, and F. González. Pamplona, Spain.

Buzan, T. and B. Buzan. 2000. *The mindmap book*. London: BBC Books.

Elmasri, R. and S. R. Navathe. 2007. *Fundamentals of database systems*. 3rd. ed. Reading, MA: Addison-Wesley.

Gómez-Gauchía, H., B. Díaz-Agudo, and P. A. González-Calero. 2004. A pragmatic methodology for conceptualization with two layered knowledge representation: A case study. In *Conceptual structures at work*, eds. H. D. Pfeiffer, K. E. Wolff, and H. S. Delugach. Paper presented at the 12th International Conference on Conceptual Structures (ICCS). Aachen, Germany: Shaker Verlag.

Gowin, B. 1987. *Educating*. Ithaca, NY: Cornell University Press.

Kelly, G. S. 1955. *The psychology of personal constructs*. New York: Ed. Norton.

Kharatmal, M. and B. Nagarjuna. 2006. A proposal to refine concept mapping for effective science learning. In *Concept maps: Theory, methodology, technology, Proceedings of the Second International Conference on Concept Mapping*, eds. A. Cañas and J. Novak.. San Jose, Costa Rica.

Kosko, B. 1986. Fuzzy cognitive maps. *International Journal of Man-Machine Studies* 24, 65–75.

McFadyen, R. 2008. Designing databases with concept maps. In *Concept mapping: Connecting educators*, eds. A. Cañas, P. Reiska, M. Åhlberg, and J. Novak. Proceedings of the Third International Conference on Concept Mapping. Tallinn, Estonia and Helsinki, Finland.

Novak, J. D. and Gowin, D. B. 1984. *Learning how to learn.* New York: Cambridge University Press.

Ohiwa, H. 2003. *KJ editor for creative work support and collaboration.* Proceedings of the First Conference on Creating, Connecting and Collaborating through Computing (C5'03) 2:9. Los Alamitos, CA, IEEE Computer Society Press.

Sien, V. Y. and D. Carrington. 2007. A concepts-first approach to object-oriented modeling. Proceedings of the Third IASTED International Conference: Advances in Computer Science and Technology, 108–113. Phunket, Thailand. ACTA Press.

Xiao, J. 2007. *Applying concept mapping technique to building super- and sub-type relationships in enhanced entity-relationship modeling.* E-proceedings of TILC2007 Conference: Transformations and Technology. Perth, Western Australia.

15

Concept Mapping in Virtual Collaboration Environments

Brian M. Moon, Jeffery T. Hansberger, and Austin Tate

CONTENTS

INTRODUCTION

Crisis response situations require collaboration across many different organizations with different backgrounds, training, procedures, and goals. Indeed, the overwhelming nature of such events calls for a diversified response that addresses the multitude of cascading effects. Compounding the challenges associated with collaboration during crisis situations is the distributed nature of the supporting organizations (in most cases, a single leader or office is not designated to integrate and advance participants from military, government, and nongovernment organizations). Thus, disparate organizations often plan and execute disparate plans. As a result, opportunities for leveraging expertise and resources across organizations are lost, and response to the crisis can appear as chaotic as the crisis itself.

Seeking more effective and efficient means to facilitate crisis response, the U.S. Army Research Laboratory's Human Research and Engineering Directorate (ARL HRED), under the direction of one of this chapter's authors (Hansberger), in 2009 launched a program to design and evaluate a virtual collaboration environment (VCE) to support a crisis response community of interest during crisis action planning activities. The ultimate goal of the program was to demonstrate the potential value in a VCE for addressing the challenges of distributed crisis response planning. More broadly, the program sought to discover implications for any distributed collaborative activity.

Among the design concepts proposed was the use of Concept Mapping in the context of the VCE. Specifically, Concept Mapping was proposed as an approach to enable the planning process, and CmapTools was proposed as one of several software toolkits for integration into the VCE.

This chapter provides an overview of the role of Concept Mapping and CmapTools in the VCE, with an eye toward highlighting the benefits and challenges discovered during a program of experimentation. In so doing, we seek to suggest the boundary conditions for successful use of Concept Mapping in virtual collaboration environments, and, more importantly, to suggest a roadmap for pushing the boundaries in the future. As such environments continue to grow, we are confident that the benefits of Concept Mapping can extend into the virtual world, as fruitfully as they have in the corporeal world.

DESIGN OF THE VCE

In addition to ARL HRED, developers of the VCE included the University of Edinburgh, University of Virginia, Carnegie Mellon University, and Perigean Technologies LLC. Together, the team created the design for an overarching approach to crisis response, i.e., information technologies, protocols, and strategies to support planning across a distributed community of interest, centered in a VCE.

The design of the VCE was guided through a cognitive work analysis (CWA) (Lintern, 2009; Vincente, 1999) for distributed collaboration. A CWA consists of multiple phases that systematically analyze the constraints across work tasks, collaborators/colleagues, organizations, and activities. A CWA typically focuses on how work can be done, compared to other types of task analyses that focus on how work should be done in a limited set of situations, which can decrease the flexibility and adaptability of the socio-technical system. The CWA identified the critical functions to facilitate distributed collaboration and allowed us to select the appropriate technology to support those functions (Pinelle, Gutwin, and Greenberg, 2003).

It also guided the design, presentation, and structure of information and processes in the three primary components of the VCE.

The VCE consists primarily of collaboration and visualization tools, and a collaboration protocol meant to guide distributed collaborative activities across the tools and diverse set of organizations typically involved in crisis response. The collaboration protocol is tied to Tuckman's (1965) "Forming, Storming, Norming, and Performing" collaboration model and how individuals communicate and collaborate through social networks (Cross and Parker, 2004). It addresses some of the unique capabilities and challenges of distributed collaboration within a virtual environment, such as virtual presence and trust, asynchronous planning, and virtual activity awareness. The next section describes the VCE toolset.

THE VCE TOOLSET

The collaboration tools and visualization tools envisioned for the VCE were intended to support a number of functions for distributed collaboration.

Collaboration

The collaboration tools consist of both a collaborative Web portal of Web 2.0 tools and a 3D virtual collaboration space. All tools were selected to support the key functions identified in the CWA, and their open source or open access nature to make them accessible and available to the wide range of organizations that make up the crisis response community. The open source/access nature also allows us the integration of new or better capabilities as new technology is developed and made available. A combination of social networking capabilities for team and activity awareness, microblogging for transmission of messages to and from users on mobile devices, and collaboration on shared and persistent knowledge through wikis are some examples.

The Open Virtual Collaboration Environment (OpenVCE.net) has been created as the means to support the community of interest in its activities. It consists of the following:

- A Web-based Community Portal (CP) for asynchronous collaboration, communication, and for creating and sharing of assets and resources. After some experimentation and discussion, a Drupal-based system augmented by a range of modules, and with the addition of MediaWiki, is used for this element.
- A virtual world 3D space to support a range of types of meetings, events, training sessions, and possibly real missions. Second Life™ and OpenSim environments are used for this element. The 3D space represents a range of collaborative spaces to facilitate meetings with audio and text communication allowing smaller meeting spaces for 5 to 25 people and larger auditoria for 100 to 400 individuals, presentations or live streaming video to a distributed audience, and sharing of information through an expo pavilion and other virtual spaces.
- An associated set of standard operating procedures (SOP) for virtual collaboration guides the use of the facilities.

A long-standing theory dealing with communication media is the social presence theory (Short, Williams, and Christie, 1976). This theory describes media along a continuum of social presence that provides a range of awareness of the people involved in the communication. Communication is most effective when the level of interpersonal involvement matches the communication medium being used. For example, face-to-face interactions have the highest level of social presence, while text-based communications have the least. The dynamic and complex collaboration activities involved within crisis response and planning requires a moderate to high level of interpersonal interactions, particularly when it is across different organizations. The use of virtual environments and avatars (computer representations of human forms) has shown higher levels of social presence than text-chat and audio conference (e.g., Sallnas, 2005).

The VCE is intended to support the higher levels of social presence through its virtual 3D spaces like the "I-Room" (Tate, Potter, and Dalton, 2009; Tate et al., 2010). An I-Room can provide support for formal business meetings, tutorials, project meetings, discussion groups, and ad-hoc interactions. The I-Room can be used to organize and present preexisting information as well as displaying real-time information feeds from other systems, such as sensor networks and Web services. It also can be used to communicate with participants, facilitate interactions, record and action the decisions taken during the collaboration.

Using the I-Room concept within virtual worlds gives collaborators an intuitive grounding in a persistent 3D space in which representations of the participants (their "avatars") appear and the artifacts and resources surrounding the collaboration can be effectively presented. Figure 15.1 shows the I-Room and present avatars.

FIGURE 15.1
Virtual world 3D space: I-Room.

Visualization

The use of Concept Maps was, primarily, as a visualization technique to provide a centralized perspective on the emergent plan without imposing centralization of the development process. The inspiration for such use came from previous work by Hoffman and Shattuck (2006), who demonstrated the potential to improve the basic process for creating, sharing, and using operational orders and operational plans for military operations. Figure 15.2 shows the vision they demonstrated: a Concept Map-based operational order.

In experiments with the U.S. Army, Hoffman and Shattuck found benefits in comprehension and efficiency for information transfer when traditional five-paragraph operational orders (OPORDs) were represented as Concept Maps and hyperlinked to other, more detailed Concept Maps that expand on the overarching order. They also discovered resistance to the notion of recasting a format deeply entrenched in army culture. To mitigate this resistance, they developed templates that call out the essential components of the OPORD that could be filled in by planners.

Other prior work also suggested the potential benefit of using Concept Maps during planning. Fourie & van der Westhuizen (2008), in exploring through experimentation the value and use of Concept Maps in the alignment process of the strategic intent of a business, found that Concept Maps are "a valuable tool in the alignment of business strategy by visually representing the strategic intent, alignment and misalignment amongst the identified concepts by different hierarchical levels of the organization. Concept Maps can visually represent the complex and abstract nature of business strategy, making it easier to plan, describe, define, craft, communicate, implement, and measure."

The vision, then, for the integrated toolset was to embed the use of CmapTools in the virtual collaboration environment in order to realize the potential benefits of both simultaneously. The next section discusses the outcome of the integration.

CONCEPT MAPS IN SECOND LIFE

Figure 15.3 shows the most basic implementation of the integration—the "projection" of Concept Maps into a virtual space within Second Life. This

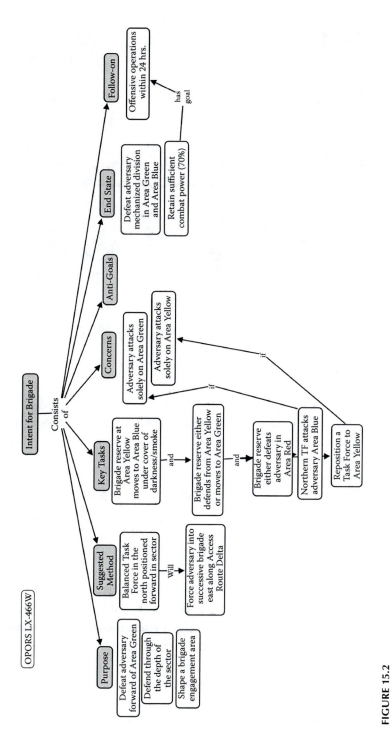

FIGURE 15.2
Concept Map-based operational order.

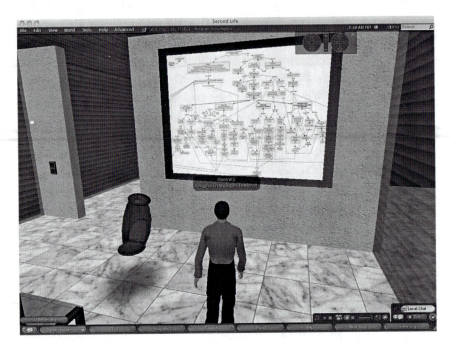

FIGURE 15.3
Concept Map projection in Second Life.

particular space was the virtual office of Perigean Technologies LLC, created by the University of Edinburgh. The Concept Map projected onto the wall in the space represented the entire VCE program, and the Concept Map is being viewed by "PerigeanTechnologiesLowbeam," one of the authors' (Moon's) avatar in Second Life.

The projection is facilitated through a media player in Second Life, which includes the capability to show images, display a Web site, run slideshows, and play media files (e.g., movies and audio). There are several approaches to projecting a Concept Map into the media player. The Concept Map can be uploaded as an image, or be shown in .html by uploading a URL (served from a CMapServer), or shown as a window from a Concept Mapper's computer using screenshare software (in our work, we used Desktop Presenter and Wirecast from Telestream, Inc.). (This basic implementation raised a number of key boundary conditions for the integration of CmapTools into Second Life.) Projecting static Concept Maps introduced one set of challenges. First, the media player screen size in Second Life is fixed. Second, the field of view in Second Life is adjustable for each avatar by the use of various camera angles. These two factors called for trial-and-error experimentation with the appropriate size and scope of the Concept Maps, i.e., we wanted to provide robust Concept Maps, but also to ensure that they were viewable with little effort on the part of the avatars. The Concept Map in Figure 15.3, while robust, required significant effort with camera adjustments on the part of the avatar to review. In many cases, the Concept Maps were simply not viewable due to resolution interactions with the media player. In the section below on Future Capabilities, we discuss a new solution to the effort issue made available by Shared Media incorporated into the release of the Second Live Viewer 2. Finding the proper size and scope of any Concept Map will likely always require a bit of trial-and-error, as a Concept Mapper searches for the right level of information to provide while trading off the limitations of screen size. Such trade-offs, however, are not confined to the virtual world, as Moon and co-authors noted in Chapter 2 of this book.

Projecting dynamic Concept Maps, i.e., Concept Maps that are shown in their evolutionary stages, presented another set of challenges. In any collaborative Concept Mapping session, it is desirable to enable all participants to view and direct, in real-time, the development of the Concept Map. Indeed, this capability underlies the development of some of the collaborative features in CmapTools (e.g., simultaneous editing). This is easily accomplished in a co-located environment with the use of a projector and screen; not so in a distributed environment. We experimented with several approaches to enable this need. First was the use of screenshare software. While this approached worked in terms of enabling dynamic projection of the emerging Concept Map (by projecting the Concept Map from a controlling Concept Mapper's computer), it was limited by security requirements for many of the avatars. Firewalls often limit the use of streamed media in government and corporate information technology environments. A second approach involved projecting the .html version of the dynamic Concept Map, which was enabled by pointing the media player at the URL of the Concept Map served by the Concept MapServer. This approach was limited in its usability due to technical issues on caching of the Web pages involved. The .html version of Concept Maps are not served dynamically. The third approach, which we used frequently, was to provide the URL of the updated Concept Maps directly to the avatars to enable them to view the HTML versions of the updated Concept Maps via a Web browser, either within Second Life or externally to it. In most cases, we simultaneously projected the Concept Map in the media player so that avatars watching only the media player viewed the current Concept Map. By serving the Concept Maps in a Web browser, we were able to finesse the size and scope issue, as Concept Maps viewed in a browser can be viewed in entirety by scrolling vertically and horizontally, which cannot be done in the media player.

With lessons learned from the basic implementation, we subjected the approach for Concept Mapping in Second Life to two experiments aimed at evaluating the entire VCE, i.e., the protocol, toolsets, and strategies. The next section highlights the experiments and the potential benefits and challenges we identified therein.

VCE EXPERIMENTATION

Two experiments were designed to investigate the effects the VCE had on a number of variables important to collaboration including patterns of communication, trust, uncertainty, and the plan itself. Experiment 1 focused only on the effect the collaboration protocol had on the dependent variables mentioned above, while Experiment 2 included the VCE in its entirety to investigate its effect on the dependent variables. Both experiments were scenario-based planning efforts for a pandemic flu outbreak and were conducted in a virtual and distributed fashion.

Experiment 1

Experiment 1 consisted of two small, distributed crisis response teams with similar expertise planning over a four-day period. The objective of this experiment was to investigate how the collaboration protocol affected collaboration and planning. The control group, therefore, did not have access to the collaboration protocol and its corresponding Web forms. The control group used an ad-hoc process to guide their actions, similar to what is seen with collaborative efforts across multiple organizations with no predefined leader. The experimental group used the collaboration protocol to guide their collaboration and planning efforts. Both planning teams used the virtual environment of Second Life to conduct their meetings and had separate but identical meeting room facilities. Both teams consisted of four members each who had experience with crisis and emergency response and planning and were presented with the same scenario.

Experiment 2 Participants and Capabilities

Experiment 2 consisted of two moderate-sized distributed crisis response teams with similar expertise planning over a four-day period. The objective of this experiment was to investigate how the VCE as a whole affected collaboration and planning. The control group for this experiment was asked to use traditional means to collaborate and communicate among their distributed members using primarily teleconference and e-mail capabilities. Like the control group in Experiment 1, they were not given a collaboration protocol to guide their collaborative and planning efforts. The experimental group used the VCE to support both their synchronous and asynchronous efforts and the collaboration protocol to guide their interactions. Similar to Experiment 1, all the participants were volunteers. The control group consisted of 9 participants while the experimental group consisted of 12 participants. Both teams consisted of roughly similar domain experts, with knowledge of biological outbreaks, and crisis and emergency response and planning.

Experimental Tasks

The participants in Experiment 1 were provided a mock scenario to initiate their activities. Briefly, they were instructed on an outbreak of "reindeer flu" (which resembled the real-world outbreak of swine flu), provided a list of 17 Emergency Support Functions (which resembled real-world functions of the Virginia (USA) Emergency Operations Center [VEOC]), and their role and task:

You will be assigned to one of these support functions in support of the VEOC's periodic review of its influenza response plan. Others on your team will also be assigned to support these roles. By the close of Experiment 1, your team should provide a plan for response to reindeer flu.

The task in Experiment 1 was purposefully vague, as we anticipated that much effort in Experiment 1 would focus in gaining familiarity with the VCE, not on substantive planning activities. In Experiment 2, tasking was more specific and the urgency of the situation was increased:

Emerging Events

There are currently two major events scheduled for late-March to take place in Hampton Roads, Virginia. The International Computer Games Conference and Exhibition, for which around 6,000 delegates and visitors from all around the world are expected, commences March 29. Given the subject of the event, there are likely to be a lot of young people amongst the delegates. The launch ceremony for a new hospital ship, for which high-ranking military personnel and government officials are expected, including a delegation from Canada who are considering commissioning a similar ship for their navy, is scheduled for March 31.

The VEOC has been tasked to provide an influenza response plan for reindeer flu. Your team will integrate with the VEOC. Once prepared, the plan will be enacted to mitigate the potential consequences to the upcoming international events. By the close of Experiment 2, your team should provide an influenza response plan for reindeer flu, specifically addressing the international events.

Proposed Uses of Concept Maps

The primary use of Concept Maps during both experiments was in support of the integration of the planning team's artifacts. By artifacts, we mean the content generated by the planning team in executing its tasks. The collaboration protocol called out a specific role for such an "Integrator: [responsible for] ensuring that task deliverables are integrated and consistent, regardless of how the tasks are performed."

Also, the collaboration protocol called for sequenced planning activities—articulation and matching of the problem dimensions and expertise of the team members, followed by specification of solutions and assignment of accountability, and completing with integration and documentation of the full plan. For each activity, the protocol recommended templates to facilitate both ease of capture of the artifacts, and to stimulate thinking at each stage.

Following Hoffman and Shattuck, integrating the details of the emergent plan in Concept Maps was a natural fit with the Integrator role. However, there were key challenges in the integration of planning artifacts from distributed planning activities across diverse contributors. First was data format. While an integrator could certainly create Concept Maps from diverse data formats, e.g., text documents, tables and spreadsheets, or audio, and

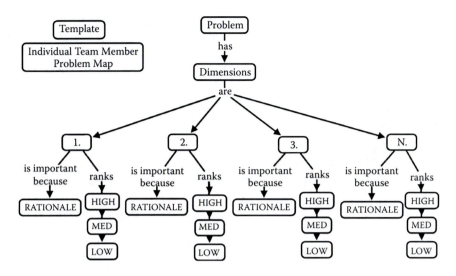

FIGURE 15.4
Protocol template in Concept Map format.

indeed such formats would likely be the types expected from a real-world sources, the collaboration protocol suggested that one route to efficiency could be through providing templates for the planners to focus their inputs into. Hoffman and Shattuck also found value in templating. This led us to the second challenge: data structure. Here we faced the competing demands of providing a data structure that (1) did not require significant training to use, (2) was usable across tools, and (3) lent itself to integration with the overall structure of the collaboration protocol. An early suggestion by Moon was to use Concept Maps for the data structuring by providing templates to the participants, as suggested in Figure 15.4.

We also decided that a representation of the collaboration protocol was vital to the efficiency and effectiveness of the participants: they needed to know where they were in the protocol, what they had accomplished, and what was ahead. The protocol structure was primarily linear, but some of the underlying rules applied across the protocol. Moreover, many steps in the protocol required input. Thus, representation as a Concept Map in CmapTools, while not a strictly "Novakian" Concept Map, offered a singular view of the entire protocol, could be resourced with the various templates and other documents, and could be used to help participants track their place along the protocol's path, e.g., by updates represented as font, or color change, or timestamp, as shown in Figure 15.5.

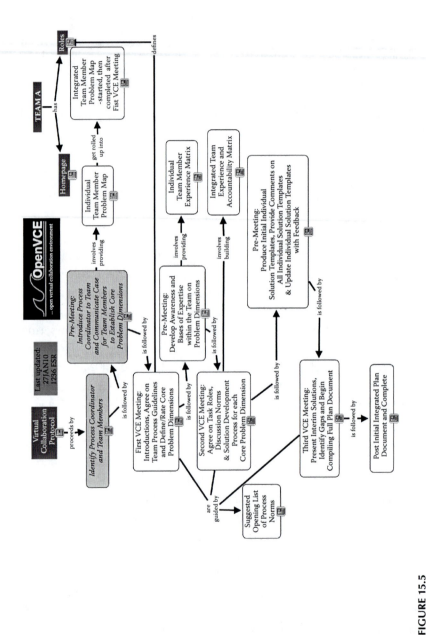

FIGURE 15.5

Collaboration protocol in Concept Map format.

We suspected that the advantage of this approach would be realized at the integration stage of the protocol, as all inputs would be in the same format and structure. Inputs could readily be integrated across participants, facilitated by the flexibility of CmapTools in manipulating data, i.e., placing, moving, and merging concepts, links, and propositions. We knew that the disadvantage, however, lay in the fact that participants would need some degree of training with CmapTools, and the data structure, i.e., the underlying set of concepts, links, and propositions, may not be as robust as necessary for use in other VCE tools.

Also, we questioned the necessity of flexibility of the Concept Maps. Because the protocol was recommended as essentially a linear process, requiring inputs that were, for all intents and purposes, tabular, the advantages did not clearly outweigh the disadvantages. It was easier to provide a capability to enable the participants to move through the protocol (linearly) and enter their inputs in tabular formats that could be automatically "rolled up" for a view on the entire team's input. Because the entire VCE experience would be new to most of the participants, we resisted the temptation to mix tools and approaches where advantages were not patently clear. The proposed Concept Mapping approach was an all-or-nothing proposition. If participants initiated with the Concept Maps, they would need to continue to use them throughout the experiment, or risk significant reformatting of their inputs midstream.

Thus, we introduced in both experiments the use of browser-based forms for the templates and a checklist for the protocol steps. These capabilities were implemented by the University of Edinburgh team, in tabular-style forms linked to the underlying collaboration portal database content, shown in Figure 15.6. Because they were so linked, they could be automatically projected into the virtual world 3D space, also shown in Figure 15.6. Note that the avatars in the 3D space are seated around a central conference table. The point of view of the space can be from the avatar's vantage point, or controlled via a camera view. Thus, any area in the space is viewable by the participant at any time.

Actual Uses of Concept Maps

Our early suspicions were realized quickly in both experiments. While the advantages of the tabular data entry were apparent as participants worked in the early steps, i.e., the individual data input steps, moving to

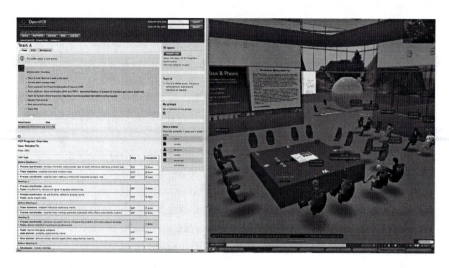

FIGURE 15.6
Integrated problem map data entry form.

integrated team activities brought the limitations of tabular formats into high relief. The VCE template forms were automatically viewable in the virtual environment, projected as slideshows in the media player. In both experiments, as participants began discussing their individual suggestions for the problem dimensions, they quickly realized that the inputs needed to be categorized, and that the categories needed to be prioritized to focus the resources of the team. Participants envisioned the categories, and made them known in the virtual environment through chat messages and voice. However, the tabular forms did not provide an easy mechanism for capturing the categories and teaming the associated dimensions under them. Manipulating the data became a serious constraint, leading to palpable confusion among the participants.

Moreover, as the discussion progressed, the initial inputs transformed. Participants clarified their statements, gave examples to illustrate their points, and reconsidered their original category classifications. They made these considerations known verbally or via chat messages, and it quickly became apparent that mechanisms to capture the team considerations— not just the individual inputs—became the primary requirement during integration.

While Concept Mapping and CmapTools were briefly introduced at the start of each experiment, the advanced uses of Concept Maps that our team had envisioned were mostly lost upon the participants, and understandably so. They needed to learn what the VCE was, what their roles were, what the scenario called for, and who their teammates were, among other things. Recognizing this, we decided to assign the role of Integrator during the first experiment to one of our team (Moon), a highly experienced Concept Mapper. While the participants ultimately were responsible for integrating their inputs, Moon supported the process by converting—on-the-fly during synchronous team meetings—their form-based inputs into Concept Maps. This was a manual task, as the data forms did not export to a data structure that Concept Maps could readily import.

This sort of on-the-fly Concept Mapping is an example of what Moon et al. describe in Chapter 2 of this book. In Experiment 1, Moon initially shared the emerging Concept Maps privately with the Process Coordinator, who was chiefly responsible for moving the team through the collaboration protocol. By introducing the Concept Maps through the process coordinator, the Concept Maps brought a level of credibility that might not have otherwise accompanied them. The Process Coordinator could immediately see the value of the Concept Maps, which were not only representing the individual inputs, but also the points of discussion, to include the categories and their priority. The team's spoken and written words were becoming the team's plan. Once introduced to the team, the Concept Maps were provided via media player projection, and URL, so that the team could track their development in the mode they desired. Figure 15.7 shows a Concept Map (the updated collaboration protocol) projected into a team meeting, as well as the chatbox, which provides the URLs. Figure 15.8 shows a working Concept Map projected.

As the team continued through the collaboration protocol, Moon continued the on-the-fly development of the Concept Maps, maintaining the connections between prior work, decisions, and the current status of the plan through the use of "nested nodes," which effectively "bottled up" the completed work and tied it directly to the new directions. Throughout the first experiment, the team completed their work in the provided forms, and used the Concept Map representations as an aide for visualizing the plan. The final Concept Map representation of the plan is shown in Figure 15.9. Of note are the crosslinks between the subsets of the plans; by showing where the subsets were related to, or dependent upon, other subsets, the plan was truly integrated. Figure 15.10 shows a subset of the plan for one of the developed categories: Containment. On the subset level, subsets were indicated by different colors, with other subsets resourced to

FIGURE 15.7
Team meeting Second Life with Concept Maps.

FIGURE 15.8
Working Concept Map projected into Second Life.

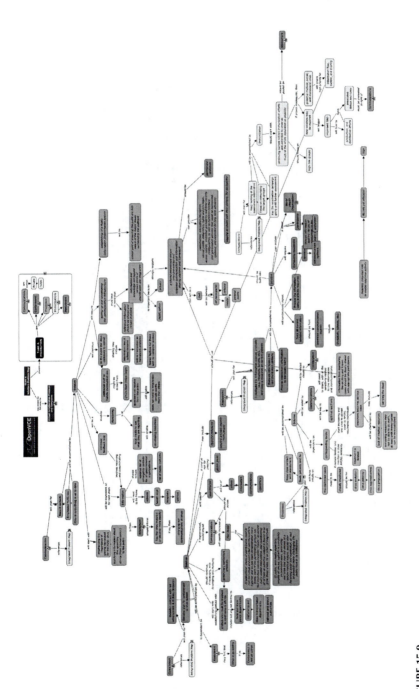

FIGURE 15.9
Integrated plan.

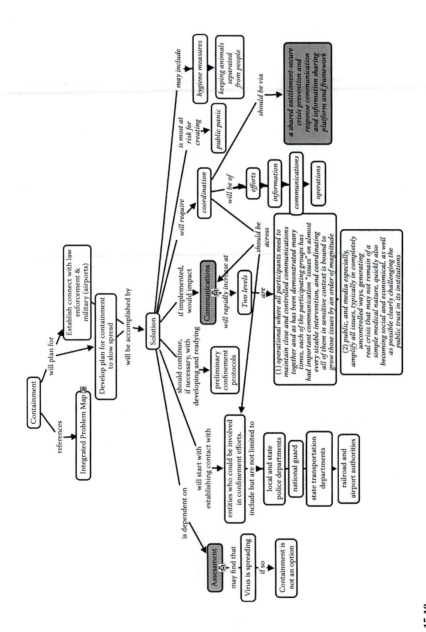

FIGURE 15.10
Subplan: Containment.

the overarching plan. Of additional note in this example is the use of italicized font, which was used to indicate data that were captured in the team meeting, but not otherwise captured in the data forms.

The final plan was drafted in a text document by the process coordinator, using both the data entries from the tabular forms and the Concept Map representation. The Concept Maps also were included as images in the text document.

During the second experiment, we observed many of the same desires in the participants: needs to categorize and prioritize, to see the big picture, and to capture the discussion and integrate new data with data already captured. And we followed essentially the same approach: data forms to capture and present initial inputs, with on-the-fly Concept Mapping to aide in organization, big picture representation, and additional data collection. The process coordinator, however, was less inclined to make use of the Concept Maps during team meetings. We were less inclined as well to "drive" the integration process using Moon as the Integrator, instead leaving the integration work for the team to accomplish. The heavy lifting of integration was accomplished by the volunteer Integrator, who chose a wiki format in which to capture the integration and allowed the team to provide additional inputs postintegration. The Concept Maps were included in the wiki.

Observations

Across both experiments, we made the following observations:

1. Concept Mapping in CmapTools clearly enables plan development, particularly during integration phases. From the moment the teams began reviewing the individual inputs, they required capabilities that are the hallmarks of Concept Mapping and native to CmapTools.
2. Deploying CmapTools in Second Life introduces important benefits to the collaboration process. From multimodal communications to use of the common projection of Concept Maps, the distributed teams made use of the combined capabilities to move through plan development in ways that are not possible using each tool singularly.
3. Deploying CmapTools in Second Life may contribute to overwhelming a planning team. While the multimodal approaches to both collaboration (e.g., verbal and chat communications, data entry forms) and visualization (e.g., projecting slideshows and Concept Maps, URLs

for Concept Maps) can introduce a range of options to planners, the options may also overwhelm them. Figure 15.7 provides only a partial sense of everything that is going on during a team meeting. To say that one is multitasking during a meeting is an understatement.

4. In-depth introductions to, and/or training in, Concept Mapping and/or CmapTools is required to mitigate observation 3. Observations 1 and 2 were made despite only brief exposure for the participants to Concept Mapping, and no exposure to CmapTools. While the benefits of Concept Mapping should be immediately apparent for planners, an appreciation for the potential uses of Concept Mapping invariably leads to more effective deployment of Concept Maps. Moreover, knowing the boundary conditions for use in Second Life is necessary to shape expectations of what is possible in order to exact maximum benefit.

5. Concept Mapping in virtual environments requires deep skill. The skills identified by Moon et al. in Chapter 2 of this book must be taken as a given for effective deployment. Indeed, even an expert Concept Mapper will likely become overwhelmed during a synchronous virtual meeting. A less-experienced Concept Mapper will struggle mightily under the weight of the multitasking.

6. Individual preferences may determine the ultimate benefits for Concept Mapping during planning, in virtual and corporeal environments. Hoffman and Shattuck discovered resistance to the notion of recasting a format deeply entrenched in army culture. We suspect this resistance is due to individual preferences. Our Process Coordinators and Integrators clearly demonstrated individual preferences for integrating the overall plan, and their preferences drove the approaches of the entire team. Nevertheless, we suspect that once properly introduced and demonstrated, planning teams will be inclined to adopt the approaches we have developed.

FUTURE CAPABILITIES

Significant new functionality in terms of shared media, shared tool use by several users simultaneously, and uses of collaborative technologies are expected in all virtual worlds intended for serious use in the future. Second Life Viewer 2, introduced in March 2010, provides a much more capable set of facilities for such tool use. For example, instead of a single media URL in each 3D space, it is now possible to make use of any URL (including those with active content, such as dynamic HTML, Flash content Web pages, JavaScript) on every separate face of every 3D object, and on avatar attachments of Head Up Display objects. We have experimented with the projection of Concept Maps into such displays, and continue to investigate how proper multiuser shared interaction with such displays can be achieved. The way in which Concept Maps are served and updated, and the means by which shared interaction takes place, will need to account for synchronous use by users with and without edit permissions to make this work in an intuitive way.

Another exciting possibility is the use 3D displays of Concept Maps, perhaps with shared media content projection and updates on the faces of the 3D elements, and interactivity via active 3D elements. These effects may truly bring to life concepts maps and make better use of the 3D space opportunities offered by virtual worlds and the virtual collaboration environment. The vision for such a capability is suggested in Figure 15.11.

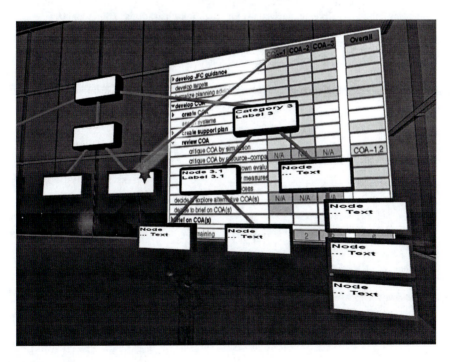

FIGURE 15.11
Future vision for Concept Maps in virtual collaboration environments.

REFERENCES

Cross, R. and A. Parker. 2004. *The hidden power of social networks.* Boston, MA: Harvard Business School Press.

Fourie, L. and T. van der Westhuizen. 2008. The value and use of concept maps in the alignment of strategic intent. In *Concept mapping: Connecting educators,* eds. A. Cañas, P. Reiska, M. Åhlberg, and J. Novak. Proceedings of the Third International Conference on Concept Mapping. Tallinn, Estonia and Helsinki, Finland.

Lintern, G. 2009. The foundations and pragmatics of cognitive work analysis: A systematic approach to design of large-scale information systems. Available online at http://www.cognitiveSystemsDesign.net.

Hoffman, R. and L. Shattuck. 2006. Should we rethink how we do OPORDS? *Military Review,* 100–107.

Pinelle, D., C. Gutwin, and S. Greenberg. 2003. Task analysis for teamware usability evaluation: Modeling shared-workspace tasks with the mechanics of collaboration, *ACM Transactions on Computer-Human Interaction (TOCHI)* 10 (4): 281–311.

Sallnas, E. 2005. Effects of communication mode on social presence, virtual presence, and performance in collaborative virtual environments. *Presence* 14 (4): 434–449.

Short, J., E. Williams, and B. Christie. 1976. *The social psychology of telecommunications.* London, U.K.: John Wiley.

Tate, A., S. Potter, and J. Dalton. 2009. I-Room: A virtual space for emergency response for the multinational planning augmentation team. Proceedings of the Fifth International Conference on Knowledge Systems for Coalition Operations (KSCO-2009).

Tate, A., Y-H. Chen-Burger, and J. Dalton, et al. 2010. I-Room: A virtual space for intelligent interaction. IEEE Intelligent Systems.

Tuckman, B. 1965. Developmental sequence in small teams. *Psychological Bulletin,* 63 (6): 384–399.

Vicente, K. J. 1999. *Cognitive work analysis.* Mahwah, NJ: Lawrence Erlbaum Associates.

16

Vying for the Use of CmapTools in Corporate Training

Carrie Ann Desnoyers

CONTENTS

INTRODUCTION

My graduate education was deeply immersed in the use of Concept Mapping. I used Concept Mapping and CmapTools software as a means to take notes in class, brainstorm, and outline and organize projects and papers. My professors used Concept Mapping to introduce new materials and as a means to evaluate students' learning and understanding. I did research on the use of Concept Maps (Cmaps) in higher education, co-authored a chapter on the use of collaborative Concept Mapping (Conceição, Baldor, and Desnoyers, 2009), and wrote and presented conference papers on the use and importance of Cmaps (Conceição, Desnoyers, and Baldor, 2008a and 2008b). By the time I had graduated and begun my career in training at a large corporation in the financial services industry, the use of Concept Mapping was so deeply imbedded in my thought and work processes that it was akin to my first cup of coffee. The transition from using Concept Maps for education to using them for training appeared seamless to me. Creating Concept Maps had completely changed my approach to learning and applying new ideas. I could not think of a better way to aid the learning and understanding of the people I would be training.

I was new to the corporate world and, admittedly, rather naïve to the processes involved in obtaining permission to procure new technologies. Seeing many opportunities to use CmapTools, I sat down at my company-issued computer to download the CmapTools software. My computer promptly informed me that I did not have the appropriate level of authorization to download a program to my computer. After seeking out my manager and explaining my plight, I was informed that only a member of the Information Technology (IT) team could download programs to a company computer. Further, if the program was not currently authorized and in use at the company, I would need to have the program investigated and approved by the software committee. This could take anywhere from three to six months. It would be more challenging than usual because the company already had "mind mapping" software that was widely used, and was consistent in the creation of "knowledge maps" using Microsoft® Visio. Because of the time and effort necessary to put forth such a request, my manager asked whether the software was truly needed.

———

CONVINCING MANAGEMENT

While I was surprised by the timeline involved with acquiring software that was free and readily available for download, I had little doubt of the positive effect that Concept Mapping would have on my trainees. To convince my manager, I tried to clearly explain the differences between mind mapping, knowledge mapping, and Novakian Concept Mapping. Mind mapping, I suggested, is commonly used to take notes, delineate facts, and show the overall structure or an idea or a subject. Knowledge mapping is used to capture procedures from start to finish, and to outline decision-making processes. The Novakian form of Concept Mapping can be used for all of these purposes, but additionally can be used as an educational tool to aid in both learning and the evaluation of learning.

To bolster my argument, I suggested an exercise. We would each create a "map" of the conversation we had just had. She would use all of the methods she was familiar with, and I would create a Cmap in the format that Novak suggests and CmapTools enables. She agreed with the idea, and we each spent about five minutes drawing our maps. We placed them side-by-side to inspect and discuss.

The two maps were remarkably different. Her map was highly linear and showed all of her thoughts in a tree-like structure. She wrote the name of each type of map at the top, and worked down the pages with straight lines connecting the ideas. The map, we agreed, could be used to show someone the topics that were discussed in our meeting. Next we investigated the Cmap that I had drawn. My Cmap contained many of the same ideas; however, they were laid out in a much different manner. The Cmap had the three different types of maps in nodes, with descriptions of the types of maps and their attributes in nodes interconnected by linking phrases in arcs. It contained not only a list of facts, but also how they were related to one another and how they were important to me and to the field of training. By examining my Cmap, one could tell not only whether I knew specific facts about the three different types of mapping, but also whether or not I had a personal understanding of the subject. Together we discussed how her form of mapping could possibly be used in some forms of rote learning as a tool for memorization, but it would not be useful as a tool to evaluate someone's learning, nor could it be used as a tool to aid in the learning process.

At the end of our conversation and map comparison, my manager started to understand some of the possibilities for using Concept Mapping and the CmapTools software in our training program. We decided to move forward with my request to have CmapTools installed on all of the instructors' computers and on the computers that our trainees would use.

CONVINCING THE SOFTWARE COMMITTEE

The software evaluation process was explained to me in three basic steps. First, we would fill out a standard online application documenting, explaining, and supporting our request. Next we would submit the request and wait to be contacted by the software committee. Once we were contacted by the committee, we would be informed if they had denied or approved our application, or if they required further information in order to make a decision.

The software request form was standard in a way that I believe that most large corporations would use a form for similar purposes. The form asked for the name of the application requested, who it was created and distributed by, and the cost of purchasing or downloading the application. In this case, the software was CmapTools v.5.03; it was created by the Institute for Human and Machine Cognition (IHMC), it was available via Web download, and there was no cost for the installation or use of the program. It also asked for an explanation of why we were unable to accomplish our goals using software already owned and in use by the company. I responded that CmapTools software is unique in that it is the only software program available that specifically supports the creation of Novakian Cmaps. While the company did have software to create mind maps or similar diagrams, these programs did not have the necessary features to create a Novakian Concept Map. In short, it was unfair to compare two programs that were created with very different outputs.

The form then requested information on what the program was designed to do and how we planned to use it to further the company and our department's mission. Answering this question took some thought. I tried to keep my response as simple and accurate as possible. We would use it to further the company's mission both by teaching trainees to use Cmaps to aid in their learning process, and to more accurately evaluate the trainee's understanding of the material.

Finally, the form asked specifically how this software would create profit or positive outcomes for the company. I answered this by explaining that creating Cmaps in training classes would help our trainees better understand the material being presented to them. These Cmaps could then be evaluated by the instructors. Trainees whose Cmaps indicated that they were unclear on certain concepts or materials could then be provided additional, *learner-specific* training that explicitly connected new knowledge to knowledge they already had. This process would lead to employees who were well-trained and better equipped to do their jobs successfully, which in turn would lead to fewer errors, higher customer satisfaction, and ultimately more business for the company.

About six weeks later, I received a message from the software committee inviting me to discuss our request in a phone conference. During the 10-minute phone conference, I was asked to explain my request in more detail. I explained that there were three main reasons underlying my request: (1) to use Cmaps in training as an educational tool and resource, (2) CmapTools enabled both linear and nonlinear thinking and mapping, and (3) my graduate-level education and concomitant research clearly demonstrated that Concept Mapping was well-suited to the theories and practice of adult education.

I explained the variety of potential uses for aiding learning. As an instructional design tool, CmapTools software could be used by instructors sharing new and important material with trainees, to provide structure to the presentation and to act as a visual aid. Visual learners in particular would benefit from the use of Concept Mapping through instructors' use of the Cmaps in presentations. All learners would benefit from creating Cmaps during training sessions as a means of note taking, brainstorming, and group collaboration. Among the trainees, Cmaps could provide an efficient platform for sharing ideas, as a great deal more information can be displayed and shared in a Cmap format in a much shorter timeframe than in a discussion of the same length.

Most importantly however, was the use of Concept Mapping as a means to evaluate learning. I explained that CmapTools was able to create both linear and nonlinear visual representations of subject matter. It provides the Cmap constructor with the ability to add information in any order and to make connections between all of the different ideas in the Cmap. Such representations can be used by an instructor to evaluate where a learner currently fell along the learning continuum.

Finally, I spoke of two aspects of adult education theory that Concept Mapping can positively influence. I explained that learning for adults was different than learning for children. In order for adult learners to absorb and understand new information, it is important to include means to connect new information being learned to current knowledge. In creating Cmaps, trainees will draw connections between the information they have recently received and things that they already know. It is critical that adults make sense of this new information by seeing how it relates to things that they already know. Moreover, it is extremely important that adults understand how the material they are learning is relevant to their life. In creating a Cmap of the information they are learning, and making connections to their current knowledge, trainees will see how this new information will directly affect their life and their career.

At the end of the conference call, the committee explained that they had also received requests for other types of mapping software and were trying to understand the differences between and the uses for each one. They requested that I do a short analysis of several mapping software programs and present my findings to them. To facilitate the analysis, the committee authorized the

IT department to download three mapping programs onto my desktop, and I was given three weeks to "test drive" them and report my findings.

MAPPING SOFTWARE COMPARISON

The three mapping software programs that I was asked to compare were CmapTools, Mindjet's MindManager® and FreeMind.* While other mapping programs were available (cf., Okada et al., 2008), these would allow comparison between two free programs, and between free and proprietary software. I began this process by familiarizing myself with all three programs. I had used CmapTools extensively in the past and, therefore, concentrated on the other two programs. I took the tutorials that came with the programs, and reviewed all information I could find on the programs' Web sites. I searched for help information and reviews posted online by users of MindManager and FreeMind. As the last stage of my testing process, I created a Novakian Concept Map with CmapTools, and then tried to recreate the same map using the other two. I compared the final maps to one another and came up with a list of attributes and features of the products. I then created a table to show the results of my comparison study, shown in Table 16.1.

I sent the table I had created to the software committee for their review. Within a week I was contacted and asked to take part in another phone conference with the committee members. During this conference, I reviewed my findings and explained how they supported my initial request for the company to procure the CmapTools software. I started with cost—FreeMind and CmapTools are free, Mindjet is not. I pointed them to Mindjet's catalog for their review. My findings showed that all three programs can be used to capture, organize, and store text and ideas. All of the programs could be effective tools for brainstorming as well. All three software programs give users the ability to create maps in full color with both hyper linking and graphic capabilities.

I pointed out, though, that Concept Mapping helps users to define the meaning of ideas and concepts, not just list facts. CmapTools was the only

---

* * Mindjet: http://mindjet.com/;   FreeMind: http://freemind.sourceforge.net/wiki/index.php/ Main_Page

TABLE 16.1

Mapping Software Comparison

	CmapTools	MindManager	FreeMind
Available for free download	Yes	—	Yes
Tutorial map available	Yes	Yes	Yes
Online tutorials and demos	Yes	Yes	—
Tech support offered	Yes	Yes	—
Personalized training available	Yes	Yes	—
Nodes containing concepts	Yes	Yes	Yes
Linking phrases show relationships between concepts	Yes	—	—
Non-hierarchical mapping	Yes	Yes	Yes
Hierarcical mapping	Yes	—	—
Linear mapping	Yes	Yes	Yes
Non-linear mapping	Yes	—	—
Full color/graphic capabilities	Yes	Yes	Yes
Hyperlink capabilities	Yes	Yes	Yes
Multimedia links	Yes	w/add on	—
Asynchronous collaboration possible	Yes	Yes	Yes
Synchronous collaboration possible	Yes	w/add on	—
Uses:			
Capture, organize and store text	Yes	Yes	Yes
Brainstorming	Yes	Yes	Yes
Define meaning	Yes	—	—
Create knowledge models	Yes	—	—
Evaluation of learning/knowledge	Yes	—	—

one of the three that could be used to create Knowledge Models (Cañas, Hill, and Lott, 2002; IHMC, 2010). CmapTools would allow instructors to evaluate their trainees' learning through assessment of their Cmaps. CmapTools allows users to create maps using both nodes, i.e., shapes that contain ideas or concepts, and arcs, i.e., lines with linking phrases showing the relationships between ideas and concepts. MindManager and FreeMind are effective tools for nonhierarchical and linear mapping techniques, while CmapTools gives users the ability to create linear, nonlinear, hierarchical, and nonhierarchical maps. CmapTools inherently enables users to link multimedia components to their Cmaps as well, and I noted that MindManager includes a similar feature as an add-on. CmapTools enables users to create online synchronous maps, making classroom collaboration for training sessions and presentations a viable option. While FreeMind's online tutorials and demonstrations for users are limited to screenshots, both CmapTools and Mindjet provide extensive resources for self-training.

Regarding technical support, I reported that CmapTools and FreeMind provide indirect technical support (i.e., FreeMind developers run a Help forum, and CmapTools developers post Release Notes and Known Issues). Mindjet, by comparison, provides both indirect and direct technical support, the latter made available through their Maintenance and Support plan packages. I also commented on the spectrum of training possibilities. While I knew of no training programs associated with FreeMind, I noted that Mindjet offered "Live Demonstrations" and a "Custom Implementation Package" that provides customized training. Customized training on the application of CmapTools was available through Perigean Technologies LLC (Novak, 2010, p. 103). The trade-off they needed to consider, I suggested, was between the not insignificant cost differential and level of technical and training support necessary to realize the potential benefits I had outlined.

RESOLUTION

After discussing my findings, the software committee expressed interest in not only downloading CmapTools software onto the computers used for training, but to create a mass download package available to all employees. I was invited to serve as a software expert to the committee on mapping software, and to serve as a reference to new users in the company. The software is being packaged for company-wide distribution. While the process is slow going, it is successful. The virtues of Novakian Concept Mapping and the CmapTools software are becoming apparent across a spectrum of users, from trainers and instructional designers to the trainees themselves. As of the writing of this chapter, the longer-term impacts have yet to be realized.

Looking back at my experience, I realize that the impact of the exercise I conducted with my manager was significant, and perhaps should have served as a model for the rest of my efforts. If you are vying for the use of CmapTools in your company and facing opposition or difficulty, perhaps the answer lies in presenting the information in the form of a Concept Map (Figure 16.1)!

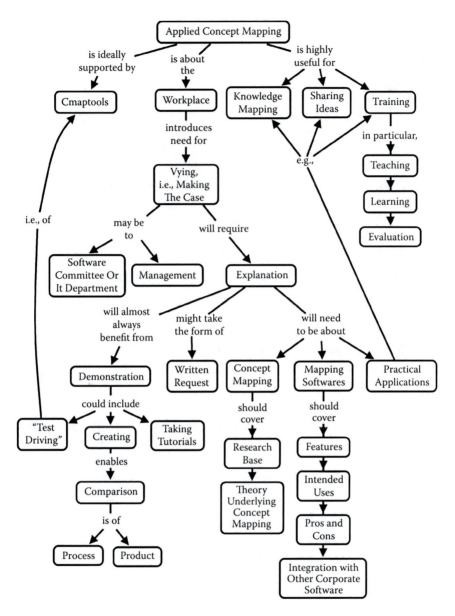

FIGURE 16.1
Vying for the use of CmapTools.

REFERENCES

Cañas, A., G. Hill, and J. Lott. 2002. Support for constructing knowledge models in CmapTools. Technical Report IHMC CmapTools 93-02. Pensacola, FL: IHMC.

Conceição, S. C. O., M. J. Baldor, and C. A. Desnoyers. 2009. Factors influencing individual construction of knowledge in an online community of learning and inquiry using concept maps. In *Handbook of research on collaborative learning using concept mapping*, eds. R. Marriott and T. Torres. Hershey, PA: IGI Global.

Conceição, S. C. O., C. A. Desnoyers, and M. J. Baldor. 2008a. Individual construction of knowledge in an online community through concept maps. In *Concept mapping: Connecting educators*, eds. A. Cañas, P. Reiska, M. Åhlberg, and J. Novak. Proceedings of the Third International Conference on Concept Mapping. Tallinn, Estonia and Helsinki, Finland.

Conceição, S. C. O., M. J. Baldor, and C. A. Desnoyers. 2008b. Concept maps used in a community of learning as tools for individual construction of knowledge. Paper presented at the 20th Annual University of Wisconsin-Milwaukee School of Education Research Conference, Milwaukee, WI.

IHMC. 2010. http://cmapskm.ihmc.us/rid=1064009710027_1421983319_27104/CmapTools-KnowledgeModels.cmap

Novak, J. 2010. *Learning, creating, and using knowledge: Concept maps as facilitative tools in schools and corporations*. New York: Routledge.

Okada, A., S. Shum, and T. Sherborne. 2008. *Knowledge cartography: Software tools and mapping techniques*. London: Spinger-Verlog.

Index